NEW APPROACHES TO EVALUATING COMMUNITY INITIATIVES:
Concepts, Methods, and Contexts

EDITED BY

James P. Connell
Anne C. Kubisch
Lisbeth B. Schorr
Carol H. Weiss

Roundtable on
Comprehensive Community Initiatives
for Children and Families

The Aspen Institute

ROUNDTABLE ON
COMPREHENSIVE COMMUNITY INITIATIVES
FOR CHILDREN AND FAMILIES
The Aspen Institute
345 East 46th Street
Suite 700
New York, New York 10017-3562
(212) 697-1261
FAX (212) 697-2258

Copyright © 1995 by
The Aspen Institute
Washington, D.C.

Published in the United States of America
in 1995 by The Aspen Institute

Printed in the United States of America

ISBN: 0-89843-167-0

Library of Congress Card Catalog Number: 95-76785

Contents

Acknowledgments

The activities of the Roundtable on Comprehensive Community Initiatives for Children and Families are currently funded by eight foundations: the Ford Foundation, the Robert Wood Johnson Foundation, the Pew Charitable Trusts, the Foundation for Child Development, the Annie E. Casey Foundation, the W. K. Kellogg Foundation, the John D. and Catherine T. MacArthur Foundation, and the Spencer Foundation.

The work of the Committee on Evaluation is part of the ongoing efforts of the Roundtable and is therefore funded, in part, through the sources listed above. It has also received specific grant funds from the following sources: the U.S. Department of Health and Human Services, the U.S. Department of Housing and Urban Development, the Pew Charitable Trusts, the Ford Foundation, and the Annie E. Casey Foundation.

The authors, editors, and publisher are solely responsible for the accuracy of the statements and interpretations contained within this publication. Such interpretations do not necessarily reflect the views of the contributing foundations or of the federal government.

The editors would like to thank Alice Tufel for her insightful and conscientious editing, and Danny Wright for overseeing the design and printing of the volume. Both worked with grace under pressure.

Preface

About the Roundtable on Comprehensive Community Initiatives for Children and Families

The Roundtable on Comprehensive Community Initiatives for Children and Families is a forum in which persons involved in the current generation of community-based cross-systems reform efforts can engage in open and detailed discussion about the challenges they face and the lessons they are learning. It also provides a venue where they can work on issues of common concern. Originally called the Roundtable on Effective Services for Children and Families, its members were first convened under the auspices of the National Academy of Sciences (NAS) in 1992. Agreeing that improving outcomes for children and families in poor communities would require more than improving the quality and quantity of human services, the group expanded its purview and membership to include a greater focus on community development and economic opportunity. In 1994, the Roundtable moved out of the NAS and became a policy program of The Aspen Institute.

The Roundtable now has 30 members, including foundation officers, program directors, experts in the field, and public officials who are engaged in cross-system, geographically targeted initiatives. (The Roundtable members appear in a list following this preface.) It is co-chaired by Harold A. Richman, the Hermon Dunlap Smith Professor of Social Welfare Policy and director of the Chapin Hall Center for Children at the University of Chicago, and Lisbeth B. Schorr, director of the Harvard Project on Effective Services and author of *Within Our Reach: Breaking the Cycle of Disadvantage* (New York: Doubleday, 1988).

Roundtable members meet biannually to share lessons they are learning and to work on common problems they are facing. Each meeting includes updates to the group on current initiatives and new developments in the field as well as structured discussions, based on commissioned papers or formal presentations by outside experts, which have thus far revolved around the four general themes of financing, governance, community-building, and evaluation.

About the Steering Committee on Evaluation

In 1994, the Roundtable created a Committee with the goal of helping to resolve the "lack of fit" that exists between current evaluation methods and the need to learn from and judge the effectiveness of comprehensive community initiatives (CCIs). Committee members were selected so as to bring three different perspectives to the work: (1) program-level and policy-level experience related to the design, implementation, and evaluation of CCIs; (2) current social science research findings about individual, family, and community change and the relationships among those three levels of change; and (3) theories and methods from the field of evaluation. Committee members are listed at the end of this preface.

The Committee met twice during 1994 and designed an 18-month project, running through December 1995, that aims to develop new approaches to CCI evaluation that could be of use to program designers, funders, managers, and participants. Specifically, the work of the Committee will attempt to define the key conceptual building blocks that underlie the current generation of CCIs, specify the hypotheses or theories of change that are guiding the CCIs, assess and present the state of the research on which those theories of change are or should be based, identify the types of measures that could reasonably be used to track CCI progress and indicate progress toward outcomes, and present a set of guidelines or alternative approaches to designing evaluations of CCIs.

About This Volume

As a first step in the Committee's work, a set of papers was commissioned to begin to lay out some of the key issues and challenges associated with the evaluation of CCIs. The papers served as the launching point for an intensive five-day working session of Committee members and several invited guests in August 1994, out of which the detailed Committee work plan emerged. Those initial papers, and an additional paper by Claudia Coulton, have now been revised and are assembled in this volume for wider distribution.

With this publication, the Committee aims to introduce some of the challenges facing CCI designers, funders, managers, and evaluators. It is not intended to be an exhaustive review of all of the problems associated with the design, implementation, or evaluation of innovative anti-poverty programs, nor does it present definitive solutions to current problems. Rather, this book is intended to help those who are currently struggling with these issues to understand, give context to, and frame their own dilemmas with greater clarity. It also aims to ground further discussion and work in the field and, indeed, has already served this purpose for the Committee itself.

The challenges associated with the evaluation of comprehensive community initiatives might strike some as a mélange of arcane issues that relate only to a small fraction of anti-poverty efforts under way across the country today. Or, they might appear to represent some of the most intriguing intellectual and methodological dilemmas in the field of social and economic development that are being surfaced as a result of the cutting-edge nature of the current generation of comprehensive community initiatives. We warn any unknowing readers that this volume is quite clearly intended for those who identify with the latter perspective.

> *James P. Connell*
> *Lisbeth B. Schorr*
> *Carol H. Weiss*
> Co-chairs, Steering Committee on Evaluation
>
> *Anne C. Kubisch*
> Director, Roundtable on Comprehensive
>   Community Initiatives for Children
>   and Families

The Roundtable on Comprehensive
Community Initiatives
for Children and Families

The Steering Committee on Evaluation

About the Authors

J. LAWRENCE ABER is director of the National Center for Children in Poverty at the Columbia University School of Public Health, where he is also an associate professor of psychology and public health. He conducts basic research on the effects of family and community poverty and violence on the development of children and youth. His applied research focuses on rigorous process and outcome evaluations of innovative programs and policies for children and families at risk, including welfare-to-work programs, violence prevention programs, and comprehensive service programs.

PRUDENCE BROWN is associate director of the Chapin Hall Center for Children at the University of Chicago. Formerly deputy director of the Urban Poverty Program at the Ford Foundation, her expertise covers issues of family and neighborhood development, urban policy, and strategic grantmaking. She has been involved with comprehensive community initiatives as a designer and funder, a documenter, and an evaluator.

JAMES P. CONNELL is a developmental psychologist and research methodologist. He has written extensively on school, family, and community factors influencing child and adolescent development in urban areas. He is co-founder and director of research of the Institute for Research and Reform on Education, a member of the Social Science Research Council's Working Group on Communities and Neighborhoods, Family Processes, and Individual Development, and is currently completing a senior fellowship at Public/Private Ventures. He is co-chair of the Roundtable's Steering Committee on Evaluation.

CLAUDIA COULTON is professor and co-director of the Center for Urban Poverty and Social Change at Case Western Reserve University. Through the Center she works with community-based organizations and initiatives to reduce poverty and related conditions in urban neighborhoods. Among her research interests are the effects of community environments on children and families and measuring community change.

JENNIFER HILL is a graduate student in statistics at Rutgers University.

ROBINSON G. HOLLISTER, JR. is the Joseph Wharton Professor of Economics at Swarthmore College. He has written extensively on labor and employment training issues. In 1966–67, he was Chief of Research and Plans for the Office of Economic Opportunity. He was co-principal investigator for the evaluation of the National Supported Work Demonstration and Chair of the Committee on Youth Employment Programs, National Academy of Sciences, which assessed the effectiveness of youth employment and training programs.

ANNE C. KUBISCH is the director of the Roundtable on Comprehensive Community Initiatives for Children and Families at the Aspen Institute. Previously, she was the deputy director of the Ford Foundation's Urban Poverty Program, where she was responsible for grants supporting comprehensive community initiatives and reforms in human service delivery systems. She also has extensive experience working on economic development and human rights issues in Latin America and Africa, including three years as the head of the Ford Foundation's office in Lagos, Nigeria.

ALICE O'CONNOR is an historian and a National Science Foundation postdoctoral fellow at the Center for the Study of Urban Inequality at the University of Chicago. She is currently working on a book on the history of poverty research and policy since the 1920s. Among her recent publications is "Community Action, Urban Reform, and the Fight Against Poverty: The Ford Foundation's Gray Areas Program," forthcoming in the *Journal of Urban History.*

LISBETH BAMBERGER SCHORR is a lecturer in social medicine at Harvard University, and director of the Harvard University Project on Effective Services. She has woven together many strands of experience with social policy and human service programs to become a national authority on improving the future of disadvantaged children and families. Her 1988 book, *Within Our Reach: Breaking the Cycle of Disadvantage,* analyzing successful programs for children, has become highly influential with policymakers, practitioners, and advocates for more effective human services. Ms. Schorr is the co-chair of the Roundtable on Comprehensive Community Initiatives for Children and Families, and co-chair of the Roundtable's Steering Committee on Evaluation.

GARY WALKER is president of Public/Private Ventures, a national not-for-profit organization located in Philadelphia that develops and evaluates promising youth policy strategies in community, educational, and employment settings. Mr. Walker was previously senior vice president of the Manpower Demonstration Research Corporation (MDRC), and formerly a Wall Street attorney. He writes and speaks extensively on ways that public policy and the private sector can improve opportunities and outcomes for disadvantaged youth.

CAROL HIRSCHON WEISS is a professor in the Harvard University Graduate School of Education. She has published eight books and almost 100 journal articles and book chapters. Her work on evaluation includes *Evaluation Research: Methods for Assessing Program Effectiveness,* published by Prentice-Hall, which has sold approximately 150,000 copies, and *Evaluating Action Programs,* published by Allyn and Bacon. She has been a congressional fellow, a guest scholar at the Brookings Institution, a fellow at the Center for Advanced Study in the Behavioral Sciences, and a member of advisory boards of over a dozen journals. She is co-chair of the Roundtable's Steering Committee on Evaluation.

Introduction

Anne C. Kubisch, Carol H. Weiss,
Lisbeth B. Schorr, James P. Connell

The idea of comprehensive community development is not new. Its roots lie in the settlement houses of the late nineteenth century and can be traced through the twentieth century in a number of neighborhood-based efforts, including the fight against juvenile delinquency in the 1950s, the War on Poverty in the 1960s, and the community development corporation movement of the last thirty years (Halpern 1994).

The current generation of efforts, referred to in this volume as "comprehensive community initiatives" (CCIs), was begun in the late 1980s and early 1990s, primarily by national or community foundations. While varied, they all have the goal of promoting positive change in individual, family, and community circumstances in disadvantaged neighborhoods by improving physical, economic, and social conditions. Most CCIs contain several or all of the following elements and aim to achieve synergy among them: expansion and improvement of social services and supports, such as child care, youth development, and family support; health care, including mental health care; economic development; housing rehabilitation and/or construction; community planning and organizing; adult education; job training; school reform; and quality-of-life activities such as neighborhood security and recreation programs. Moreover, most CCIs operate on the premise that the devolution of authority and responsibility from higher-level auspices to the neighborhood or community is a necessary aspect of the change process. (For overviews of current CCIs and

1

of the field, see American Writing Corporation 1992; Eisen 1992; Fishman and Phillips 1993; Gardner 1992; Himmelman 1992; Jenny 1993; Rosewater et al. 1993; Sherwood 1994; and Stagner 1993.)

THE EVOLUTION OF COMPREHENSIVE COMMUNITY INITIATIVES

The emergence of CCIs over the last few years can be attributed to the convergence of several trends:

- Human services professionals were recognizing that fragmentation and categorization of social services and supports were limiting program success.

- Experience in several domains was revealing the high cost and uncertain success of remediation, and a search for effective prevention strategies was emerging.

- Community development experts were recognizing that, with some notable exceptions, physical revitalization had come to dominate activities on the ground, but that "bricks and mortar" alone were not achieving sustained improvements in low-income neighborhoods.

- For both pragmatic and ideological reasons, public–private partnerships and local action were being promoted as complementary or even alternative approaches to relying on "big government" to solve social problems.

It would be a mistake, however, to suggest that the rationale for comprehensive community-based intervention has been grounded solely in a frustration with unsuccessful social interventions. There was and continues to be a sense that we know a great deal about "what works" for at-risk populations and that if we could manage to concentrate and integrate resources and program knowledge in particular communities over a sustained period of time, we could demonstrate that positive outcomes are indeed "within our reach" (Schorr 1988). This call for cross-sector, cross-system reform has been further justified by recent social science research that has begun to identify the linkages and interconnectedness among the various strands of an individual's life, and of the importance of family and neighborhood influences in determining individual-level outcomes. Thus, CCIs are the offspring of a marriage between program experience and academic findings, and they offer hope at a time when skepticism about the efficacy of strategies to help those most in need is high.

Whether or not interest in and commitment to the current wave of comprehensive community initiatives are sustained by the public and private funding communities, the principles that underlie them will surely continue to infiltrate social policy. The last two years alone have seen a large number of new federal initiatives that have adopted a comprehensive, community-based approach—including new efforts aimed at teen pregnancy prevention, youth employment and training, and crime prevention, as well as the more broad-based Empowerment Zones/Enterprise Communities. The states also have taken on the task of reforming their service delivery, education, and economic development activities to make them more responsive to families and communities (Chynoweth et al. 1992). And, national and local foundations have launched a significant number of experiments based on the principles of comprehensiveness and community-based change (Rosewater 1992).

Why CCIs Are So Hard to Evaluate
The attributes of CCIs that make them particularly difficult to evaluate include horizontal complexity, vertical complexity, the importance of context, the flexible and evolving nature of the interventions, the breadth of the range of outcomes being pursued, and the absence of appropriate control groups for comparison purposes.

Horizontal Complexity. Although each comprehensive community initiative is unique, they all are based on the notion of working across systems or sectors. They aim to revitalize the community physically by building or improving housing, to strengthen the system of social supports for children and families, to improve schools and other education and training centers, and to promote economic activity within the community and access to economic opportunity outside the community. Given this complex array of activities, what should the evaluator seek to measure?

One option is to track progress in each of the individual program areas. Not only would that be an extensive task, but it may miss the essence of the initiative: the general reason that program designers and funders are willing to consider a comprehensive range of potential interventions is that they believe that a certain synergy can be achieved among them. By focusing on discrete program components, the evaluator might ignore the effects of their interaction. Moreover, if the CCI director believes that evaluation will be based exclusively upon program-level outcomes, his or her own management strategies may become narrowly focused. But tracking and measuring "synergy" is a problem that the methodologists have yet to solve.

Vertical Complexity. CCIs are seeking change at the individual, family, and community levels, and are predicated on the notion that there is interaction among those levels. For example, a key assumption is that improvements in community circumstances will improve outcomes for individuals. But social science research is only beginning to identify the forces that influence these community-level circumstances and which among them, if any, are amenable to intervention. Moreover, our understanding of the specific pathways through which community-level variables affect individual outcomes is still rudimentary, making it difficult for evaluators to judge whether an initiative is "pulling the right levers." Finally, because there is little good information about how low-income urban communities work, how these communities evolve over time, and how to detect and measure community improvement, it is difficult to learn about change in the other direction—that is, how improvements in individual and family conditions affect the wider community.

Contextual Issues. By definition, the current CCIs are community-focused. Although most are designed with an appreciation for the need to draw upon political, financial, and technical resources that lie outside the community, there is a broader set of circumstances and events that may have a direct bearing on the success of CCIs but that CCIs have little power to affect. The macroeconomic climate may be the best example: it becomes especially difficult to strengthen disadvantaged communities when the economy is undergoing changes that have significant negative consequences for low-wage and low-skilled workers. The racial and cultural barriers facing minority populations is yet another important condition that may well constrain the ability of CCIs to make substantial improvements in individual or community circumstances. A host of other political, demographic, and geographic factors may also apply.

Flexible and Evolving Intervention. CCIs are designed to be community-specific and to evolve over time in response to the dynamics of the neighborhood. The "intervention," therefore, is flexible, constantly changing, and difficult to track. As it unfolds and is implemented, it may look very different from its design document. Even in multi-site initiatives where all communities have the same overall charge, the approach and the individual program components may vary significantly from place to place.

Broad Range of Outcomes. CCIs seek improvements in a range of less concrete domains for which there are few agreed-upon definitions, much less agreed-upon measures. For example, as mentioned above, most CCIs operate on the premise that authority and responsibility must shift from higher-level sponsors to the neighborhood or community in order to effect change. They have fairly explicit goals about community participation, leadership development, empowerment, and community building. They also aim for significant changes in the ways institutions operate in the community, and many seek reforms in government agency operations at the municipal, state, or federal system level as well. But operationalizing those concepts, and then measuring their effects, is difficult.

Absence of a Comparison Community or Control Group. The community-wide and community-specific characteristics of CCIs rob the evaluator of tools that many consider essential to assess the impact of an initiative. Since CCIs seek to benefit all members of a community, individuals cannot be randomly assigned to treatment and control groups for the purposes of assessing impact. In addition, finding an equivalent "comparison" community that is *not* benefiting from the initiative, and with which outcomes in the target community can be compared, is an alternative tool fraught with methodological and logistical problems. As a result, it is extremely difficult to say whether changes in individual or community circumstances are the result of the initiative itself or whether they would have occurred in the target population in any case.

Addressing the Challenge of Evaluating CCIs

The challenge of evaluating comprehensive community initiatives warrants the attention of practitioners, scholars, policymakers, funders, and initiative participants for three main reasons:

1. CCIs embody many of the most promising ideas to promote the well-being of disadvantaged individuals and communities in the United States today. A number of audiences—from national policymakers to individual community residents—have a stake in knowing whether and how CCIs work.

2. CCIs are testing a range of important hypotheses about individual development, family processes, and community dynamics. If the CCIs are well evaluated, the findings will have implications for our understanding of human behavior and will suggest important directions for further research as well as for broad policy directions.

3. CCIs offer an opportunity to expand and redefine the current boundaries of the field of evaluation, perhaps to address similar challenges posed by other complex, interactive, multi-system interventions. Evaluators are continually challenged to meet the demand for information—whether for accountability or for learning purposes—more effectively and efficiently. The evaluation of CCIs raises, in new and more complex ways, fundamental questions about how to ascertain the ways in which an investment of resources has "paid off."

Yet, at this time, the field is faced with enormous difficulties in making judgments about CCIs and in learning from them and other similarly complex interventions. This has several important consequences. First, knowledge is not being developed in a way that could inform new comprehensive programs or, at a broader level, guide the development of major new social policies. Second, CCI funders are not able to determine with any degree of certainty whether their initiatives are succeeding and merit continued investment. Third, program managers are not getting adequate information about how the initiatives are working and how to modify them in order to improve their impact. And finally, the communities themselves are receiving little feedback from the efforts that they are investing in the program.

The mismatch between prevailing evaluation approaches and the needs of CCIs has produced a situation where program designers, funders, and managers have been faced with imperfect options. One such option has been to limit the design and scope of the program by, for example, narrowing the program intervention and specifying a target population, in order to make it easier to evaluate. A second option has been to resist outcome-oriented evaluation out of a fear that current methodology will not do justice to a complex, nuanced, long-term intervention. In this case, monitoring events associated with the initiative serves as the principal source of information. A third option has been to accept measures or markers of progress that are not wholly satisfactory but may provide useful feedback. These include documenting "process" such as undertaking collaborative planning activities, measuring inputs, conducting selective interviews or focus-group discussions, establishing a community self-monitoring capacity, and selecting a few key indicators to track over time. In actuality, the CCIs have generally selected from the range of strategies presented in this third option, often combining two or more in an overall evaluation strategy that aims to give a textured picture of what is happening in the community, but may lack important information and analysis that inspires confidence in the scientific validity and generalizability of the results.

The Contribution of this Volume

Taken together, the papers in this volume suggest that CCIs are difficult to evaluate for reasons that relate both to the design of the initiatives themselves and to the state of evaluation methods and measures. They also suggest that work can be done on both fronts that will enhance our ability to learn from and to judge the effectiveness of CCIs and, ultimately, other social welfare interventions.

The first paper, by Alice O'Connor, puts today's CCIs and the problems of their evaluation in historical context by reviewing the experiences of the juvenile delinquency programs of the 1950s, the Gray Areas, Community Action and Model Cities programs, and the community development corporation movement. The next two papers focus on evaluation problems that emerge as a result of the complex design of CCIs and suggest new ways of approaching the task. Carol Weiss outlines the promise of CCI evaluations that are based on their own "theories of change" and discusses how such an approach would serve the multiple purposes of evaluation. James Connell, J. Lawrence Aber, and Gary Walker then present a conceptual framework, based on current social science research and theory, that could inform the program-based theories that Weiss describes. Both papers conclude that theory-based evaluation holds promise for CCIs. The next two papers address methodological problems associated with CCI evaluation. Robinson G. Hollister and Jennifer Hill focus on the absence of control groups or comparison communities for CCI evaluation purposes and discuss the problems that arise as a result. Claudia Coulton's paper focuses on measurement dilemmas. She describes some of the problems that she and her colleagues have had using community-level indicators in Cleveland and strategies they have adopted to assess community programs in that city. The final paper, by Prudence Brown, brings the volume to a close by recommending that evaluators take new roles with respect to CCIs, roles that engage the evaluator in the initiative more than has traditionally been the case.

EVALUATING COMPREHENSIVE COMMUNITY INITIATIVES: A VIEW FROM HISTORY

In the first paper, Alice O'Connor gives an historical context for the volume by critically reviewing where the field of evaluation and the field of comprehensive, community-based development have converged and diverged over the last three decades. She points out that it was in the 1960s that evaluation came to be recognized as a distinct research field and that an evaluation industry was born, strongly influenced by the "hard" sciences, in particular the traditional scientific search for quantifiable outcomes. The New Jersey Income Maintenance Experiment, launched in 1967, was the first of the large-scale controlled experiments, testing various versions of the package with randomly assigned individuals, and that experience informed a large number of subsequent social experiments that have had considerable policy impact, notably in the area of welfare reform.

The community-based social action programs that emerged during the same period, like today's CCIs, did not lend themselves to that type of evaluation. The documentary evidence from the social welfare and anti-poverty programs of the 1950s, 1960s, and 1970s reveals less attention to the programs' actual or potential impact on the urban problems they were designed to address than to generating knowledge about the origins of and remedies to unhealthy individual behavior or community environments, documenting changes in institutional relationships, and providing feedback to guide program implementation. Nonetheless, from the evaluations and other analyses produced at the time, O'Connor succeeds in drawing a number of important lessons for current CCIs, ranging from, for example, the difficulty in achieving public agency coordination, to the critical role of race, to addressing the tensions created when an initiative has long-term goals but needs to be able to demonstrate results in a relatively short time.

Throughout her paper, O'Connor cautions us that the barriers to developing effective evaluation strategies have been as much political and institutional as they have been substantive. Moreover, she warns: "[N]o matter how rigorous the scientific method, evaluative evidence will play only a limited—and sometimes unpredictable—role in determining the political fate of social programs. In the past, decisions about community-based initiatives—or about welfare reform, for that matter—have been driven not, primarily, by science but by the values, ideologies, and political interests of the major constituencies involved." As a result, she concludes with a strong recommendation that evaluations of today's initiatives focus on the "contextual factors" that influence their success or failure—that is, on identifying the economic, political, and other conditions at the federal and local levels under which CCIs can be most effective.

ADDRESSING DESIGN-RELATED DILEMMAS IN THE EVALUATION OF CCIs

Two of the papers in this volume—by Carol Weiss and by James Connell, J. Lawrence Aber, and Gary Walker—offer promising avenues for addressing some of the problems that emerge as a result of the complex objectives and designs of CCIs. Because CCIs are broad, multi-dimensional, and responsive to community circumstances, their design features are generally underspecified at the outset of the initiative. The absence of a well-specified and clearly defined intervention makes the evaluation task extremely difficult.

Carol Weiss posits that, even when the design is not clearly specified or linked to ultimate goals from the start, a large number of implicit "theories of change" underlie the decisions that program designers and funders have made in the process of launching CCIs. In her paper, Weiss challenges the CCI designer to be specific and clear about the premises, assumptions, hypotheses, or theories that guide decisions about the overall structure and specific components of the initiative. She suggests that once these theories are brought to the surface, they can drive the development of a plan for data collection and analysis that tracks the unfolding of events. Evaluation would then be based on whether the program theories hold during the course of the CCI. With this approach, testing the program's "theories of change" is offered as a means of assessing the progress and the impact of the intervention.

Weiss gives examples of the kinds of hypotheses that she sees underlying many of the CCIs: a relatively modest amount of money will make a significant difference in the community; the involvement of local citizens is a necessary component of an effective program; the neighborhood is a unit that makes sense for improving services and opportunities; comprehensiveness of services is indispensable; and benefits provided to an individual family member accrue to the entire family. In each case, she shows how those hypotheses can be played out through a series of micro steps to a set of desired ends. The types of data that an evaluator would need to collect in order to confirm the underlying theory become clear, as do the points at which specific hypotheses can be tested.

Weiss offers four reasons for pursuing theory-based evaluation for CCIs. First, it provides guidance about the key aspects of the program on which to focus scarce evaluation resources. Second, CCIs are not only attempting to test the merits of particular configurations of services, economic development activities, and so forth—they are also testing a broader set of assumptions about the combination and concentration of efforts that are required to make significant and sustained improvements in the lives of disadvantaged people. Theory-based evaluation will tell whether those assumptions, on which many specific program decisions are based, are valid and, if they are not, where they break down. Third, this approach to evaluation helps participants in the initiative reflect on their assumptions, examine the validity and practicality of those assumptions, and ensure that a common understanding exists about the theories that are being put into practice. Fourth, Weiss suggests that validating—or disproving—fundamental theories of change has the potential to powerfully affect major policy directions.

While Weiss's paper contains examples of some of the theories of change that underlie the *structural* or *operational dimensions* of current CCIs, the next paper, by Connell, Aber, and Walker, complements Weiss's suggestions by demonstrating how current thinking and research in the social sciences can inform the development of the theories of change that underlie the *program dimensions* of initiatives. The authors present a framework for understanding how community dimensions affect outcomes for individuals both directly and indirectly. The paper focuses on young adolescents as a case, but the framework that the authors present can and will be applied to future research on young children and families and on older youth as well.

The authors identify and define three desired outcomes for youth: economic self-sufficiency, healthy family and social relationships, and good citizenship practices. They review social science research on factors influencing those outcomes and conclude that community variables— physical and demographic characteristics, economic opportunity structure, institutional capacities, and social exchange and symbolic processes—affect the outcomes, directly in some cases, but mostly indirectly through their effects on social mediators and developmental processes. The key developmental processes are defined as learning to be productive, learning to connect, and learning to navigate. According to the authors, recent research has made considerable progress in demonstrating how the social mediators of family, peers, and other adults affect those developmental processes and ultimately the desired outcomes for youth.

By organizing and presenting the research in this way, the authors can spin their general theory of change into ever-more specific micro steps that give guidance for program design. As an example, they focus attention on the part of the framework that addresses the relationships between youth and adults and they demonstrate how program decisions would be made based on the framework's hypothesized pathways.

Thus, the research-based framework that Connell, Aber, and Walker present can help guide program designers in developing their theories and thereby facilitate the evaluation task. Moreover, this basic research can also help spur progress on some of the current challenges to developing the measures that could be used to track CCI activities and outcomes.

DETERMINING AND MEASURING THE EFFECTS OF CCIs

The Absence of a Comparison Community or Control Group

Evaluators point to a fundamental problem in the evaluation of CCIs: it is virtually impossible to establish a "counterfactual" to a comprehensive community initiative—that is, to set up a situation that would permit an evaluator to know what would have happened in the same community in the absence of the intervention. As Hollister and Hill note in their paper, the traditional approach to evaluation compares outcomes for the population that is affected by the initiative with outcomes in communities that do not receive the initiative and, from that comparison, draws conclusions about its effects. The way to obtain the best comparison, closest to what the situation would have been in the same community without the initiative, is through random assignment of similar communities either to receive the intervention or to serve as "controls." Hollister and Hill refer to random assignment as the "nectar of the gods" and say that "once you've had a taste of the pure stuff it is hard to settle for the flawed alternatives." Researchers, the policy community, and funders have come to expect the high standards of validity associated with experimentation. However, funders have not selected communities for CCIs randomly, nor are they likely to do so in the future, and in any case appropriate communities are too few in number and CCIs are too idiosyncratic to justify randomization at the community level. Another traditional approach is random assignment of individuals within a community to treatment and control groups (or alternative treatment groups), as a way to draw valid conclusions about the impact of the intervention. Yet, since CCIs aim to affect all residents in the community—and many CCIs depend on this "saturation" to build support for the initiative—random assignment of individuals is not an option.

In their paper, Hollister and Hill examine alternative approaches for establishing a counterfactual that might have relevance for the evaluation of community-wide initiatives—such as constructing comparison groups of individuals, selecting comparison communities, and examining the community pre- and post-intervention—and assess the experience of various experiments that have used these alternative approaches. They conclude that none of these alternatives serves as an adequate counterfactual, "primarily because individuals and communities are changing all the time with respect to the measured outcome even in the absence of any intentional intervention." Moreover, little effort has been made up to this point to develop a statistical model of community and community change that might serve as a theoretical counterfactual.

Hollister and Hill conclude that there are no clear second-best methods for obtaining accurate assessments of the impact of a community-wide intervention. They turn their attention, instead, to steps that can be taken to facilitate the development of better methods of CCI evaluation. In particular, they point to the need for high-quality information about how communities evolve over time through, for example, better small-area data, improved community-records data, panel studies of communities, and better measures of social networks and community institutions. Such improvements would not only assist evaluators on the ground, but would also help researchers understand and model community-level variables. In time, a statistical model of a community undergoing "ordinary" change might be able to serve as an appropriate comparison for communities undergoing planned interventions.

Identifying and Measuring Outcomes

Documenting outcomes and attributing them to the intervention should be, of course, a key element of any evaluation. For those who believe in the promise of CCIs, the challenge is to demonstrate with some degree of certainty that they are achieving positive change within a time frame that assures continued financial investment on the part of public and private funders and continued personal investment on the part of staff and community residents.

But, as all of the papers in this volume suggest, CCIs are operating at so many levels (individual, family, community, institutional, and system) and across so many sectors that the task of defining outcomes that can show whether the initiatives are working has become formidable. Although a number of indicators are currently in use to assess the impact on individuals of services and supports, many key child, youth, and adult outcomes are still not appropriately measured, and indicators of family- and community-level outcomes are poor. Those problems are compounded in CCIs by the fact that, although they seek long-term change, short-term markers of progress—for example, interim outcomes, measures of institutional and system reform, and indicators of community capacity—are important for sustaining commitment to the initiatives. Finally, even if appropriate measures could be defined, CCI evaluators encounter a range of obstacles in devising cost-effective and nonintrusive ways of obtaining accurate data and in ensuring compatibility of data that come from various sources.

Claudia Coulton discusses the data dilemmas in some detail in her paper. She writes from her experience working with existing community-level indicators in Cleveland and points out the conceptual, methodological, and practical challenges associated with using them. She also describes the strategies that she and her colleagues have adopted to obtain information, in spite of those constraints, that have been useful in the design and evaluation of community initiatives, with special attention to indicators of child well-being. She focuses on two kinds of measures: outcome-oriented and contextually oriented measures.

When *outcome-oriented indicators* are sought, communities are treated as units for measuring the status of resident individuals according to various social, economic, health, and developmental outcomes. At the community level, these kinds of data are most likely found in agency records and other administrative sources. The types of measures that are most readily available relate to the health and safety of children and can be obtained from sources such as birth and death certificates, official reports of child maltreatment, trauma registries in hospitals, and police departments. Measures of social development are more difficult, but Coulton reports success using teen childbearing rates, delinquency rates derived from court records, and teen drug violation arrest rates from police department records. Measures of cognitive development can be developed for communities in collaboration with the local school system. The economic status of families can best be obtained from the census, but, because the census is decennial, Coulton and her colleagues have been working to develop a model for estimating poverty rates in noncensus years using variables derived from Aid to Families with Dependent Children (AFDC) and food stamp use.

Contextually oriented indicators include measures of community structure and process, such as overall income levels or the presence or absence of strong social support networks, that are presumed to affect resident children and families either positively or negatively. As a result, they are particularly relevant for the evaluation of CCIs. Unfortunately, the sources for these types of indicators at the community level are limited. Many come from the census and are therefore only available in ten-year intervals. This is especially true for information about economic status.

Coulton explains the potential relevance of information about the age and family structures of a community, residential mobility, environmental stress as measured by such indicators as vacant and boarded houses, and incidence of personal crime. She also stresses the importance of seeking data that describe not only the negative but also the positive contextual influence of communities such as supports for effective parenting and community resources for children.

Coulton describes a range of other community-level data problems, including disagreement about the geographic boundaries for a community and reporting bias in agency data, and concludes her paper with a set of recommendations for improving community-level indicators. She argues for community residents and leaders to be involved in designing the appropriate geographic units to be studied and the types of indicators that should be sought, and for mechanisms that make the information accessible and usable to community residents.

THE PURPOSE OF EVALUATION
AND THE ROLE OF THE EVALUATOR

The complex nature of comprehensive community initiatives and the state of the field of evaluation combine to suggest a reconsideration of the objectives of CCI evaluations and of the role of the CCI evaluator. All of the papers in this volume touch upon this issue, and the last paper, by Prudence Brown, addresses it directly. A brief review of the key purposes and audiences that evaluations are meant to serve will help to set the stage for the direction that Brown recommends in her paper.

A main purpose of evaluation is *impact assessment*. All who are involved in an initiative—most especially the funders who are investing their money and the community members and staff who are investing their time and energy—have a need to know the degree to which it is working.

Accountability is a second purpose of evaluation, and this may become increasingly important if the call for decategorization of funds and devolution of authority to the local level is successful. In this case, there would likely be a trade-off between more flexible funding schemes and increased accountability, especially for outcomes (Gardner, forthcoming).

A third purpose aims to ensure that lessons from experiments are learned in a systematic way so that they can be applied to the next generation of policies, programs, and research. Alice O'Connor points out that history suggests that this process of *social learning* through evaluation is uncertain. Yet, this purpose of evaluation is particularly relevant for CCIs because they represent the operation of a new generation of social ideas.

Fourth, if an evaluation is so designed, it can become a program component of a CCI and serve the initiative's goals through *community building*. The right kind of evaluation can build the capacity of initiative participants to design and institutionalize a self-assessment process and, through that, support an ongoing collaborative process of change.

Prudence Brown's paper focuses on yet another purpose of evaluation that has become increasingly important in today's CCIs: evaluation can play an important "formative" function, affording a way to examine the ongoing implementation of the initiative and providing *information for mid-course correction* that can strengthen the initiative's chances for success. Because CCIs are new and experimental, evaluators are being called upon more and more to perform this function.

Brown's paper reviews the pros and cons of a more participatory role for the evaluator and concludes that a greater-than-normal degree of engagement in these multifaceted community initiatives is warranted. Indeed, it may be inevitable, since the multiple tasks with which the evaluator is likely to be charged cannot be performed well without meaningful interaction with the initiative participants. These tasks include defining and articulating the underlying theories of change, tracking and documenting the implementation of the initiative, identifying interim and long-term outcome measures to assess its effectiveness, collecting the relevant data, determining whether outcomes can be ascribed to the intervention, and analyzing the implications for the field. Brown notes, however, that this high degree of involvement in the initiative does not "release the evaluator from the right or obligation both to maintain high standards of scientific inquiry and to make judgments and recommendations as warranted," and suggests that funders, especially funders of multi-site initiatives, should experiment with different methods for obtaining the highest-quality information.

CONCLUSION

We believe that the readers of this volume will come away feeling hopeful. The broad conclusion of this set of papers is that CCIs represent an important and promising opportunity to test the best of what we believe has been learned from recent social programs and economic development efforts to improve the lives of children and families: (1) they combine the social, economic, and physical spheres; (2) they recognize the critical role of "community-building" and community participation; (3) at the same time, they recognize that poor communities need financial, political, and technical resources that lie outside the community; (4) they recognize that improvements in the public sector's systems of support must be complemented by private- and nonprofit-sector activities; (5) they recognize that the changes that are sought will require sustained investment over a long period of time.

Taken together, the papers in this volume convey the following messages.

To the **program designers**, they say: You are on the right track. Working simultaneously on a variety of fronts seems to offer the greatest promise of success. But, comprehensiveness should not be a cover for imprecision or for the absence of rigorous thinking. You still need to be clear about your goals and about your theories of change. You need to articulate your theories to all who are involved in the initiative. You need to be able to use negotiation around your theories as a vehicle for engaging all stakeholders in the process. And you need the theories to serve as the foundation for your evaluation.

To the **methodologists**, they say: We understand that random assignment is the best way to control for selection bias and gives you the greatest confidence in ruling out alternative, nonprogram-related explanations for how an outcome was achieved. But, given the nature and magnitude of the problem that we are trying to combat, we cannot limit our research questions and programmatic approaches to those for which random-assignment demonstration research is best suited. We are prepared to redefine standards of certainty in a search for meaningful answers to more relevant, complex, and multi-dimensional questions, and we need your help. But we are not coming empty-handed. We offer sound and well-articulated theories to inform the conversation. You can help us give our theories of change a scientific and more formal representation. You can also help us develop the measures to track whether our theories are holding up and encourage the collection of relevant data. Finally, you have an important role to play in legitimizing theory-based evaluation to the policy and funding communities.

To the **program evaluators**, they say: Your role is dramatically different in this new generation of interventions. You are part of the team that will work to define the program theory and you need to develop the tools that will facilitate that process. You will also need to develop valid measures of an initiative's success and help negotiate agreement on them among stakeholders. Your measures can certainly include input and process dimensions, but you also need to focus on outcomes. You need to develop methods to analyze both quantitative and qualitative data in a way that will deliver scientifically credible conceptual and statistical information on an initiative's progress. And your methods need to be cost-effective and respectful of those who are being evaluated.

To the **social science research community**, they say: You have told us quite a bit about the critical features of services, supports, and interventions that lead to improved outcomes for children and youth. But we need to know more about families. And we need much more information about communities, especially about how disadvantaged communities function and evolve and what it means to "build" a community. You must help us understand what the mediating factors are between the environment and family and individual outcomes, and how to influence them. This includes knowing much more about the elements that work best together to reinforce a trend toward positive outcomes and the conditions under which they are most likely to succeed.

To the **funding and policy community**, they say: You need to continue to press for evidence that the initiative is accomplishing the objectives for which it has been funded, but you must be mindful of the fact that significant change takes a long time. You need to become comfortable with the fact that the efforts that you fund may be necessary but not sufficient to achieve improved outcomes. For this reason, you should be thinking creatively about how several initiatives in the same community, operating under separate auspices and supported by separate funding, might be encouraged to agree to be held jointly accountable for achieving improved outcomes that none could achieve alone. You also need to re-assess your standards of "certainty" and "elegance" in evaluations of these initiatives, because your pressures for evaluations to conform to a narrow set of methods may not only distort program design and operations but may also suppress information that is both rigorous and relevant. Finally, of all the stakeholders in these efforts, you are best placed to influence the larger environments and conditions that bear upon an initiative's likelihood of success, and you should focus your energies in that direction.

◊   ◊   ◊   ◊   ◊

With the above messages in mind, what should be the next steps for the Roundtable's Steering Committee on Evaluation and for the larger community of individuals and organizations working directly with CCIs and on their evaluation? This volume suggests work on several fronts.

We need to work with program designers, funders, managers, and participants to identify and articulate both the programmatic and operational theories of change, whether explicit or implicit, that are guiding their efforts. We also need to construct frameworks, based on current theory and research findings, that lay out, as specifically as possible, the ways in which community-level and individual-level variables are known to affect one another. These two lines of information can then be brought together to develop richer and more specific "theories of change" about how to effect meaningful improvement in the lives of residents of disadvantaged communities, theories that are solidly grounded in both practice and research and that can guide evaluation strategies.

Development of evaluation methods would then focus on (1) tracking the extent to which CCIs put their assumptions into practice and (2) identifying and analyzing the linkages between CCI activities and desired outcomes. We must seek to identify the data, qualitative and quantitative, that will be necessary to indicate advancement on both of those dimensions as well as promising new strategies for analyzing those data. And finally, these "new" approaches need to be applied to operating initiatives to ascertain how well they serve the purposes of assessing impact, ensuring accountability, encouraging social learning, and guiding program modification and improvement.

The Roundtable's Evaluation Committee plans to pursue the implications of these papers in the year ahead and hopes that their publication will enable many other interested individuals and agencies to do so as well. The Roundtable welcomes comments, suggestions, and accounts of experience that could contribute to this process.

NOTE

The authors wish to thank Alice O'Connor, Robert Granger, and J. Lawrence Aber for their helpful comments on earlier drafts.

REFERENCES

American Writing Corporation. 1992. "Building Strong Communities: Strategies for Urban Change." Report of a conference sponsored by the Annie E. Casey Foundation, Ford Foundation, and Rockefeller Foundation, Cleveland, Ohio, May 1992.

Chynoweth, Judith K., Lauren Cook, Michael Campbell, and Barbara R. Dyer. 1992. "Experiments in Systems Change: States Implement Family Policy." Final Report to the Ford Foundation and United Way of America. Washington, DC: Council of Governors' Policy Advisors.

Eisen, Arlene. 1992. "A Report on Foundations' Support for Comprehensive Neighborhood-Based Community-Empowerment Initiatives." Report sponsored by East Bay Funders, the Ford Foundation, The New York Community Trust, the Piton Foundation, and the Riley Foundation, March 1992.

Fishman, N., and M. Phillips. 1993. "A Review of Comprehensive Collaborative Persistent Poverty Initiatives." Paper prepared for the Poverty Task Force of the Donor's Forum of Chicago, June 1993. Mimeographed.

Gardner, Sid. 1992. "Elements and Contexts of Community-Based, Cross-Systems Reforms." Paper prepared for Discussion by the Roundtable on Effective Services [now the Roundtable on Comprehensive Community Initiatives for Children and Families], October 1992. Mimeographed.

_____. Forthcoming. "Reform Options for the Intergovernmental Funding System: Decategorization Policy Issues." Roundtable on Comprehensive Community Initiatives for Children and Families, Working Paper No.1. Queenstown, Md.: The Aspen Institute.

Halpern, Robert. 1994. "Historical Perspectives on Neighborhood-Based Strategies to Address Poverty-Related Social Problems." Paper prepared for the University Seminar on Children and Their Families in Big Cities, Columbia University, New York, April 11, 1994. Mimeographed.

Himmelman, Arthur T. 1992. "Communities Working Collaboratively for a Change." Minneapolis: The Himmelman Consulting Group. Mimeographed.

Jenny, Patricia. 1993. "Community Building Initiatives: A Scan of Comprehensive Neighborhood Revitalization Programs." Paper prepared for The New York Community Trust, New York City, September 1993. Mimeographed.

Rosewater, Ann. 1992. "Comprehensive Approaches for Children and Families: A Philanthropic Perspective." Washington, DC: Council on Foundations.

Rosewater, Ann, Joan Wynn, et al. 1993. "Community-focused Reforms Affecting Children and Families: Current Foundation Initiatives and Opportunities for the MacArthur Foundation." Paper prepared by the Chapin Hall Center for Children, University of Chicago, April 1993. Mimeographed.

Schorr, Lisbeth B. 1988. *Within Our Reach: Breaking the Cycle of Disadvantage.* With Daniel Schorr. New York: Doubleday.

Sherwood, Kay. 1994. "Comprehensive Community Planning Initiatives: A List of Foundation-Sponsored Projects." Paper prepared for the Foundation for Child Development and the Chicago Community Trust, December 1994. Mimeographed.

Stagner, Matthew. 1993. "Elements and Contexts of Community-based Cross-systems Reform: An Update." Paper prepared for Discussion by the Roundtable on Effective Services [now the Roundtable on Comprehensive Community Initiatives for Children and Families], October 1993. Mimeographed.

Evaluating Comprehensive Community Initiatives: A View from History

Alice O'Connor

Although both community-based initiatives[1] and evaluation research have been prominent in the fight against poverty since the 1960s, they have taken distinctly divergent paths over the past three decades. Evaluation research has grown steadily in prestige since the 1960s, its results featured prominently in debates over the Family Support Act of 1988 (Wiseman et al. 1991; Manski and Garfinkel 1992). The field built its reputation for scientific objectivity and policy relevance on experimental design and has been preoccupied with its requisites: finite, measurable program goals; discernible program components; the ability to control for internal and contextual contingencies; and generalizability across locality. Community-based initiatives, in contrast, have been largely abandoned by the federal government, left to rely on foundations and other private sources for their chief means of support. If anything, these initiatives have increased their emphasis on the "intangibles" of community building such as strengthened social bonds, their conviction that the whole of the intervention is more than the sum of its parts, and their determination to become immersed in the needs and strengths unique to their communities. While groups such as the Roundtable continue to search for appropriate evaluation methodologies, a deep-seated skepticism persists in policy circles about the efficacy of community-based initiatives.

This paper explores the roots of this impasse—and, perhaps, some ways out of it—in an examination of past experience in evaluating a variety

23

of community-based initiatives designed to combat poverty. It starts out by discussing the historical relationship between community-based initiatives, social scientific knowledge, and policy, and then reviews past evaluation strategies to examine what has been learned, both about the capacity of community-based initiatives to combat poverty and about the institutional and political capacity to learn from their experience. This review indicates that past evaluation efforts have yielded important findings and insights about community-based initiatives. At the same time, it serves as a reminder that evaluation is conducted within a political context, in which decisions are driven more by values, political interests, and ideology than they are by scientific evidence (Aaron 1978). Moreover, the practice of evaluation is itself a profoundly political and value-laden process, involving judgments about the validity of program objectives and choices about how progress can be measured (Weiss 1993). Recognizing the political nature of evaluation does not mean that evaluators cannot come up with valid assessments of program effectiveness. However, it does suggest that evaluators need to be aware of the context within which they are conducting their work, the function that evaluation can and should play in programs and policies, and the values and assumptions that they themselves bring to the evaluative enterprise. Finally, an analysis of the historical record points to the questions that have not been asked as well as those that have been asked in past evaluation efforts, and points to issues that will need to be addressed in efforts to create more effective evaluative paradigms for community-based initiatives.

COMMUNITY INITIATIVES, KNOWLEDGE, AND POLICY

Community-based initiatives and evaluation research can be seen as two different strands of an approach to social change that relies on the purposeful application of knowledge—whether knowledge takes the form of experience, scientific investigation, or both—as a strategy for social improvement. Long before evaluation research existed as a field within the social sciences, community reformers regarded their efforts as social experiments, part of the process of accumulating knowledge about the nature of social problems and their solution (Bremner 1956; Carson 1990; Davis 1984). Similarly, in its earliest years American social science was motivated by the cause of social reform (Haskell 1977). Community-based interventions and evaluation research have also been shaped by similar historical forces and processes, three of which have been especially important in their evolution as separate fields: professionalization, which has contributed to increased specialization in the production of knowledge on the one hand and in the design and implementation of social welfare programs on the other; the growth of the welfare state and the new demands for knowledge it created; and changes in the social, economic, and political context within which both community-based interventions and evaluation have been developed. The shaping influence of these historical forces can be seen in a brief overview of community-based social change efforts, and their changing relationship to knowledge and policy, since the late nineteenth and early twentieth centuries.

Community-Based Initiatives

Comprehensive community intervention has been used as a strategy for responding to a variety of social problems since the Progressive Era, and its history encompasses such diverse efforts as the settlement house movement, neighborhood-based projects to combat juvenile delinquency in the 1930s and again in the 1950s, the Community Action and Model Cities programs during the War on Poverty, and the wide range of community-based economic development projects, including community development corporations (CDCs), that have emerged in recent decades (Halpern 1994). What links these diverse initiatives together is a set of assumptions and operating principles that have proved remarkably stable in the face of changing circumstances. These include:

- *An analysis of social problems that emphasizes their environmental origins, their complexity, and their interrelatedness:* Over the course of the twentieth century, environmentalist explanations have pointed to a number of external factors to explain social inequality and behavioral "pathology," some more difficult to measure than others. Thus, economic and social conditions, neighborhood environment, family structure and processes, and group culture have all been identified as explanatory factors. In the face of the periodic resurgence of eugenic and other biologically based explanations for inequality, those who adhere to environmentalist explanations have insisted that individual and group differences stem from outside forces and hence are susceptible to intervention.

• *A recognition of the importance of the geographically bounded area, whether rural small town or urban neighborhood, as the basis of communal social bonds, as a manageable landscape for achieving social reform, as a laboratory for social experimentation, and as a legitimate unit for social scientific analysis:* At times these functions have overlapped or co-existed in tension with one another within the ideological framework of community-based social reform.

• *An emphasis on institutions as key leverage points for stimulating change, both in individuals and in society at large:* The institutional approach has taken two main forms in community-based reform movements. One, exemplified by the settlements and by community action agencies in the 1960s, embraces institutional innovation as a goal, and often establishes new or "parallel" institutions in order to stimulate innovation. The other works within existing institutions, often the school, to reform or coordinate institutional practices. The emphasis on institutions stems in part from the need to steer a path between individual and social change goals, from the conviction that existing institutions are not set up to address local needs, and from a desire to make lasting changes in the community.

• *A faith in knowledge as the basis of planning, public education, and learning for the sake of social betterment:* This, too, has been expressed in many different ways in community-based initiatives, with some quite consciously basing their programs on social science theory and evaluation, and others relying on experience.

• *A belief that the isolation of the poor is a key factor in causing and perpetuating poverty and social inequality:* Concepts of social isolation have expressed themselves in many different ways in the history of community-based intervention—middle-class settlement workers or "neighbors" saw their presence in poor communities as a form of cultural uplift for the poor; initiatives based on organizing and empowerment strategies have sought to combat the political isolation of poor communities. In those and other forms, the concept of social isolation can be linked to a strategy that embraces the principle of local participation as a means of individual transformation, of transcending social differences, and of building essential resources from within the community.

Applied in various ways, primarily in low-income urban settings, these principles and assumptions have translated into an approach to social change that seeks to be comprehensive, firmly rooted in the community, participatory, and informed by accumulated knowledge, either in the form of ongoing research or experience (Davis 1984; Trolander 1987; Carson 1990; Bremner 1956; Halpern 1994). And yet, this characterization perhaps suggests more coherence in action principles than actually was there. In fact, community-based initiatives have historically faced persistent dilemmas—balancing individual with social change objectives, revitalizing poor communities while increasing outward mobility for residents, combining the requisites of social experimentation with immediate community priorities—that have caused some ambiguity in defining objectives and designing programs.

Community-based initiatives have undergone important changes over the course of the twentieth century. In earlier decades, they were tied to local reform movements and often worked through nongovernmental institutions (NGOs). Beginning in the 1950s, community-based initiatives were linked more directly to efforts to reform urban governing structures, which were seen as too narrow and fragmented to deal with the complex of changes brought about by "metropolitanization." Reacting to the "bricks and mortar" and downtown business orientation of federal urban renewal policy, advocates of the approach known as "community action" called attention to the "human face" of redevelopment and insisted on a reorientation of the bureaucracy to respond to the needs of the inner-city poor. That led to a series of experiments designed to stimulate local government reform—often from a position outside of local governing structures—which were eventually absorbed into the War on Poverty (O'Connor, forthcoming). The 1970s marked a retreat from looking to reformed governing institutions as "change agents" and devolution to the states and localities for dealing with community needs. This period also featured a turn to market forces as instruments of reform, as government looked for ways to "privatize" service delivery and CDCs formed public/private alliances to create markets in ghetto neighborhoods. Those trends have continued into the 1990s.

The past three decades have also brought important changes in the role and production of knowledge related to community-based initiatives. One of the most important changes has been the emergence of national sponsorship for community-based reform, and with it the emergence of national audiences for the results of evaluation. Thus, from the Progressive Era through the 1920s the application of community-based social research was, for the most part, immediate and localized (although widely recognized reform-movement leaders such as Jane Addams did reach a national audience) (Carson 1990). Gradually, under the auspices of the emerging social work profession and New Deal initiatives, the use of social scientific theory to plan and evaluate local community-based programs for a national audience began to take hold (Trolander 1987). The Chicago Area Project, for example, combined social work practice with sociological theories of neighborhood ecology to train neighborhood workers and community organizers for juvenile delinquency prevention programs. Launched by Clifford Shaw of the Illinois Institute for Juvenile Justice and sociologist Ernest Burgess of the University of Chicago, the Project grew out of a decade's worth of "Chicago School" research on poor neighborhoods, which convinced Shaw that delinquency could be tied to a breakdown or weakness in neighborhood socializing institutions, especially the family, brought about by pressures from the industrial economy and immigration. Informed by this theoretical perspective, the Project targeted three neighborhoods, and focused its efforts on developing capacity in existing and newly established neighborhood institutions to respond to delinquency and provide alternative activities for gang-prone youth. In a practice that would later be replicated in anti-delinquency programs of the 1950s, the Project recruited "curbstone counsellors"—young male graduate students or former delinquents "gone straight"—to act as role models and mentors for local youth. Though not formally evaluated in terms of the outcomes it produced, the Project provided models for replication and was used as evidence to bolster the ecological theories that would inform the next generation of community-based initiatives (Halpern 1994). In this sense, the Project could be seen as an experiment in the application of social scientific theory to human problems, as well as in delinquency prevention practice. Some of the New Deal agencies, such as the Farm Security Administration, also sponsored community-based experiments that were grounded in social scientific theory (Gilbert 1994; Kirkendall 1966; Baldwin 1968).

With a growing emphasis on using community-based initiatives as demonstration experiments for national policies, the 1950s ushered in a transformative period in the use of research, placing greater importance on learning for the sake of widespread replication, and introducing new, less community-based standards for evaluating program success. Local demonstrations in juvenile delinquency prevention, housing, and mental health services were funded by the National Institute of Mental Health, the Children's Bureau, and other federal agencies to inform national policy initiatives. Major foundations also funded demonstration projects in areas such as education reform with an eye to learning for the sake of national policy (Lageman 1989). Reflecting the growing faith in scientific knowledge that characterized the immediate post-World War II years, social science became a more important component of these centrally orchestrated local demonstration projects: beyond informing the initiatives, social scientists would be part of the national planning team as program monitors, evaluators, and liaisons with the outside funders. At the same time, social science would be called upon to judge programs according to standards generated by the national funders: Did the initiative address a problem of national significance? Could it be replicated? Did it achieve the outcomes funders were reaching for? As evaluation came to be associated with "outside" priorities, local administrators became more skeptical about its value for their indigenous concerns.

Evaluation:
Policy, Science, and Politics

In addition to changes in the nature, purposes, and sources of support for community-based initiatives, developments in policymaking, in the social sciences, and in the politics of evaluating social action programs were also important to the changing relationship between research and community-based programs. Beginning in the 1960s, the introduction of a new federal planning and budget system, the shaping of evaluation as a science, and the political use of evaluation in legislative battles over social welfare together created an environment that favored the development of quantitative experimental design techniques and discouraged sustained attention to theories and methods—including ethnographic, combined quantitative/qualitative, comparative case studies, and theory-based techniques—that might have contributed to better understanding of comprehensive community-based initiatives.

During the New Deal and continuing throughout the post-WWII years, federal government expanded into the unfamiliar terrain of social welfare, steadily escalating the demand for social scientific expertise while also making new demands on knowledge. Evaluation became part of program planning in several New Deal agencies, taking the form of program monitoring and, in a smaller number of cases, impact assessment using control groups (Deutscher, n.d.). It was not until the 1960s, however, when the Johnson Administration mandated the adoption of the Planning-Programming-Budgeting System (PPBS) in all executive branch agencies, that the policy environment became ripe for more widespread use of the experimental, outcomes-oriented research that is most often associated with scientific evaluation. This bureaucracy-wide introduction of PPBS was an attempt to introduce rationality and long-range planning into the otherwise chaotic annual budget process. Following detailed instructions and strict timetables set by the Bureau of the Budget, each agency was to establish an internal process for "setting goals, defining objectives, and developing planned programs for achieving those objectives" as "integral parts of preparing and justifying a budget submission" (Bureau of the Budget 1965, 1). This system placed a premium on cost-benefit analysis of existing programs as well as on the range of alternative programs, on "objectives and planned accomplishments" expressed in "*quantitative* non-financial terms," and, above all, on an "output-oriented . . . program structure . . . which presents data on all of the operations and activities of the agency in categories which reflect the agency's end purposes or objectives" (Bureau of the Budget 1965, 2, 6; emphasis in original). Increasingly, this process would be handled at the agency level by separate divisions for research, planning, and program evaluation, staffed by social scientists or career bureaucrats who were one step removed from actual program administration; indeed, PPBS assumed "[t]he existence in each agency of an *Analytic* capability which carries out continuing in-depth analyses by permanent specialized staffs of the agency's objectives and its various programs to meet these objectives" (Bureau of the Budget 1965, 2; emphasis in original). Evaluation, once informal and often carried out by program staff or locally hired consultants if at all, would now be recognized as a separate function, to be undertaken by professionally trained social scientists using scientific methods. Moreover, PPBS demanded a particular *kind* of evaluation: focused on program outcomes rather than processes, stated in quantitative terms, analyzed in categories that corresponded with policy goals that were generated from the top.

Partly fueled by the expansion of government demand for evaluation, it was also in the 1960s that evaluation became more widely recognized as a distinct research field, informed by theoretical frameworks and, eventually, undergirded by a set of institutions devoted to evaluation training and practice (Rossi 1994). Reflecting a more generalized social scientific tendency to emulate the "hard" sciences, the social science research community responded to the growing policy demand for quantitative outcomes research by adapting the methods of controlled experimentation that had been developed over several decades and applied in engineering and psychological research after World War II, and that had been used in educational research beginning in the 1920s (Haveman 1987; Campbell and Stanley 1966). The idea behind the experimental approach was to approximate a laboratory setting as closely as possible, so that analysts could establish the cause and effect of particular interventions with some precision and with a measure of statistical validity. In the absence of ideal laboratory conditions, wherein researchers can manipulate most of the variables, evaluations of human interventions became an exercise in control: establishing comparable "control" groups to determine what would happen in the absence of intervention; "controlling" for contextual factors or natural processes not directly tied to the intervention; keeping careful control over sampling, measurement, testing, and other evaluative techniques to avoid the introduction of bias. More important than understanding the management and substantive program content of the interventions was the ability to identify a measurable set of inputs and a corresponding set of outputs. Such "black box" evaluations would have little to say about how and under what conditions programs were implemented, nor much about the configuration of components within the intervention. They were designed to answer, that is to say, exactly the questions that were assuming priority in the policy world of PPBS.

Of course, quantitative experimental design was not without critics among evaluation practitioners, and was by no means the only method used in the profession. Mirroring similar disputes in the social sciences, advocates of more qualitative approaches criticized quantitative researchers for their positivist assumptions and de-contextualized world view (Rossi 1994; Quane 1994). Even the most steadfast practitioners of experimental design became more realistic about its limitations, and began to develop more flexible, "quasi-experimental" techniques while also calling for theory-based and combined qualitative/quantitative approaches (Weiss 1972a; Cook and Campbell 1979; Quane 1994). Evaluators' experience in assessing the social action programs of the 1960s could only reinforce this tendency toward flexibility, by underscoring the mismatch between experimental theory and program reality: program goals were complicated and hard to measure; local administrators were often uncooperative; true experimental design was politically if not technically impossible; and the results were used out of context and for political purposes (Weiss 1972b; Rossi and Williams 1972). The findings from early social action program evaluation were no more encouraging: program impacts, if positive at all, were small when compared to program costs. These findings caused particular dilemmas for evaluators who, committed to program objectives, were unable to substantiate their convictions with the hard numbers policymakers were asking for (Weiss 1993).

If such doubts might have created an opportunity for developing more integrated methods for evaluating community-based social action programs, the political realities of evaluating Great Society programs quickly squelched it. In efforts to keep control over the new social programs, Congressional monitors, too, discovered the merits of cost-benefit accounting and quantitative outcomes-oriented evaluation. Soon after the War on Poverty was launched and with increasing regularity thereafter, legislators began to mandate regular evaluation—even specifying the use of control groups and experimental design as a condition of continued funding. Social scientists invested their intellectual capital in the kind of research that would have a payoff in policy circles, developing quantitative and experimental techniques for use in negative income-tax experiments, employment and training research, and, beginning in the early 1970s, welfare reform schemes designed to combine work and welfare. Both within and outside the profession, the political constituency for evaluation research was built around the large-scale, experimental approach, and power was ceded to the "quants" (Rossi 1994). With the help of foundations and federal contracts, a substantial research industry was created to carry out this type of research. As funding agencies retreated from community action, evaluators had little reason to develop and gain scientific legitimacy for qualitative, process-oriented, and theory-based methods that would be more appropriate for evaluating community-based initiatives.

PAST EVALUATION EFFORTS

Despite the divergent paths taken by research and community action, much of contemporary value can be learned from past experiences with evaluating community-based social programs. In addition to some important findings about the potential of local initiatives in the fight against poverty, a selective review of evaluations over the past three decades says a great deal about the function and politics of evaluation, underscoring the point that the job of the evaluator is complex and multi-layered. (See Prudence Brown's chapter in this volume.) And although evaluators have not exactly made great methodological or theoretical inroads in their approach to comprehensive, community-based programs over the past thirty years, the variety of approaches that have been used is indicative of the methods and critical issues that must be pursued in future efforts. In addition, a review of past experience highlights some crucial questions that have been raised but not pursued by evaluation—and must be if the current generation of reformers is going to learn about whether and how community initiatives can achieve what they set out to do.

Evaluation as "Social Learning":
Gray Areas and Juvenile Delinquency

In the mid-1950s the Ford Foundation initiated a series of experiments in urban areas, the capstone of which was the "Gray Areas" program started in 1961. These experiments grew out of the Foundation's effort to respond to the "urban crisis" brought about by deindustrialization, white middle-class suburbanization, and the massive in-migration of poor minorities. They were variously designed to promote metropolitan governance and planning structures, create new community-based mechanisms for dealing with juvenile delinquency, increase the capacity of inner-city schools to educate "culturally deprived" newcomer populations, and improve employment and human services to the inner-city poor (O'Connor, forthcoming). Combining research, local planning, and community action, many of the experimental programs attempted to reform local government agencies to coordinate and make services more responsive to the needs of the inner-city poor. Alternatively, the initiatives set up new institutional structures designed to overcome the fragmentation and other problems associated with government bureaucracies. As the culmination of this series of experiments, the Gray Areas program was the product of an extended period of social learning in which continual program evaluation played a central role.

The chief architect of Ford's urban programs was a Harvard-trained public administrator named Paul Ylvisaker, who had most recently been an aide to Philadelphia reform mayor Joseph Clark. Aware that the staff was working from limited knowledge and experience with what would work in hard-pressed inner-city areas, Ylvisaker was deliberately experimental when he first set out to define the Foundation's urban program, funding a variety of locally planned initiatives aimed at different points of intervention. "We are confronted with the task of dealing with problems which have no criteria upon which to base decisions," he noted in a speech to a group of urban grantees in 1963. "We have to deal with the unknown. We have to have an experimental period, searching for the unknown, and then justify this activity" (Ylvisaker 1963). The purpose of such experimentation was as much to test the underlying problem analysis as it was to explore new methods for responding; lessons from earlier, more tentative urban interventions would be used to help refine and bring focus to the overall urban program. Thus, having started out with a somewhat vague notion that the "urban crisis" required government reorganization along metropolitan lines, Ylvisaker shifted his focus over time to what he called the "people problems" that were being ignored in government reform movements and in "bricks and mortar" urban-renewal efforts. These "people problems" were embodied in the "newcomer" populations: black, Puerto Rican, and Appalachian white migrants from rural backgrounds who were seen to suffer from low skills, low educational achievement, and overall "cultural deprivation." They were geographically concentrated in the urban "gray areas," neighborhoods in between the central city and the suburbs that in bygone days had served as staging grounds for immigrant upward mobility. The key to restoring this historic function still lay in governance, only now it was not for the purposes of metropolitan planning but to force social service agencies to be more comprehensive, coordinated, and responsive to the needs of the newcomers. Having thus narrowed the focal point for the urban program, the purpose of local experimentation then became a search for the institution that the Foundation could use as an "entry point" to stimulate comprehensive reform in the gray areas. Following short-lived attempts to use school systems and housing as the point of intervention, Ylvisaker's search eventually led him to the conclusion that such institutions did not exist and would have to be invented, leading to the creation of nonprofit organizations to provide the needed coordinating functions (O'Connor, forthcoming).

Although it was given rhetorical emphasis, evaluation remained a vaguely defined component of the Foundation's urban experiments. Individual programs were required to establish "self-evaluation" mechanisms, usually with the help of local universities, and they were periodically visited by staff members and outside consultants. Little effort was made to introduce any uniformity or validation process to these self-evaluations, however. Much more important to the social learning process was a different, less formal type of evaluation carried out by staff members and a changing cast of "expert" consultants appointed by Ylvisaker to "accompany" the process of program development, serving as what he called a "gadfly committee" to observe and generate new ideas. This eclectic group of experts included recognized scholars such as Peter Marris and Lloyd Ohlin, urban "practitioners" such as Chicago city planner Clifford Campbell, former mayors who shared Ylvisaker's reform ideas, and journalists. With few marching orders, they conducted site visits, participated in staff meetings, and helped to plan special training programs and conferences that brought grantees together, and eventually served as advisors to the grantees as well as to the Foundation. This dual function did not raise a problem because, as Ylvisaker saw it, evaluation should involve the local project directors, the expert consultants, and the funders in a constant dialogue that would result in steady program improvements; the evaluation team members were to act as "teachers and learners" for "people on both sides of the table." In this sense, evaluation was a collective process (Ylvisaker 1963).

In addition to fostering the intangible social learning that accompanied the programs, this unstructured evaluation process produced a wealth of narrative reports, correspondence, internal memos, and the now-classic study, *Dilemmas of Social Reform,* by Peter Marris and Martin Rein (1967). Together, these documents track the continuing learning process that informed the Gray Areas program, offering a kind of running commentary not only on how various local efforts were faring organizationally, but also on the conceptual revisions that accompanied program development. Thus, it is in these exchanges that one can detect the emergence of poverty, and the notion of a "vicious cycle" of cultural and material deprivation, as the underlying problem definition. Similarly, these exchanges articulate the theory of institutional reform that informed the Gray Areas approach (Marris and Rein 1967; O'Connor, forthcoming). In this sense, the Foundation's social learning process offers glimmers of that kind of theory-based evaluation strategy that methodologists have been calling for since the 1970s (Weiss 1972a). They also contain crucial insights into the process of community-based social action. A number of themes in particular stand out, perhaps because they are virtual advance warnings of the kinds of problems that would later be experienced by the local efforts sponsored by the Community Action Program during the War on Poverty. One is the sheer difficulty of achieving the kind of administrative cohesion and program coordination the Foundation was looking for in its attempt to change the way local governing institutions dealt with the poor. Here, more often than not, bureaucratic rivalries and historically rooted local power struggles got in the way of comprehensive, integrated approaches, as was the case in Boston, where the housing establishment struggled with social welfare leaders for control over the program. A second important theme is that racial inequality—particularly if left unacknowledged—could serve to undermine the effectiveness of anti-poverty efforts. Third, several of the Foundation's urban programs revealed an ambivalence about the nature and importance of citizen participation. Finally, some of the programs made mistakes with the media that later got them into trouble with public expectations and perceptions (Ford Foundation 1964).

As helpful as it was in the process of program development, the Foundation's social learning process did not systematically address the question of what the programs were actually accomplishing and did little to assess the connections between programs and their stated objectives. However, given the rudimentary documentation and short time-frame they were working with, it is questionable whether evaluators could have made reasonable statements about outcomes. By the time such evidence was becoming available, the Foundation was proudly handing its experimental programs off to the government's anti-poverty initiative, for use as grantees and model programs in the community action strategy. The Foundation's short attention span was only one aspect of its broader institutional incapacity to conduct and absorb the lessons of evaluation. At about the time when Ylvisaker's staff was assessing its urban experiments, Foundation president Henry Heald established a central office of Policy and Planning, the purpose of which was to rationalize planning and to be more systematic about feeding program lessons into the federal pipeline. Given the mandate to establish Foundation-wide program-evaluation procedures, this office was widely interpreted as Heald's effort to centralize control over his independent-minded staff, and few program officers wanted any part of it (Sheldon 1974). The Gray Areas programs were still new, had taken the Foundation into unfamiliar territory, and had introduced a much more activist style of philanthropy than had been followed in the past; though willing to conduct an internal dialogue with grantees, program officers were understandably wary of what the results of outcomes-oriented evaluation would say to the trustees, let alone to the outside world. This sensitivity was not confined to the Gray Areas program, and evaluation remained a problematic issue within the Foundation for the next several years.

The reluctance to subject programs to outside evaluation and to create accountability beyond the confines of the funder–grantee relationship had its costs. In the first place, the absence of more systematic, widely agreed-upon criteria for gauging program progress meant that choosing among alternative strategies was largely subjective and politically opportunistic; local program directors did take part in the evaluative dialogue, but only the most entrepreneurial among them had much influence on decision-making. Nor did the Foundation establish a way of following up on the "early warnings" coming from the consultants' reports. Second, the Foundation staff had difficulty accepting the critical perspectives on the conceptual underpinnings of their program—perspectives that challenged its essentially behavioral notions of poverty and its failure to grapple with the structural underpinnings of Gray Area problems. Most important, because evaluation remained a dialogue among insiders, many valuable lessons were simply overlooked as the urban experiments became caught up in the federal anti-poverty efforts and the Foundation's priorities shifted from achieving local reform to providing replicable models for the War on Poverty. In the rush to promote community action as an anti-poverty strategy, those closest to the urban experiments proved willing to overlook problems that had given them reason for caution. In large degree, success was being measured in the volume of Administration visitors to the Gray Area sites; the passage of Title II, the Community Action clause of the Economic Opportunity Act of 1964, was deemed the program's "proudest achievement" (Ford Foundation 1964).

A slightly different version of evaluation as social learning can be seen in evaluations of juvenile delinquency demonstration programs in the

1950s and early 1960s. Delinquency was virtually a national obsession in the 1950s, the subject of numerous reports, special commissions, Congressional investigations, and popular fiction (Gilbert 1986). Public concern was matched by a flood of new research, much of it either challenging or building on the University of Chicago ecological theories from earlier decades. Youth organizations, universities, social welfare programs, and law-enforcement agencies—now armed with a broad spectrum of theoretical perspectives that implicated individual psychology, female-headed families, adolescent transitions, lower-class culture, and the absence of opportunity in explanations for delinquent behavior—became involved in a proliferation of community-based demonstration programs during the 1950s and '60s. Funded by the Children's Bureau, the National Institute of Mental Health, the Ford Foundation, and, later, the President's Committee on Juvenile Delinquency, these demonstrations were more firmly grounded in theory than the Gray Areas and related urban experiments were, and the accompanying evaluation plans were meant to reflect on the validity of one or more of these theories. However, as part of relatively short-lived and sometimes elaborate demonstration projects, these evaluations could not possibly achieve the requirements of time necessary to subject theories—most of which were tied to some form of life-course framework—to empirical assessment.

If they did not exactly offer definitive backing for any single theory, the findings from these theoretically informed evaluations of delinquency programs did play a prominent role in social scientific debates over the nature of delinquency and, later, poverty. (See, for example, Miller 1968.) Ultimately, however, pragmatism and ideology—and not evaluation research—were responsible for the growing popularity of the opportunity theory of delinquency among liberal policymakers in the early 1960s, and its incorporation into the Juvenile Delinquency Control Act of 1961. This theory was propounded by sociologists Richard Cloward and Lloyd Ohlin in their book *Delinquency and Opportunity* (1960), and embodied in Mobilization for Youth, a community action program on New York's Lower East Side. It shifted attention away from deep-seated psychological and cultural factors and toward more malleable environmental conditions, arguing that the absence of a viable "opportunity structure" for social and economic advance was what pushed disadvantaged youth into delinquent behavior. With its emphasis on creating new pathways for young people to share in the American Dream, opportunity theory captured the imagination of Kennedy staff members and fit in with the ideological predilections of the new Administration. Unlike the more psychological and culturally oriented explanations, opportunity theory also pointed to concrete targets for intervention, in the form of educational, job training, and other opportunity-enhancing programs (Hackett 1970; Marris and Rein 1967).

The Gray Areas and juvenile delinquency evaluation strategies shared a common, if not widely articulated, view of evaluation as an essential part of the social learning that would guide advocates of social change as they sought out new ways of responding to urban problems. Emphasizing the educational function of evaluation, they focused on underlying concepts, on administrative processes, and on site-specific details that could only be picked up in close observation. If not entirely successful in the sense of having produced definitive evidence regarding the effectiveness of the experimental program strategies or the validity of the assumptions that informed them, these evaluations did produce a rich body of information that was certainly relevant to advocates of community-based change. In the rush to implement community action on a national scale, however, the mostly cautionary lessons from this brief period of social learning were often overlooked, and the potential lessons for evaluation methodology were never developed.

Evaluation as Impact Assessment: *PPBS and Community Action Programs*

As part of its broader strategy against poverty, the Johnson Administration established the Community Action Program (CAP) in Title II of the Economic Opportunity Act of 1964, providing funds for rural and urban Community Action Agencies (CAAs) to mobilize local resources on behalf of the poor. Modeled on the Gray Areas and Juvenile Delinquency demonstration programs, CAP was conceptualized as a mechanism for stimulating program coordination at the local level and for ensuring "maximum feasible participation" by the poor. The program was centrally administered by the Office of Economic Opportunity (OEO), which required CAAs to submit planning and action proposals, and to report regularly on their progress. Local CAAs were also encouraged to develop local capacity for evaluation. As the agency responsible for research and evaluation of the poverty program as well as for administering CAP, OEO also had the more difficult job of evaluating the impact of CAP with respect to the goals of national anti-poverty policy.

OEO's attempts to evaluate CAP should be seen as part of the overall governmental effort to evaluate the new "social action" programs in light of Great Society objectives. This posed a substantial challenge to social science and to the federal bureaucracy, which was faced with the task of generating both the knowledge and the staff necessary to implement and act on the results of evaluation. Unlike other agencies responsible for administering social programs, OEO had a sizeable research budget and had established a separate division for Research, Plans, Programs, and Evaluation (RPP&E) from its outset. This division was staffed primarily by economists and sociologists, who through a combination of primary and contracted research were responsible for meeting the diversified knowledge needs of the entire War on Poverty. In addition to basic research on poverty, RPP&E had to generate a substantial amount of information in response to the requirements of the PPBS system, and to the persistent political pressure to convince Congress and the public that the government was winning the War on Poverty. In addition to knowledge of labor markets, community processes, statistical techniques, and evaluation methodology, the RPP&E division needed versatility, political savvy, and the ability to produce under pressure from its staff. Director Joseph Kershaw and assistant director Robert Levine were both economists with previous government experience and had also worked at the Rand Corporation, where they had become familiar with the PPBS system and cost-benefit analysis; over the years, they recruited colleagues from the Department of Defense, where PPBS had first been instituted. As a result, the RPP&E staff was closely tuned in to the importance of systematic, quantitatively supported, goal-oriented data for the sake of making the case for poverty programs to the Administration and to Congress.

As one of its first steps, this office came up with what it hoped would be the road map against which its annual appropriation requests would be judged: a five-year plan that would take the country well on the way toward the ultimate goal of eliminating poverty within a generation (Levine 1970). The five-year plan retained the comprehensive vision of the War on Poverty, and included provisions for expanded community action to deal with the local political and institutional barriers to opportunity, expanded job training to reach a broader segment of the population, and a significant public job creation component to deal with structural slack in demand for low-skill workers. However, the most prominent feature of this and subsequent OEO five-year plans was fundamental reform of income maintenance policy. Whether they took the form of family allowances or a negative income tax, such ideas were quite popular among economists across the political spectrum throughout the 1960s and early 1970s, when it appeared the country had the means, and could the develop the technological know-how, to eliminate "income poverty" while simultaneously working to expand opportunities (Levine 1970). Motivated by the possibility of reform along these lines, RPP&E staff contracted with the University of Wisconsin's Institute for Research on Poverty and Mathematica Policy Research, Inc., to design and run the New Jersey Income-Maintenance Experiment, a social experiment that was unprecedented in scope and ambition (Kershaw and Fair 1976; Watts and Rees 1977). This experiment, versions of which would be launched in other urban and rural locations, was seen at the time to represent the cutting edge of evaluative policy research, using sophisticated sampling techniques and random assignment, and testing several different versions of the income package. Launched in 1967, it also coincided with officialdom's preference—bordering on a creed, to hear some tell it—for large-scale controlled experiments as testing grounds for proposed policy innovations. This preference, which helped to generate support for additional income maintenance, health care, work/welfare, and other social experiments in the 1970s, became especially pronounced and spread to a wider circle of policymakers in the 1980s when experimental design became the mantra of Congressional welfare reform advocates on both sides of the aisle (Wiseman et al. 1991; Fishman and Weinberg 1992; Manski and Garfinkel 1992).

While the demands of long-range planning and policy innovation created an institutional impetus for supporting large-scale quantitative experimental research on income maintenance, evaluating CAP and related social programs became increasingly tied to the political need to produce measurable results—and to produce them quickly. Such pressures were foremost in the minds of RPP&E staff members as they worked with CAP program staff to develop a comprehensive evaluation strategy beginning in late 1965. In efforts to stave off simplistic demands for mere numerical reporting, Kershaw and Levine took it upon themselves to educate program administrators and the Congress about the purpose of evaluation and the particular difficulty posed in evaluating CAP. Systematic reporting on program content, participation levels, and other gauges of program input, though essential, had to be distinguished from assessments of CAP's outputs, if not yet in terms of reducing poverty rates then in terms of reasonable interim measures. In practice, however, identifying and measuring the appropriate effectiveness indicators was not a straight-forward process. CAP as a program not only had multiple objectives, it also was responsible for administering several individual programs that them-selves had multiple objectives. This posed the immediate problem of whether impact should be assessed by focusing on the comprehensive, integrating functions unique to local CAAs, or by accumulating evalua-tions of the individual programs administered under their auspices. The former approach, which was methodologically the more challenging task, was clearly the one that captured the essence of the community action idea.

Recognizing the complexity of the task, Kershaw attempted early on in his tenure to engage the talents of top-ranked researchers and social theorists in evaluating CAP. He first approached Yale University, which, because of its academic prestige and proximity to New Haven's "model" Gray Areas/CAA, seemed ideally situated to conduct a comprehensive evaluation of a local project while also developing methodology for evaluating community-based interventions more generally. To the chagrin of OEO director Sargent Shriver, himself under the gun to testify on CAP in Congress, Kershaw envisioned a process of scholarly conferences and research that would take a minimum of two years to have any concrete payoff. The differences between Shriver and Kershaw themselves turned out to be academic: despite expressions of enthusiasm from Yale president Kingman Brewster, the University failed to take up Kershaw's offer of funding for such an undertaking, claiming that it was impossible to find the senior scholar with the ability and the commitment to take responsibility for the project (OEO 1965). Nor could Kershaw seem to persuade any other major academic institution to take it on, despite numerous overtures. As a result of a more general request for proposals, OEO eventually made individual contracts with several universities and nonprofit research orga-nizations to conduct evaluations of local CAAs, jettisoning the more ambitious effort to develop new evaluation methodologies. In the mean-time, the pressure for evidence of concrete program achievements was unyielding, whether coming from an increasingly skeptical Congress or from the need to justify budget requests to an increasingly stringent Administration. OEO thus had to make due with what it considered a partial, short-range evaluation plan combining site visits with "single component" evaluations of specific programs such as Head Start and Job

Corps. Thus, for a combination of political and academic reasons, Kershaw's hope of making a serious methodological contribution to evaluating comprehensive social action programs—and ultimately of gathering evidence to show how, in CAAs, the whole could be far more than a sum of its parts—was never seriously pursued.

The political pressures on OEO's evaluation function only intensified in 1967 when, as part of an effort to rein in the War on Poverty, Congress passed a series of amendments explicitly requiring that all OEO programs be subject to "careful, systematic and continuing" evaluation using "control groups, cost-benefit analysis, data on the opinions of participants about the strengths and weaknesses of programs," and the like, requirements that would "outstrip the capabilities" of OEO's evaluation division, according to Levine (1968). CAP and the work-training program were singled out as programs in need of published standards of effectiveness that would be used in deciding whether they would be renewed, tying evaluation of these programs even more closely to the budget allocation process than they already were under PPBS. Under these mandates, evaluation for the sake of learning, of developing methodology, and of program improvement would take a back seat to evaluation for the sake of political accountability. In response to the 1967 amendments, RPP&E revamped its evaluation practices, distinguishing between overall program effectiveness and program-specific evaluation (Levine 1968).

Increasingly, then, under the influence of Congressional critics, evaluation of politically vulnerable programs such as CAP were supposed to take on a "bottom line" quality. Though this legislative intent was well understood by OEO in the waning months of the Johnson Administration, it was not until the Nixon years that this somewhat single-minded approach to program evaluation was fully accepted as an objective. As part of a Congressionally mandated review of OEO evaluation procedures, a contractor for the General Accounting Office approvingly cited an internal OEO memo by a staff member appointed under the new regime, articulating this philosophy of evaluation and in the process drawing a sharp distinction between large-scale impact studies "based on national samples and using sophisticated research designs with control groups and longitudinal measures of change" and studies aimed at improving program operations. Leaving no doubt about which approach was preferable for policy purposes, the memo went on to say that " . . . social programs should be evaluated on the basis of a generalized quantitative technique very much like the framework within which business investment decisions are made. The ideal methodology would remove judgment from the process and, in essence, permit the public authorities to settle society's problems by computation" (Resource Management Corporation 1969, 23, 30). Achieving this ideal type of evaluation would require more far-reaching changes at OEO than those initiated by Levine, the report indicated. And those changes had direct implications for the future of CAP: one of the chief obstacles to more "effective" evaluation in the past, it found, was the OEO's dual mandate as an operating and an "R&D" organization. The implication was that one of those functions would have to be relinquished.

Prior to the release of the Government Accounting Office (GAO) report, Levine and his staff had managed to get a start on the overall impact assessment of CAP called for in the 1967 legislation, and the fate of those efforts as the Nixon Administration took over are revealing with regard to the uses of evaluation under changing political conditions. This overall impact assessment was based on eight case studies conducted by separate outside contractors, and a national impact assessment jointly conducted by The University of Chicago's National Opinion Research Corporation (NORC) and Barss Reitzel and Associates, Inc., of Cambridge, Massachusetts. As noted by Joseph Wholey in his study of federal evaluation policy, little effort had been made to coordinate the design of the case studies and they were generally regarded to be of limited value in the larger assessment task (Wholey et al. 1970). The NORC/Barss Reitzel efforts, however, held more potential interest, for they were based on a national sample of 100 CAAs, and included multiple-survey, personal interview, and observational techniques. The study's objective was to determine CAP's effectiveness in stimulating local institutional change, as measured by indicators such as the changes in the size and demographic make-up of the population served by local agencies, changes in the demographic composition of various community boards, and the number of agency referrals generated by CAAs. Its major finding was that CAAs did indeed bring about local institutional change, and that those dedicated to community mobilization and empowerment had a greater impact on local institutions than did CAAs serving primarily as local service coordinators. Reporting on these findings, the authors were careful to point out that change was well within the law and the boundaries of political acceptability; CAAs were making the system work better, without unduly shaking up the status quo. However, the question of whether institutional change translated into better services and employment outcomes for the poor was left open to interpretation in the early reports from the study (Vanecko 1970; Vanecko and Jacobs 1970). In a separate analysis based on face-to-face interviews with a range of community respondents drawn from the same sample, a Barss Reitzel study expressed more skepticism about the anti-poverty effect of the CAAs, claiming that on the "gut issues" of jobs, income, and political power, CAAs had little actual impact (Barss Reitzel and Associates, Inc. 1969).

By the time the results of these various studies were available, the Nixon OEO was in place, and the future of both CAP and OEO were in doubt. Convinced that the future for OEO was in acting principally as a social "R&D" laboratory rather than in the actual administration of politically vulnerable programs, OEO director Donald Rumsfeld and his successors acceded to the phase-out of CAP and the transfer of administrative responsibility for Head Start and other programs to the appropriate outside agencies. OEO's research agenda reflected the Administration's priorities: reforming income maintenance was one and assuring the continuation of the Negative Income Tax (NIT) experiments was another; community action was not, and OEO would not follow up on the effort to learn from the CAP experience. However, the OEO research staff under the Nixon Administration was responsible for "drafting . . . a replacement for the current Title II of the Economic Opportunity Act. . . . " (Redenius 1970, 1). In the process of gathering a range of evidence to support the recommendations they would make, the staff contracted with the Institute for Research on Poverty to conduct a comprehensive and synthetic review of the eight case studies that had been done, and to review the findings that were then coming out from the NORC/Barss Reitzel study. The legislative timetable would not wait for an eight-case CAP synthesis, as it turns out, but sociologist Myron J. Lefcowitz did conduct a review of the NORC study. In a thorough critique, Lefcowitz called the findings into question, noting that the investigators had not adequately specified their indicators of institutional change, and had relied on simple correlational findings rather than more rigorous causal analysis to draw their conclusions. Nor did the study address the issue of the magnitude of change that resulted from various practices. These and other methodological flaws made the study virtually useless for policy purposes, he concluded. However, he added, "there can be little doubt that the material available . . . is one of the social scientific mother lodes of the decade" (Lefcowitz 1969, 1).

While Lefcowitz's critique was heavily influenced by the standards of cost-benefit analysis and experimental evaluation research, his documentation of methodological and analytic flaws was convincing. Equally plausible were his conclusions regarding the political issues raised by this and other assessments of CAP, which, he suggested, could account for problems in the study. One was the "tremendous time pressure to weave a story from a mass of data," for which OEO "could not wait for the year or two necessary to do the proper analytic job. The Community Action Program is continuously under the political gun and any evidence that would justify its past performance and legitimate its future continuance was and is essential" (Lefcowitz 1969, 1). But political considerations had also influenced the substance of the evaluations findings, Lefcowitz suggested, noting a "strain" in the analysis to show that CAP "is accomplishing something and not upsetting the system" (1969, 1). What Lefcowitz may not have anticipated was the political use to which his own report on the evaluation might be put.

Soon after submitting the Lefcowitz report, it became clear to Harold Watts, the director of the Institute for Research on Poverty (IRP), that OEO's motivation in commissioning the review was political. "We have now moved to the point where your office has a lack of interest in (or even impatience with) this task and seems to me to want us to shoulder at least some 'line responsibility' for formulation of new policy direction," he wrote in a pointed memo to Assistant OEO director John Wilson. "Moreover, there seem already to be presumptions about that direction which we are expected to validate (endorse, sanctify?)," he continued. "Namely, the direction seems to be how do we cool out the CAP operation and make a nice, well-behaved (emasculated?) service-distribution mechanism" (Watts 1970, 1). For technical but, more important, for political reasons, then, there was no serious and sustained effort to learn from the evaluations of the CAP program.

That the War on Poverty yielded neither a thoroughgoing assessment of the impact of CAPS nor any significant methodological inroads into evaluating comprehensive community interventions represents a significant lost opportunity, a loss due to political pressures, to a lack of academic engagement in the issues, and to the fact that there was insufficient organized political interest in establishing whether and how a sustained investment in CAP could contribute to anti-poverty goals. Even the evaluations that were conducted—partial or flawed though they may have been—had considerable value in clarifying the difficult methodological issues that would have to be addressed: how to operationalize the many and conflicting goals of CAP; how to measure the existence and extent of such complex, long-range processes as institutional change; identifying appropriate interim indicators for measuring progress against poverty; and developing the appropriate framework for comparing findings across sites. Equally significant, an unfortunate and artificial distinction between policy-relevant outcome evaluation and program-relevant operations monitoring began to take hold and became institutionalized as Congress increased the pressure for the "bottom line" on OEO programs. An RPP&E staff that was initially open to exploring new ways of assessing CAP's impact—and even to questioning some of the precepts of PPBS—never got the chance.

Evaluation as Policy Learning:
The Case of Model Cities

As CAP was getting under way, the Administration was also trying to breathe new life into its national urban policy by establishing priorities for the newly established Department of Housing and Urban Development (HUD). In 1965 LBJ appointed a special task force for this purpose, chaired by Massachusetts Institute of Technology (M.I.T.) urbanist Robert C. Woods, and instructed its members to be bold and innovative, leaving the legislative politics to the White House. With the sense of urban crisis looming, exacerbated by recurring incidents of racial unrest in impoverished inner cities, the task force came up with a set of recommendations designed to make up for the failings of urban renewal and to avoid the political mistakes of the anti-poverty program. Included in its report was a proposal for what would become the Model Cities program: grants to a designated number of demonstration cities to concentrate and coordinate existing federal resources for physical and social development in inner-city neighborhoods. The task force recommended that a total of 66 cities be chosen as experimental sites, which would be eligible for the full range of existing categorical grants on a "priority" basis, a new block grant administered by HUD to provide for planning and implementation of comprehensive redevelopment plans in poor neighborhoods, and technical assistance from a federal coordinator working as a liaison with local agencies. While the bulk of the funding would come from existing social welfare, housing and employment programs administered by the

Departments of Health, Education, and Welfare (HEW), HUD, and Labor, HUD would be designated as the "lead agency" responsible for getting cooperation from the others in making grants available. To avoid some of the tensions that had been created by making Community Action Agencies independent of mayors, the Model Cities Demonstration Agencies would be run by the mayor's office, and the mechanisms for assuring citizen participation would be left up to the localities. The task force recommendations also included proposals requiring racial integration in new federally funded housing units. The estimated cost of the program was $2.3 billion in new appropriations for the planning grants, with an anticipation that as much as $12 billion would be available through the existing categorical grant programs. Through these measures, the task force hoped to achieve a concentration of resources in the neediest areas, coordination of fragmented social welfare and housing programs, local flexibility in the use of categorical grants, and a federal commitment to careful experimentation: the program envisioned one year for planning and five for implementation (Haar 1975).

The proposed legislation arrived in Congress with several handicaps that made it difficult to build a solid constituency behind the program. Critics saw it as a proposal from "on high," cooked up by an overly secretive task force set on adding yet another array of programs to an already overwhelming domestic agenda. Mayors, though generally supportive, insisted that the projected funding levels were much too low. Others worried that it would drain money from cities not in the program. The Administration, on the other hand, was trying to restrict new requests for domestic programs, aware of escalating costs in Vietnam and wary that Congressional willingness to approve additional spending had already been stretched to its limits. By the time it got through Congress, the Model Cities legislation had been expanded to twice the number of cities, its appropriation cut to $900 million, and its initial life span reduced from six years to two years. The bill had also been gutted of racial integration requirements, and designated no central federal coordinating authority, not even offering clarifying language for how the program was to be implemented. Equally significant, the legislation was now being pitched as the Administration's response to Watts, to the Kerner Commission Report, to the threat of future "long hot summers"; Model Cities would appease the inner city. All of this left a sense of deep ambivalence about the ultimate purposes of the program: was it a national experiment, to guide future urban policy, or was it simply another way of providing aid to "distressed"—and dangerous—areas? One thing seemed certain to the original architects of the Model City idea: what had started out as an ambitious effort to demonstrate what could be achieved by concentrating substantial resources and know-how in disadvantaged neighborhoods was in danger of becoming simply another bureaucratic mechanism for helping cities to use available resources—however inadequate—more efficiently (Haar 1975; Frieden and Kaplan 1975).

The same ambivalence and vagueness of purpose that accompanied the watered-down Model Cities program was reflected in efforts to institute evaluation procedures once the legislation was passed. In contrast to the trend initiated in other Great Society legislation, neither the task force nor Congress had paid much attention to evaluation, and no money had been set aside for it. Thus, it was up to administrators in HUD, working within a new bureaucracy, with virtually no trained staff and little idea of the appropriate methods, to come up with an evaluation plan for a program whose ultimate purposes were uncertain. More immediately damaging to the evaluation cause were the deep divisions within HUD over the function and control of evaluation. The Model Cities Administration (MCA) was established under HUD's jurisdiction as the agency responsible for implementing the new legislation. Its evaluation staff came up with an elaborate plan that reflected the legislation's experimental intent, seeking to learn from the experience of the initial demonstration sites for the purpose of refining the program in future rounds while also trying out a variety of evaluation methodologies. This plan was premised on the notion that evaluation was an integral part of the program design and implementation; optimally, local programs would be designed with the needs of policy evaluation in mind. Included in the MCA's proposed evaluation plan were documentations of the local planning processes, assessments of existing and prospective local information systems, and measures of Model City's local impact as indicated by changes in neighborhood attitudes, levels of citizen participation, institutional change in the targeted neighborhoods, and improved economic and social conditions for local residents. Reflecting HUD's limited internal capacity to conduct such an ambitious, multi-pronged evaluation plan, the MCA staff proposed that it be conducted by outside contractors.

In what turned out to be a protracted and ultimately fruitless internal bureaucratic struggle, the HUD deputy undersecretary's office objected to the plan, arguing that the MCA should have control over implementation but not over evaluation, which was more properly a function of a separate monitoring and oversight office. Indicating a very different orientation to evaluation, the undersecretary's office criticized the MCA plan for jumping the gun; evaluation would not even be relevant until after the cities had begun implementing their plans (Haar 1975).

Eventually, the MCA did receive funding for Model City evaluation, only then to be thwarted when it attempted to issue requests for proposals (RFPs). The lingering bureaucratic tensions were ultimately settled by the changeover to the Nixon Administration, which incorporated Model Cities into its broader "new federalism" policy. Strengthening local capacity—and not learning for the sake of a future, expanded federal policy—became the rationale for Model Cities. Within that framework, the immediate needs of program implementation became the standard for determining the kinds of evaluation studies HUD would undertake, placing emphasis on troubleshooting and internal management issues. As a result, the national, broader impact evaluation plan was never implemented.

The Model Cities experience nevertheless did suggest important lessons for efforts to implement a national strategy of community-based intervention. Two of them stand out as especially pertinent for this discussion. First, Model Cities illustrated on a federal scale what the Gray Areas experience did on the local level: agency coordination is very difficult and should not be taken for granted. Never clearly designated and given no leverage to act as the "lead agency" for the effort to mobilize the categorical grants available through various federal agencies, HUD ran into tremendous difficulties in getting the other agencies to cooperate for the sake of concentrating resources. Second, Model Cities offers a stark example of the problems built into the demonstration model of social programming, problems also evident in the Gray Areas, Juvenile Delinquency, and in subsequent demonstration programs. Inevitably, these demonstrations have run into tensions between the goals of experimentation for the sake of replication, policy revision, and future program improvement, and the goals of effective local management—tensions that arise not from an inherent incompatibility between these goals, but from the existence of differing priorities among different players in coordinating multi-level programs. Thus, national funders want to know how local demonstration sites are furthering national policy objectives, and try to be sure that local programs are designed to test the relationship between intervention strategy and outcome. Local program directors, while often sharing the need and desire to learn about the relationship between intervention and outcome, often find that the needs of the experiment might conflict with the local responsibilities of the program. These tensions have been played out in the evaluation process, raising basic questions about who should have responsibility for evaluation, how criteria for success will be determined, and to what end evaluation results will be used. There is no clear answer to these dilemmas, but the Model City and subsequent experiences suggest the need for critical reexamination of arrangements for funding and learning from local programs.

Finally, Model Cities is, in the words of one recent analysis, "a lesson in the dissipation of limited resources" (Edelman and Radin 1991, 53). As such, it points to another potential pitfall in the use of local demonstrations for the purpose of policy learning. Time and again, proposed multi-site demonstrations have been stretched thin in the legislative process, expanding to cover a large number of Congressional districts even as appropriation levels are pared down. Such inadequately funded experiments only reinforce skeptics' expectations when they fail to achieve the ambitious goals of federal policymakers.

Evaluation and Context:
Community Development Corporations

Almost from its inception, the War on Poverty was subject to a critique of its assumption that poverty could be eliminated without significant job creation, a critique coming from within the ranks of the Administration as often as from outside commentators. This criticism took on added weight as the extent and impact of inner-city joblessness were highlighted in such "events" as the debate over the Moynihan Report, civil unrest, and extended hearings on inner-city conditions headed by Senators Javits and Kennedy in 1966. One product of those hearings was an amendment to the Equal Opportunity Act providing federal funds for the Special Impact Program (SIP) for economic development in neighborhoods and communities where "dependency, chronic unemployment and community deterioration" (Abt Associates 1973, 6–7) converged, and under this program to support a project in New York's Bedford Stuyvesant neighborhood that promised to add job creation and economic development to the mix of services and housing the federal government was trying to achieve in Model Cities. Like CAP and Model Cities, the projects funded under SIP were designed to target the neediest neighborhoods, concentrate available resources, and coordinate interventions in a total, comprehensive approach. Unlike the other efforts, however, the strategy in Bedford Stuyvesant and other neighborhoods aimed directly at regenerating the local economy through community economic development and at creating its own infrastructure of community-based services rather than seeking to reform government bureaucracies. At the center of several of the community-based development efforts was the community development corporation (CDC), a private entity, often combining nonprofit and for-profit branches, set up with multiple purposes, such as building housing and other neighborhood infrastructure, providing job training and technical assistance to local small businesses, and leveraging public and private funds for community-building. To a greater degree than past community action efforts, the CDC also represented an effort to build on several genuinely "home grown" movements—many of them headed by minorities—to promote comprehensive redevelopment and to control the future of the community. Over the next few years, federal funds were extended to approximately forty urban and rural CDCs under SIP and its successor programs, although overall funding levels remained relatively low. The Ford Foundation and others also established a major philanthropic presence in community-based economic development, lobbying for Congressional funding and providing direct support for major CDCs in the late 1960s, and then moving to create intermediaries to provide technical and financial support in the 1970s. In the 1980s, Ford once again began to provide direct subsidies for "emerging" CDCs, partly in response to severe federal funding cutbacks (Halpern 1994; Peirce and Steinbach 1987; Vidal 1992).

From the start, federally sponsored community development in impoverished areas was burdened by inadequate funding levels and a cumbersome administrative set-up, which presented particular challenges for evaluation. Centrally administered by OEO, the SIP program actually consisted of a series of development projects that were proposed by several different agencies, including the Departments of Labor, Agriculture, Commerce, and OEO itself. Working with relatively small sums of money, a specially designated OEO committee would choose a number of projects from among these proposals for funding, using as criteria the legislative requirements that the programs be targeted on areas of concentrated poverty, that they show promise of stimulating local economic development and employment, and that they be large enough to have a significant impact on the community. Given the limitations of funding, the OEO also "made an early decision to use this money to test and evaluate rigorously the various approaches with a view to finding out the best means of utilizing the operating impact programs," according to then-OEO director Bertrand Harding (Harding 1968). If evaluators were thus to play a prominent role in the SIP strategy, they also had to respond to a number of challenges, as noted in the evaluation RFP issued by OEO. One was the multiplicity of agency sponsors and the varying emphases they brought to the program. A second was the "complexity of the poverty impact indicators" (OEO 1968), which would require measures not only of job creation and other aspects of economic opportunity, but also of changes in neighborhood environment, attitudes, and other less tangible effects. A third difficulty, according to the instructions for potential evaluators, was the "shortness of time" (OEO 1968) available for evaluation. In order to meet Congressional reporting requirements, OEO needed "hard data" within one year of issuing the evaluation contract, and suggested that evaluators might have to settle for reports on "before" rather than "after" data (Harding 1968). As it turned out, time would also be a frustrating factor in the OEO effort to conduct rigorous evaluation of the anti-poverty impact of community economic development strategies: by the time longer-range measures would have been available, OEO was being dismantled and responsibility for SIP re-assigned.

In light of these administrative and political realities, the early CDC movement did not put much emphasis on basic research and knowledge-generating activities. Evaluations commissioned by the funding agencies, the Ford Foundation, and other sponsors generally relied on individual case studies, ranging from the highly technical to the highly anecdotal. Little was done to develop comparative frameworks that would help to inform or draw lessons from these ongoing case studies. In part, the relatively low priority given to research and evaluation can be attributed to the activist roots and pragmatic ethos that have pervaded the CDC movement, along with an understandable impatience with social scientific concepts not grounded in local reality. But it is also the case that government and other funding sources did not invest significant resources in CDC evaluation, for lack of persistent political pressure to do so, and in the absence, following the demise of OEO, of consistent centralized administrative accountability for their contribution to anti-poverty goals.

A third barrier has to do with the *kind* of evaluation required to understand the impact of CDCs. As the efforts most explicitly designed to change the economic and physical environment in poor communities, CDCs called for the kind of contextual analysis that was not being pursued in evaluation research at the time.

This conclusion can be drawn from three studies, two conducted in the early 1970s and one in the mid-1980s, that did attempt to develop broader frameworks for assessing CDC performance and effectiveness as an approach to reducing neighborhood poverty. One, conducted by Abt Associates in the early 1970s, was an evaluation of SIP commissioned by OEO. Using statistical measures of CDC growth rates, job-creating capacity, average wage rates in the jobs created, and resident attitudes and perceptions in urban and rural CDCs, the study attempted to measure the potential for "appreciable and continuing impact" on the local area, and to determine how particular characteristics of CDCs influenced their effectiveness. While most of the SIP program grantees showed only limited success in the various performance indicators, the Abt study concluded that CDCs did have the potential to achieve appreciable impact and that their commitment to the comprehensive approach to community needs and citizen participation made them more effective than other types of minority business ventures as local economic development agencies (Abt Associates 1973). In another study, commissioned by the Ford Foundation in 1973, the Urban Institute attempted to develop a framework for assessing individual CDC performance standards based on quantifiable "milestones" of profitability, production levels, and efficiency set for each of their major program areas. Using case studies of Bedford Stuyvesant, The Woodlawn Organization (TWO) in Chicago, and The Zion Non-Profit Charitable Trust in Philadelphia, the evaluation found that the CDCs varied considerably in their areas of strength, and although they showed some progress, they generally fell short of the milestones set by the evaluation team. Despite or perhaps because of these somewhat discouraging findings, the report concluded that CDCs were viable community institutions that could not be judged solely in terms of profitability or efficiency indicators. Calling for alternatives means of assessing the effectiveness of CDCs, the report pointed out that they were uniquely vulnerable to external political and economic conditions; evaluation would need some way of taking the effects of such externalities into account (Urban Institute 1976).

By the time the Urban Institute completed its report, the policy climate for CDCs had changed considerably: the economy was in decline, OEO had been dismantled and the Special Impact Program transferred to the Community Services Administration, housing programs were at a virtual standstill, funding for CDCs from all sources was in decline, and the emphasis among funders was increasingly on weaning them away from direct subsidy to promote self-sufficiency. "The combination of directions in federal policy and national economic trends paints a very serious and bleak picture for both CDCs and the communities they serve," the Urban Institute authors concluded (Urban Institute 1976, 130). Nor was any attempt made to follow up on either of the early attempts to develop frameworks for assessing and monitoring CDCs on anything more than a strictly localized basis. In this sense, the failure to develop an overall evaluation strategy can be seen to reflect more than the culture of the movement or the difficulty of comparison. It was an acknowledgment of the federal retreat from direct involvement in poor communities, the end of the short-lived experiments of the 1960s. It was also an expression of skepticism about social science research, a retreat from the Great Society notion that applied research could be used to make and improve policies. While thousands of community-based anti-poverty initiatives continued their work, there was no longer a clearly identifiable audience, no visible bureaucratic or political demand, for broadly based evaluations that would assess local interventions as contributors to national anti-poverty policy.

Thus, in the mid-1980s a third effort to assess the overall anti-poverty potential of CDCs had no empirical or theoretical base on which to build. Undertaken by the Community Development Research Center of the New School for Social Research, this third effort involved a study based on a national sample of 130 successful CDCs. Characterizing its findings as "exploratory" in nature, a report issued in 1992 described a record of moderate success according to quantitative indicators of housing production, commercial real estate, and, to a lesser extent, small business development, linking success to a number of CDC characteristics, such as size, quality of leadership, and record of past success. Also important to CDC success, the report emphasized, were several contextual factors, including the overall conditions of the neighborhoods they served, the existence of a local network of CDCs, and local political and institutional support (Vidal 1992). Relying as it did on numerical indicators of success in each area of CDC activity, this report did not address the issue of how the CDC acted as a comprehensive, multi-faceted neighborhood presence rather than simply a sum of its programs, nor did it address the question of how effectively CDCs were meeting neighborhood needs. Housing represented the least risky of the economic development activities pursued by CDCs, but did housing development respond to community needs and priorities? These and related issues continue to be explored in subsequent, related research, suggesting that this study will continue to be an important empirical base for future evaluative inquiries.

CONCLUSIONS AND LESSONS

This historical review suggests three major conclusions that should help to guide contemporary efforts to evaluate comprehensive community-based initiatives. Drawing attention to the political barriers that have hampered effective evaluation, to the persistent dilemmas facing community-based initiatives, and to the relatively limited role that scientific evaluation has played in determining the fate of past community-based initiatives, these conclusions suggest concrete ways to develop new strategies for conducting, learning from, and building a constituency for the results of evaluation.

First, the barriers to developing effective evaluation strategies for community-based initiatives have been political and institutional as much as they have been methodological and substantive. This paper focuses on the former; others in this volume address the latter in more detail. Not all of these political and institutional barriers are easily susceptible to change. However, there are steps that researchers, foundations, program administrators, and others interested in the future of community-based initiatives can take to improve the situation, even as they work on developing better methods for measuring program impact and effectiveness. One is to create legitimacy—among social scientists as well as policymakers—for the theory-based, qualitative, contextual, and integrated quantitative/qualitative techniques that are necessary for assessing community-based initiatives. Related to that is the need to create incentives and opportunities for evaluators to explore these and other appropriate methodologies, in collaboration with local program directors and community residents. A particularly useful step in this direction would be to engage current theorists of community and neighborhood effects in the project of evaluation and developing evaluation methodologies. In addition, funding agencies should examine their own internal procedures for evaluating community-based initiatives, asking, among other things, whether those procedures are based on a shared and realistic set of expectations for program achievement, whether local programs and funding agencies have the flexibility to absorb the lessons from evaluation, and whether evaluation strategies adequately respond to the knowledge needs of various collaborators and "stakeholders" in community-based initiatives. Only by responding to these varied needs can a broad-based constituency for continuing evaluation efforts be built and sustained.

Second, evaluators should explore in greater depth the persistent dilemmas that community-based initiatives have encountered over the years, in the hope of promoting historical as well as cross-initiative learning, and for the pragmatic purpose of helping funders and practitioners to think through these recurring dilemmas. One example of a recurring dilemma experienced by leaders of community-based initiatives is the tension between the need to maintain a comprehensive vision of problems and objectives and the practical demand to focus, whether on a discernible set of problems and goals or on a clearly defined geographic area. A second persistent frustration for community-based initiatives has been the difficulty of achieving agency coordination and institutional reform, as illustrated particularly in continuing conflict between the "bricks and mortar" and the human service bureaucracies at the federal and local levels. A third persistent difficulty has been in achieving genuine integration among the individual components that make up community-based initiatives—making the whole more than a sum of its parts. Appropriate responses to these and other built-in dilemmas could be illuminated by historical and comparative analysis. By the same token, the recurrence of common problems across time and space may provide the basis of a comparative framework for conducting cross-site evaluations.

Third, several useful models for evaluating comprehensive community-based initiatives are suggested by past experience, each of them offering lessons in the role evaluation can usefully play in program and policy, as well as insights into the programs themselves. But experience also raises a cautionary note for evaluators: no matter how rigorous the scientific method, evaluative evidence will play only a limited—and sometimes unpredictable—role in determining the political fate of social programs. In the past, decisions about community-based initiatives—or about welfare reform, for that matter—have been driven not, primarily, by science but by the values, ideologies, and political interests of the major constituencies involved. Historically, comprehensiveness and citizen participation have been pursued in community-based initiatives because they make sense, they are strategies that grow out of a long tradition of local democratic activism, because experience shows that the "piecemeal" categorical alternatives are not effective, and because they embody values that are worthwhile ends in themselves. Analysts have yet to produce scientific evidence about whether these strategies "work" in terms of measurable outcomes. Developing the appropriate methods and indicators to assess the impact of community-based initiatives remains an important goal (Schorr 1994). Nevertheless, it is also important to keep in mind that evaluation results are only part of what governs program and policy design.

I will conclude, then, by suggesting that a more "policy-relevant" type of evaluation research should be asking questions that have hitherto not been adequately pursued in evaluation design: questions that focus a little less on how community-based initiatives can achieve modest goals while working against incredible odds and much more on changing those odds by identifying the socioeconomic conditions and policy environments under which local initiatives can be more effective vehicles for change. Such evaluation would be more contextual in nature, making social, economic, political, and geographic factors integral parts of the evaluation equation, rather than trying to control for them. It would actively explore how contextual factors influence the nature and effectiveness of community-based initiatives on several levels: Are the programs informed by theories about the relationship between individuals, institutions, and the larger environment? Do such factors as local labor markets, degree of political support for the initiative, strength of the local philanthropic and nonprofit sector, and degree of ethnic and class heterogeneity in the targeted neighborhood create opportunities and/or constraints in program effectiveness? What contextual factors does the initiative attempt to change? In devising ways of answering those and related questions, such evaluations would also take advantage of the recent increase in social scientific interest in macro- and micro-level contextual analysis, as seen in the resurgence of literature exploring "neighborhood effects" on poverty and in efforts to measure such intangible concepts as group or neighborhood-based social networks and social capital. And such contextual analysis would of necessity be historical, examining how the legacy of past community activism has shaped the current generation, using lessons from experience to build comparative, longitudinal frameworks for evaluation, and understanding the initiatives as products of a particular configuration of historical circumstances that may help as well as hinder them.

In addition to exploring such issues as how community-based initiatives fare in varying macro-economic circumstances, contextual analysis would focus on local governance issues, exploring, for example, the links between metropolitan and region-wide development plans and the economic fate of poor neighborhoods. Conversely, such analyses would provide empirical means of assessing prospective policies for the impact they would have on poor neighborhoods and on the possibility for generating job creation and resource development in those neighborhoods. In these and other ways, a more contextual approach would shift the lens of evaluation away from a sole focus on individual initiatives and onto the economy and the policy environment, away from the behavior that takes place within poor communities and onto the choices being made—or not being made—by policymakers and funders. In effect, a more contextual approach to evaluation would take stock of one of the most important lessons from historical experience: that even the most effective community-based initiatives cannot, by themselves, reverse the interacting economic, social, and political trends that have generated growing inequality. This is an important starting point for a discussion of future directions in evaluating, and learning from, community-based initiatives.

NOTES

An earlier version of this paper was presented at the Workshop on Comprehensive Community Initiatives held at the Aspen Institute in August 1994. I am grateful to the workshop participants for their helpful comments. I am especially indebted to Anne Kubisch, Donald Schon, and Lisbeth Schorr for their detailed and thought-provoking comments.

I would also like to thank the Ford Foundation for permission to quote from sources in its archival holdings.

1. Throughout this essay, I use the term "community-based initiatives" to refer to a diverse range of programs, including the Progressive Era settlement house movement, a variety of community action programs sponsored by foundations and the federal government in the 1950s and '60s, Model Cities,

community development corporations, and the comprehensive cross-systems reform efforts that have emerged in several communities over the past few years. Without diminishing the differences among these very diverse initiatives, my analysis suggests that they share several common assumptions and pose similar evaluation challenges.

REFERENCES

Aaron, Henry J. 1978. *Politics and the Professors: The Great Society in Perspective* Washington, DC: The Brookings Institution.

Abt Associates. 1973. "An Evaluation of the Special Impact Program: Final Report." Cambridge, Mass.: Abt Associates.

Baldwin, Sidney. 1968. *The Rise and Decline of the Farm Security Administration* Chapel Hill: University of North Carolina Press.

Barss Reitzel and Associates, Inc. 1969. "Community Action and Institutional Change." An Evaluation Prepared for the Office of Economic Opportunity, July.

Bremner, Robert. 1956. *From the Depths: The Discovery of Poverty in the United States.* New York: New York University Press.

Bureau of the Budget. 1965. *Bulletin # 66-3* (October 12). Austin, Tex.: Lyndon Baines Johnson Library Archives.

Campbell, Donald T., and Julian C. Stanley. 1966. *Experimental and Quasi-Experimental Designs for Research* Chicago: Rand McNally.

Carson, Mina. 1990. *Settlement Folk: Social Thought and the American Settlement Movement, 1885–1930.* Chicago: University of Chicago Press.

Cloward, Richard A., and Lloyd E. Ohlin. 1960. *Delinquency and Opportunity: A Theory of Delinquent Gangs.* New York: Free Press.

Cook, Thomas D., and Donald T. Campbell. 1979. *Quasi-Experimentation: Design and Analysis Issues for Field Settings* Skokie, Ill.: Rand McNally.

Davis, Allen F. 1984. *Spearheads for Reform: The Social Settlements and the Progressive Movement 1890–1914* New Brunswick: Rutgers University Press.

Deutscher, Irwin. n.d. "The Evaluation of Social Programs: Some Consequences of Historical Insensitivity, Naiveté and Contempt." Unpublished paper.

Edelman, Peter B., and Beryl A. Radin. 1991. "Effective Services for Children and Families: Lessons from the Past and Strategies for the Future." In *Effective Services for Children and Families: Report of a Workshop* Washington, DC: National Academy Press.

Fishman, Michael E., and Daniel H. Weinberg. 1992. "The Role of Evaluation in State Welfare Reform Waiver Demonstrations." In *Evaluating Welfare and Training Programs,* ed. Charles F. Manski and Irwin Garfinkel. Cambridge: Harvard University Press.

Ford Foundation. 1964. "Public Affairs: Gray Areas Program." Unpublished Report #2845, Ford Foundation Archives, September.

Frieden, Bernard J. and Marshall Kaplan. 1975. *The Politics of Neglect: Urban Aid from Model Cities to Revenue Sharing* Cambridge: M.I.T. Press.

Gilbert, James. 1986. *Cycle of Outrage: America's Reaction to the Juvenile Delinquent in the 1950s.* New York: Oxford University Press.

Gilbert, Jess. 1994. "Democratic Planning in the New Deal: The Federal-County Agricultural Planning Program." Paper presented at the Newberry Library Rural History Seminar, Chicago, February 1994.

Haar, Charles M. 1975. *Between the Idea and the Reality: A Study in the Origin, Fate and Legacy of the Model Cities Program.* Boston: Little, Brown.

Hackett, David. 1970. Oral History Interview, Boston, Massachusetts, July 22, 1970. John F. Kennedy Memorial Library.

Halpern, Robert. 1994. *Rebuilding the Inner City: A History of Neighborhood Initiatives to Address Poverty in the United States.* New York: Columbia University Press.

Harding, Bertrand. 1968. Letter to Senator Joseph S. Clark, May 1968. Harding Papers. Austin, Tex.: Lyndon Baines Johnson Library.

Haskell, Thomas. 1977. *The Emergence of Professional Social Science: The American Social Science Association and the Nineteenth Century Crisis of Authority.* Urbana: University of Illinois Press.

Haveman, Robert. 1987. *Poverty Policy and Poverty Research: The Great Society and the Social Sciences.* Madison: University of Wisconsin Press.

Kershaw, David, and Jerilyn Fair. 1976. *The New Jersey Income-Maintenance Experiment.* Vol. 1. New York: Academic Press.

Kirkendall, Richard. 1966. *Social Science and Farm Politics in the Age of Roosevelt.* Columbia: University of Missouri Press.

Lageman, Ellen C. 1989. *The Politics of Knowledge: The Carnegie Corporation, Philanthropy and Public Policy.* Chicago: University of Chicago Press.

Lefcowitz, Myron. 1969. "CAP Evaluation: Some Comments." Unpublished paper. Madison, Wisc.: Institute for Research on Poverty Archives.

Levine, Robert A. 1968. "Memorandum to RPP&E Staff," January 1968. Madison, Wisc.: Institute for Research on Poverty Archives.

———. 1970. *The Poor Ye Need Not Have with You.* Cambridge: M.I.T. Press.

Manski, Charles F., and Irwin Garfinkel, eds. 1992. *Evaluating Welfare and Training Programs.* Cambridge: Harvard University Press.

Marris, Peter, and Martin Rein. 1967. *Dilemmas of Social Reform: Poverty and Community Action in the United States* New York: Atherton Press.

Miller, Walter. 1968. "The Elimination of the American Lower Class as National Policy: A Critique of the Ideology of the Poverty Movement of the 1960s." In *On Understanding Poverty: Perspectives from the Social Sciences* ed. Daniel P. Moynihan. New York: Basic Books.

O'Connor, Alice. Forthcoming. "Community Action, Urban Reform, and the Fight Against Poverty: The Ford Foundation's Gray Areas Program."*Journal of Urban History.*

Office of Economic Opportunity (OEO). 1965. "Yale University." OEO Agency Files. Austin, Tex.: Lyndon Baines Johnson Library.

_____. 1968. "Request for Proposals for Evaluation of the Special Impact Program." Harding Papers. Austin, Tex.: Lyndon Baines Johnson Library.

Peirce, Neal R., and Carol F. Steinbach. 1987. *Corrective Capitalism: The Rise of America's Community Development Corporations.*New York: Ford Foundation.

Quane, James. 1994. "Back From the Future: Can Evaluation Survive Dissention in the Ranks?" Paper presented at the Annual Conference of the American Evaluation Association, Boston, Massachusetts, November 2–5, 1994.

Redenius, Richard. 1970. "Memorandum to John Wilson," March 20, 1970. Madison, Wisc.: Institute for Research on Poverty Archives.

Resource Management Corporation. 1969. "Evaluation of the War on Poverty: Status and Prospects at the OEO." Santa Monica, Calif.: Resource Management Corporation.

Rossi, Peter H. 1994. "The War Between the Quals and the Quants: Is a Lasting Peace Possible?" In *The Qualitative -Quantitative Debate: New Perspectives,* ed. C. C. Reichardt and S. F. Rallis. New Directions for Program Evaluation, No. 61. San Francisco: Jossey-Bass.

Rossi, Peter H., and Walter Williams, eds. 1972. *Evaluating Social Programs: Theory, Practice and Politics.* New York: Seminar Press.

Schorr, Lisbeth B. 1994. "The Case for Shifting to Results-Based Accountability." Improved Outcomes for Children Project. Washington, DC: Center for the Study of Social Policy.

Sheldon, Richard. 1974. Oral History Interview, September 30, 1974. Ford Foundation Archives.

Trolander, Judith A. 1987. *Professionalism and Social Change From the Settlement House Movement to Neighborhood Centers, 1886 to the Present.* New York: Columbia University Press.

Urban Institute. 1976. *Evaluating CDCs: A Summary Report.* Washington, DC: Urban Institute.

Vanecko, James J. 1970. "Community Organization in the War on Poverty: An Evaluation of a Strategy for Change in the Community Action Program." Final Report of a National Evaluation of Urban Community Action Programs Prepared for the Office of Economic Opportunity. Chicago: National Opinion Research Center.

Vanecko, James J., and Bruce Jacobs. 1970. "The Impact of the Community Action Program on Institutional Change: Assistance to Community Organization as a Successful Strategy." Joint Report from NORC and Barss Reitzel and Associates, Inc. Chicago: National Opinion Research Center.

Vidal, Avis C. 1992. *Rebuilding Communities: A National Study of Urban Community Development Corporations.* New York: Community Development Research Center.

Watts, Harold. 1970. "Memorandum to John Wilson," April 1970. Madison, Wisc.: Institute for Research on Poverty Archives.

Watts, Harold W. and Albert Rees, eds. 1977. *The New Jersey Income-Maintenance Experiment.* Vols. 2 and 3. New York: Academic Press.

Weiss, Carol H. 1972a. *Evaluation Research: Methods for Assessing Program Effectiveness.* Englewood Cliffs, N.J.: Prentice-Hall.

_____, ed. 1972b. *Evaluating Action Programs.* Boston: Allyn and Bacon.

_____. 1993. "Where Politics and Evaluation Research Meet." *Evaluation Practice* 14, no. 1: 93–106.

Wholey, Joseph S., John W. Scanlon, Hugh G. Duffy, James S. Fukumoto, and Leona M. Vogt. 1970. *Federal Evaluation Policy: Analyzing the Effects of Public Programs.* Washington, DC: Urban Institute Press.

Wiseman, Michael, P. L. Szanton, E. B. Baum, R. Haskins, D. H. Greenberg, and M. B. Mandell. 1991. *Research and Policy: A Symposium on the Family Support Act of 1988.* Madison, Wisc.: Institute for Research on Poverty.

Ylvisaker, Paul. 1963. "Remarks to the Conference on Urban Extension," October 1963. Staff Speeches Collection, Ford Foundation Archives. New York: Ford Foundation.

Nothing as Practical as Good Theory: Exploring Theory-Based Evaluation for Comprehensive Community Initiatives for Children and Families

Carol Hirschon Weiss

The topic on the table is the evaluation of comprehensive cross-sector community-based interventions designed to improve the lot of children, youth, and families.[1] These types of initiatives draw on a history of experience, from the Ford Foundation's Gray Areas Program in the early 1960s, continuing through the federal programs of the President's Committee on Juvenile Delinquency, the large Community Action Program of the War on Poverty, the Model Cities Program, community development corporations, services integration programs, and others. Most of the government programs incorporated requirements for systematic evaluation; for foundation-supported programs, evaluation was more sporadic and informal. None of the programs was satisfied that it had achieved either maximal *program* benefit from its efforts or maximal *evaluation* knowledge about program consequences from the evaluations it undertook.

In recent years a new generation of comprehensive community initiatives (CCIs) has been funded. Supported in large part by private foundations, the initiatives aim to reform human service and collateral systems in geographically bounded communities. They work across functional areas—such as social services, health care, the schools, and economic and physical redevelopment—in an effort to launch a comprehensive

65

attack on the social and economic constraints that lock poor children and families in poverty. They bring local residents into positions of authority in the local program, along with leaders of the larger community, public officials, and service providers. Examples of foundation-sponsored initiatives include Annie E. Casey Foundation's New Futures Initiative, Pew Charitable Trusts' Children's Initiative, and the Ford Foundation's Neighborhood and Family Initiative. Recent federal programs, such as the Empowerment Zone and Enterprise Community Initiative, include some parallel features.

A number of evaluations have been undertaken to discover the effects of the recent initiatives. Much effort has gone into developing appropriate outcome measures that can indicate the degree of success—or at least progress—in attaining desirable results. The evaluation strategies being used and proposed have tended to follow standard evaluation practice, emphasizing quantitative measurement on available indicators of outcome, sometimes supplemented by case studies. Influential members of the foundation community have wondered whether these evaluation strategies fit the complexity of the new community initiatives and the knowledge needs of their practitioners and sponsors.[2]

It is in this context that I suggest an alternative mode of evaluation, theory-based evaluation. In lieu of standard evaluation methods, I advance the idea of basing evaluation on the "theories of change" that underlie the initiatives. I begin by describing this evaluative approach and discussing its advantages. I then make a preliminary attempt to elucidate the theories, or assumptions, on which current initiatives are based. Although this is a speculative enterprise, its aim is to suggest the kinds of questions that evaluation might address in the current case. The paper concludes with some issues concerning the feasibility of theory-based evaluation and a discussion of steps that might test its utility for the evaluation of CCIs. The paper is meant as a contribution to the discussion of how evaluation can derive the most important and useful lessons from current experience.

THEORY-BASED EVALUATION

The concept of grounding evaluation in theories of change takes for granted that social programs are based on explicit or implicit theories about how and why the program will work (Weiss 1972, 50–53; Shadish 1987;

Chen 1990; Lipsey 1993). The evaluation should surface those theories and lay them out in as fine detail as possible, identifying all the assumptions and sub-assumptions built into the program. The evaluators then construct methods for data collection and analysis to track the unfolding of the assumptions. The aim is to examine the extent to which program theories hold. The evaluation should show which of the assumptions underlying the program break down, where they break down, and which of the several theories underlying the program are best supported by the evidence.

Let me give a simple example. There is a job-training program for disadvantaged youth. Its goal is to get the disadvantaged youth into the work force (thus forestalling crime, welfare dependency, drug use, and so forth). The program's activities are to teach "job-readiness skills"—such as dressing appropriately, arriving on the job promptly, getting along with supervisors and co-workers, and so on—and to teach job skills. What are the assumptions—what is the theory—underlying the program?

The theory obviously assumes that youths do not get jobs primarily because they lack the proper attitudes and habits for the world of work and they lack skills in a craft. The program's sponsors may or may not have considered alternative theories—for instance, that high youth unemployment rates are caused by forces in the larger economy and by the scarcity of entry-level jobs with reasonable long-term prospects; or that youth unemployment is a consequence of youths' lack of motivation, their families' failure to inculcate values of work and orderliness, health problems, lack of child care, lack of transportation, a lack of faith in the reality of future job prospects, or ready access to illegal activities that produce higher financial rewards for less work.

Those responsible for the program may have rejected (implicitly or explicitly) those alternative theories, or they may believe that alternative theories are not powerful enough to overwhelm their own theory, or they may believe that other interventions are concurrently addressing the factors that their work neglects.

At the program level, the program theory is based on a series of "micro-steps" that make important assumptions—for example:

- Training for attractive occupations is (or can be) provided in accessible locations.

- Information about its availability will reach the target audience.

- When young people hear of the program's availability, they will sign up for it.

- They will attend regularly.

- Where necessary, stipends (and perhaps child care) will be available to youth while they are in training.

- Trainers will offer quality training and they will help youth learn marketable skills.

- Trainers will attend regularly and provide helpful and supportive counsel.

- Youth will learn the lessons being taught about work habits and work skills.

- Youth will internalize the values and absorb the knowledge.

- Having attained the knowledge and skills, the youth will seek jobs.

- Jobs with adequate pay will be available in the areas in which training was provided.

- Employers will hire the youth to fill the jobs.

- The youth will perform well.

- Employers will be supportive.

- Youth will remain on the job and they will become regular workers with good earnings.

When we examine the theory, we can see how many of the linkages are problematic. At the program level, we know that the quality of instruction may be below par. It can be difficult to recruit young people to job-training programs. Many attendees drop out of the programs; others attend erratically. In some job-training programs, the promised jobs fail to materialize; either the skills taught do not match the job market or employers do not hire the trainees. Many young people get jobs but leave them in a short time, and so on. There are a host of reasons why the benefits originally expected from job-training programs are usually so small—in the best cases resulting in perhaps a 5 to 10 percent higher employment rate among program participants than among people who do not participate. The San Diego welfare-to-work program, the Saturation Work Initiative Model, was heralded in policy circles as a great success after two years, on the basis of evidence that about 6 percent more of the program participants than of the control group were employed after two years (Hamilton and Friedlander 1989). A five-year follow-up indicated that some of the difference between trainees and controls faded out over time (Friedlander and Hamilton 1993).

In fact, one reason for the current emphasis on community-based cross-systems reform is the need to deal with multiple factors at the same time—education, training, child care, health care, housing, job creation, community building, and so on—to increase the chances of achieving desired effects. The initiatives aim to work on the whole array of needs and constraints, including those that create opportunities, connect young people to opportunities, and prepare them to take advantage of opportunities.

The Case for Theory-Based Evaluation

Why should we undertake evaluation based on analysis of program theory? Basing evaluations on theories of the program appears to serve four major purposes:

1. It concentrates evaluation attention and resources on key aspects of the program.

2. It facilitates aggregation of evaluation results into a broader base of theoretical and program knowledge.

3. It asks program practitioners to make their assumptions explicit and to reach consensus with their colleagues about what they are trying to do and why.

4. Evaluations that address the theoretical assumptions embedded in programs may have more influence on both policy and popular opinion.

Focusing on Key Aspects of the Program. No evaluation, however well funded, can address every question that might be of interest to someone. With the current constraints on evaluation funding, the opportunity to look at a wide range of program processes and outcomes is further limited. In any evaluation of a program as complex as the current initiatives for children, youth, and families, careful choices need to be made about where to put one's evaluation energies. Central hypotheses about the program appear to represent potential issues that evaluation should address.

If good knowledge is already available on a particular point, then we can change its label from "hypothesis" or "assumption" to something closer to "fact," and move along. However, where a central tenet of the program is still in doubt, or in contention, then it might represent a question for which evaluation is well suited.

Generating Knowledge about Key Theories of Change. A whole generation of anti-poverty programs has proceeded on the basis of kindred assumptions, and we still lack sound evidence on the extent to which the theories hold up in practice. Many "effective services" programs, which began from somewhat different premises, have come to believe that "you can't service people out of poverty" (Schorr 1994), and have moved toward the same kinds of theories. Some assumptions have persisted since the Ford Foundation's Gray Areas Program. Although a great many evaluations were conducted on the community-based anti-poverty programs (including those in education, health, mental health, housing, community organization, and social services of many kinds), there has not been much analysis of the underlying assumptions on which they were based.

Effort was put into looking at outcomes—for example, school attendance, unemployment rates, and feelings of self-esteem. In later years increased attention was directed at studying how the programs were carried out—for example, styles of service and length of contact. Considerable knowledge accumulated about processes and outcomes. A small number of analysts have sought to synthesize the knowledge, but many of them have subordinated the synthesis to their own interpretations of the causes and cures of chronic poverty (for example, Bane and Ellwood 1994; Jencks 1992; Wilson 1987; Schorr 1988, 1991; Haveman 1977; Haveman and Wolfe 1994).

Creating a useful synthesis of the findings of evaluation studies on community-based programs has been difficult to do. The original evaluation studies used a large assortment of indicators, periods of follow-up, sources of data, methods of study, definitions, and perspectives. Their research quality also varied widely. To add them up presents the familiar apples-and-oranges problem. Meta-evaluation, the quantitative technique that aggregates the results of different studies into an overarching conclusion, is suitable for studies of a single type of program, where the quantitative measures of program effects can be converted into a common metric of effect size. To synthesize the results of the hodgepodge of evaluation studies available on community-based cross-sector interventions at this point would require substantive knowledge and analytic skills of rare discernment.

Nevertheless, important questions about the implicit hypotheses of community-based programs endure. It would be very useful to direct new evaluations toward studying these theoretical hypotheses, so that knowledge accrues more directly on these key matters.

Making Explicit Assumptions, Defining Methods, and Clarifying Goals. A third benefit of theory-based evaluation is that it asks program practitioners to make their assumptions explicit and to reach consensus with their colleagues about what they are trying to do and why. Without such a conversation, it is likely that different participants have different tacit theories and are directing their attention to divergent—even conflicting—means and ends. Imagine, for example, a preschool teacher who believes in unconditional affection and nurturance for the children in her care, working under a supervisor who requires that the children demonstrate cognitive achievement (numbers, colors) before they can receive approval. At the extreme, the assumptions and practices of the teacher and the supervisor may be so divergent that their efforts tend to cancel each other out.

When they are asked to explicate the theories on which the program is based, the discussion among practitioners—and between them and program designers, managers, sponsors, community leaders, and residents—is likely to be difficult at first. Usually they haven't thought through the assumptions on which the program is based but proceed intuitively on the basis of professional training, experience, common sense, observation, and informal feedback from others. Although reaching a consensus will be no mean feat, it is expected that discussion will yield agreement among program stakeholders and that the theories will represent a common understanding.

When the evaluator seeks to elicit formulations of program theory from those engaged in the initiatives, they may begin to see some of the leaps of faith that are embedded in it. Program developers with whom I have worked sometimes find this exercise as valuable a contribution to their thinking as the results of the actual evaluation. They find that it helps them re-think their practices and over time leads to greater focus and concentration of program energies.

Influencing Policy. Evaluations that address the theoretical assumptions embedded in programs may have more influence on opinions, both elite opinion and popular opinion.

Theories represent the stories that people tell about how problems arise and how they can be solved. Laypeople as well as professionals have stories about the origins and remedies of social problems (poor people want to work but the jobs have disappeared; services make people permanently dependent). These stories, whether they arise from stereotypes, myths, journalism, or research knowledge, whether they are true or false, are potent forces in policy discussion. Policies that seem to violate the assumptions of prevailing stories will receive little support. Therefore, to the extent that evaluation can directly demonstrate the hardiness of some stories (theories) and the frailty of others, it will address the underlying influences that powerfully shape policy discourse.

In a sense, all policy is theory. A policy says: If we do A, then B (the desired outcomes) will occur. As evaluative evidence piles up confirming or disconfirming such theories, it can influence the way people think about issues, what they see as problematic, and where they choose to place their bets. The climate of opinion can veer and wiser policies and programs become possible.

◊   ◊   ◊   ◊   ◊

In sum, the theory-driven approach to evaluation avoids many of the pitfalls that threaten evaluation. It helps to ensure that the developments being studied are good reflections of the things that matter in the program and that the results identified in the evaluation are firmly connected to the program's activities (Chen and Rossi 1987). Tracking the micro-stages of effects as they evolve makes it more plausible that the results are *due to* program activities and not to outside events or artifacts of the evaluation, and that the results generalize to other programs of the same type. These are strong claims, and inasmuch as only a few large-scale theory-based evaluations have been done to date, it is probably premature to make grandiose promises. But certainly tracing developments in mini-steps, from one phase to the next, helps to ensure that the evaluation is focusing on real effects of the real program and that the often-unspoken assumptions hidden within the program are surfaced and tested.

THEORIES OF CHANGE UNDERLYING CCIs: A FIRST TAKE

The comprehensive initiatives with which we are engaged are extraordinarily complex. What services they will undertake, how they will manage them, how they will conduct them, who will be involved—all these facets are to be determined on the ground in each community, with the full participation of the unique constellation of individuals in positions of business, political, and community leadership, and professional service. Unlike the job-training example that I have given, it is almost impossible to develop a plausible set of nested theoretical assumptions about how the programs are expected to work. In one community the assumptions might have to do with a series of steps to coordinate existing services available from the public and private spheres in order to rationalize current assistance, and then fill in the gaps with new services. Another community might have theories related to the empowerment that accrues to local residents who gain a strong voice in the organization and implementation of social programs for the community, and the consequent psychological and political mobilization of residents' energies. One initiative may focus on enhancing the quality of life of *individuals* with the expectation that individuals in more satisfactory circumstances will create a better community. Another initiative may put its emphasis on building the community and its social networks and institutions, in the hope that a better community will make life more satisfying for its residents.

It is challenging, if not impossible, to spell out theories of change that apply across the board to all the existing foundation-sponsored initiatives and to such federal programs as Empowerment Zones and Enterprise Communities. They differ among themselves in emphasis, managerial structure, and priorities. They allow for complex interactions among participating entities; they give great autonomy to local community efforts;

they foresee a process of long-term change; they do not even try to foresee the ultimate configuration of action. But if we cannot spell out fine-grained theories of change that would apply generally, we can attempt to identify certain implicit basic assumptions and hypotheses that underlie the larger endeavor. That is what the rest of this paper is about.

An Examination of Assumptions

I read a collection of program documents about community-based comprehensive cross-sector initiatives for children, youth, and families (Chaskin 1992; Enterprise Foundation 1993; Pew Charitable Trusts, n.d.; Rostow 1993; Stephens et al. 1994; Walker and Vilella-Velez 1992), and here I outline the theoretical assumptions that I discerned. These assumptions relate to the service-provision aspects that appear to underlie confidence that the initiatives will improve the lot of poor people. (I limit attention to service provision here, even though additional assumptions, including those about structure and institutional relationships, are also important.) Some of the assumptions on which the initiatives appear to be based are well supported in experience; others run counter to the findings of much previous research. For most of them, evidence is inconclusive to date.

Assumption 1: You can make an impact with limited funds. A relatively modest amount of money (on the order of half a million dollars per community per year) will make a significant difference. Even though the War on Poverty in its heyday was spending massively more money than that, the assumption here appears to be that this money can stimulate activity on a broad array of fronts that will coalesce into significant change. Perhaps it is assumed that much has been learned from prior experience that can now be exploited.

1. *The money will leverage money already available in the community for public and private services.* One possible assumption may be that the carrot of additional money will stimulate greater willingness among public and private agencies to coordinate existing services. Each of the agencies serving the community may be willing to give up some of its autonomy and control in return for some additional money from the initiative, and engage in more collaborative action. Agencies are customarily short of uncommitted funds, and even minor infusions of money can be assumed to divert them to new ends or new means. A further assumption is that the resulting coordination will yield large benefits (see the third point in Assumption 3, below).

2. *Another possible way in which the additional money can be expected to leverage current expenditures is by funding the creation and ongoing operation of a high-powered board of community leaders (elected officials, business people, voluntary association leaders), service professionals, and local residents.* This board will have the clout to persuade service providers to be more respon-sive to community needs, to coordinate more effectively, and to plug up the gaps in service provision. Because of its stature, and the stature of the national foundation that stands behind it, the board can convene meetings and conferences among important segments of the community and exercise its influence to ensure that coordination is succeeded by true collaboration across sectors. The funds, in this formulation, provide for the staff work for a steering body of influential elites (including "elites" from among the residents), and the theory would posit that it is the influence of the elites that succeeds in attaining coordination and funding new services.

3. *A third way in which modest resources from the initiative might stimulate action would be by funding a central entrepreneurial staff.* It might be assumed that this staff would have the savvy to locate needs and opportu-nities in the community. For example, a shooting episode in a local school might spark public concern about serious violence, and the entrepreneurial staff might seize upon this opportunity to press for further services from the schools and the police, and for greater cooperation between them, as well seek additional funding for enhanced services. Or the occasion of a search for a new school superintendent might provide the initiative staff an oppor-tunity to set forth their agenda for what a superintendent should do, and therefore for the kind of person to be hired. If the "new" money supported an activist staff who could locate windows of opportunity and fashion ap-propriate agendas for action, it might be assumed to have multiple payoffs.

4. *Money could also be used to fund research, analysis, and evaluation.* The intent here would be to marshall the experience of earlier change efforts, to monitor the programs and projects supported by the initiative, to analyze opportunities, costs, and benefits, and to evaluate the consequences of action. The assumption would be that people respond rationally to the presentation of formal, systematic evidence, and that they use it to improve the work they are doing. It implies that research evidence helps to overcome preferences based on other grounds. For example, the assumption is that service staff will heed analysis showing that a particular program has been unsuccessful with a particular kind of family, and change their approach to service, despite such factors as their familiarity with traditional ways of

work, the structure of the service organization that supports accustomed practice, expectations from collateral agencies, professional convictions and allegiances, political pressures, and so on.[3]

Assumption 2: An effective program requires the involvement of local citizens. This assumption can rest on any of several grounds, or on a combination of them.

1. *Local residents bring local knowledge, representativeness, and legitimacy.* Local residents on a board may be expected to have a better understanding of local needs, and therefore be able to direct the program toward things that matter to the people on the site. Local residents on a board may be expected to have greater legitimacy to local residents, who will then be more trusting of actions that emerge from the local initiative and be more likely to give those actions their support.

Local residents on the board may also be expected to be "representative" of the community. Even if they are not elected, they may be seen as democratically empowered to speak in the name of the whole community. All communities have existing divisions (by ethnicity, age, gender, recency of migration, economic status, education, aspiration, law-abidingness, and so on), and poor communities have at least their share. Still, in some way the local residents invited to serve on the board may be viewed by the business and professional members of the board as manifesting the "general will" of the poor community.

Another scenario is that local residents on the board may be expected to be effective spokespersons to outside funders and other influentials. An articulate person who has spent three years on welfare and worked her way off can be expected to speak with conviction and be heard with respect, and thus may be effective in public relations and fund raising.

2. *It is expected that resident members of the board will be eager and effective participants.* They will want to participate on the board on a voluntary basis. They will attend meetings regularly. They will have the skills to deal with the matters that come before the board. They will have the time to give to participation. They will be conscientious in learning about matters up for discussion. If they are expected to represent the community, they will make at least some kind of bona fide attempt to canvass opinion in the community. They will be able and willing to articulate their preferences in a group that includes better-educated and higher-socioeconomic-status members.

3. *Local residents on the board will not bring serious limitations to the task.* They will not try to work the initiative for their own personal benefit (beyond an acceptable range). For example, they will not give their relatives priority in hiring regardless of qualifications or appropriate initiative property for their personal use.

4. *A further hypothesis might be that the more participants the better.*[4] Extensive representation of residents is valuable because it brings to the table a wider range of ideas and experiences, and increases the diversity of opinions considered in planning and operations. Even though increased diversity is likely to generate conflict and slow the pace of action, nevertheless it enriches plans and ideas.

Assumption 3: Urban neighborhoods are appropriate units on which to focus program attention. Another assumption is that an urban neighborhood is a unit that makes sense for improving services and opportunities. Even though it is not a political subdivision, an urban neighborhood has natural boundaries that residents pretty much agree upon and that distinguishes it from nearby areas. It has social coherence so that residents feel at least some sense of common destiny. There is a real "community" and people who can speak for the community.

1. *Physical space.* Although assumptions on this topic are only hinted at in the documents I read, there may be theories about the improvement of physical space in the neighborhood. For example, improvement in outdoor physical space, such as improved street lighting, might be expected to lead to a reduction in crime and a reduction in fear of crime. As another example, improvement in the esthetics of the street, such as fill-in structures for snaggle-tooth blocks, will improve community morale. Or, expansion and improvement of recreational areas will provide play space and outlets for the energies of youth, with the expectation that this will reduce their engagement in illicit activity. Or turning rubbish-strewn empty lots into gardens will provide constructive activities for young people, give them a sense of pride in the neighborhood and even perhaps some potentially marketable skills, and give pleasure to residents.

Improving the housing stock can be expected to have a host of positive effects, so long as residents can afford the units that become available. Upgrading existing housing units and building additional units might be expected to improve the health of family members: such improvements will provide space and privacy so that tensions are reduced and family relationships improve; children will have space to do homework and therefore will be more conscientious about it and thus do better in school; better cooking facilities will be available, which can be expected to improve nutrition; and so forth. If very-low-priced units (or rooms) are created, the numbers of homeless people on the streets can be expected to be reduced, with improvement in their lives and enhancement of the esthetics of the neighborhood.

2. *Economic development.* A series of assumptions are embedded in expectations for economic development of the neighborhood. Investment and loans for businesses and housing might be assumed to result in increased income for residents (if it is assumed that they are the ones employed in the businesses) and better housing conditions (assuming they get priority in the new or rehabbed housing) and increased income might be expected to lead to new enterprises (since residents are now more affluent consumers), which in turn are expected to create jobs and lead to prospering local retail and perhaps small craft and manufacturing businesses. Local businesses will employ local workers, and thereby give hope to potential trainees in job-training programs and students in educational programs.

3. *Social development.* With the neighborhood as the unit for planning, services, economic development, and physical rehabilitation, further development of the positive aspects of the neighborhood can be expected in the form of local clubs and associations, religious congregations, schools, and informal interactions. Why should this happen? Perhaps because of symbiosis. An upward spiral of development might be expected because many of the separate activities will be successful and thus contribute to rising hope, satisfaction, optimism about the future, and a sense of common destiny. The bedrock hypothesis is that the visible success of early efforts will set off a chain of optimism and rising expectations.

Perhaps another theoretical strand would be that social and physical development can lead to a safer environment. Fewer people would commit crime; police would be more zealous about catching criminals; and crime rates would go down. People would feel safe to walk on the streets; instead of hiding behind their double-locked doors, they would engage in the kinds of social activities that bring liveliness and culture to the neighborhood.

4. *Social services.* A serious theoretical premise is that services can be effectively coordinated on a neighborhood level. Even though each separate service reports to a "downtown" bureaucracy, neighborhood caregivers from health, welfare, employment, policing, probation, sanitation,

health inspection, and education will be motivated to coordinate their services. They will not be constrained by the standard operating procedures of their agency, its longstanding regulations, traditions, and culture. They will embrace coordination, not sabotage the program's operation. In fact, staff should press for changes in bureaucratic rules that will accommodate residents' wishes for integrated services, family-centered care, and cuts in red tape. They can even be expected to press for co-location of services if and where this is one of the residents' priorities.

Downtown bureaucracies are expected to accede to such pressures for greater decentralization of services and increased coordination at the neighborhood level, even when it reduces the authority of the central bureaucracy. This unusual organizational behavior may have its origins in the fact that a high-ranking representative from each social service department serves on the board of the initiative, and these representatives will promote the objectives of the initiative neighborhood within their own organizations. Perhaps there is also pressure from the city's elected officials to accommodate the initiative (why?) or to respond to residents' demands because of their enhanced political organization and electoral mobilization. (If the latter is part of the theory, we need to adumbrate the set of assumptions about how political organization and electoral mobilization develop from the initiative's activities.)

Assumption 4: Neighborhood action will achieve the initiative's goals. A collateral hypothesis is that neighborhood involvement is sufficient to achieve the goals of the initiative, by using the influence of the neighborhood to leverage other resources. Additional action would be desirable at federal, state, and city levels or by corporations, banks, and supra-neighborhood private voluntary associations other than those involved. But while added resources and interventions would be beneficial, an important assumption is that the initiative board and staff operating at the neighborhood level are sufficient to mobilize resources necessary to make the program successful.

Assumption 5: Comprehensive services will lead to success. Comprehensiveness of services is indispensable. The assumption is that many prior failures in programming were due to single-strand narrow-band programs. Each program addressed one need of a poor child, youth, or parent, but failed to recognize the extent to which families were trapped in a web of constraints that single programs did not reach. No one program is sufficient to alleviate the multiple problems of a family suffering from low income, debt, poor health, lack of preschool day care, school failure of another child, and overcrowded, dilapidated housing. Only services across the whole range of need will help such a family escape from poverty.

1. *The nested assumption is that comprehensive service is possible to establish and maintain.* Agencies and direct-service workers can take the whole family as the unit of service and provide direct assistance themselves, direct assistance from another worker in the same or a nearby location, or easy, convenient referral to needed service elsewhere. Workers will be able to do at least a quick appraisal of the kinds of service required and know the appropriate care-givers who can provide that service. They will know the rules and regulations, eligibility standards, and operating procedures of hospitals, foster care agencies, probation services, welfare agencies, employment agencies, and the like, and can not only give referrals but can also follow up to see that family members receive appropriate help. They will have had sufficient training to prepare them for this changed role.

2. *Perhaps another assumption is that professional care-givers will intervene on behalf of their clients if proper assistance is not forthcoming.* Although such intervention is likely to bring care-givers into conflict with other social service providers (physicians, teachers, social workers, and so forth), they will run the gauntlet for the sake of their clients and press the other agency to alter its practice. Presumably they will usually be successful (or else the clients will lose confidence and hope, and the care-givers themselves will lose heart).

3. *Workers in the community initiative will seek policy changes* in service agencies to which clients are referred, and in other agencies, such as transportation and sanitation, so that they can collaborate in ensuring comprehensiveness of services.

4. *Implicit, too, is the expectation that these other agencies will alter their rules, regulations, and operating procedures* to adapt to the need for comprehensive provision of service to the community. (See item 4, under Assumption 3, above.)

Assumption 6: Social service interventions will succeed irrespective of employment conditions. Interventions in the social service sphere will make headway without regard to the employment structure. Business and industry, which control the availability of most jobs in the nation, are not apt to be affected by the community initiatives (except perhaps in some distant future if the community has turned around and become a thriving market and source of able workers). Without changes in the availability of jobs, the assumption evidently is that families served by the initiative will move to the head of the job queue. They may thus displace applicants less capable of satisfying the needs of the job market.

Assumption 7: Services for adults confer benefits on children. A final set of assumptions deals with the intra-familial allocation of benefits. There is an assumption that when an adult in a family receives services, benefits accrue to younger members of the family. A mother whose asthma is relieved has more energy to devote to her children; a father who receives training and gets a job becomes a positive role model for his children and is better able to support their needs. However, it is possible to imagine feedback loops that are less benign. A mother newly enabled to get a job may leave her children with a neglectful relative; a father who gains kudos through taking a leadership role in the community may lose interest in the relatively pale rewards of family life. Actions that assist adults may not automatically redound to the benefit of their children.

◊   ◊   ◊   ◊   ◊

In seeking to tease out the underlying hypotheses of the programs, I may have omitted a number of strategic points and perhaps included some that are tangential. I hold no brief for this particular list. My aim has been to give an example of what it would mean to begin an evaluation with an explication of the theories implicit in the program. The evaluation can then be directed toward testing those theories. I do not mean "test" in the sense of experimentation or even necessarily of quantitative assessment. I simply mean asking questions that bear on the viability of the hypotheses in these particular cases, through whatever methods of inquiry are chosen.

THE PROVISIONALITY
OF THE UNDERLYING HYPOTHESES

Some of the hypotheses in the list are well supported by evidence and experience. Some are contradicted by previous research and evaluation. For example, Wilner's (1962) study of the effects of public housing on its residents failed to find any of the positive effects, compared with a matched comparison group, that had been posited. But that study was done a long time ago. Today public housing is different; neighborhoods are different; families are different. While the new high-rise public-housing projects of the 1950s represented great hopes for improvement not only in housing but also in family functioning, they proved to be disastrous in many locations. Public housing has now developed theories of the advantages of small low-rise units on scattered sites with tenant participation in management.

Another example: all the studies that I'm familiar with about coordination/integration of public social services have documented the extraordinary difficulties of changing the behavior of workers and agencies (see, for example, Arizona Department of Economic Security 1989 and State Reorganization Commission 1989). But perhaps there are success stories that give clues about necessary incentives and sanctions.

An important step will be to discuss the theories that practitioners and residents engaged in community-building initiatives actually have in mind as they go about their practice. Often their theories will be implicit rather than explicit, and it may take time for them to think through their assumptions about how their work will lead to the effects they seek. Nevertheless, the feasibility of theory-based evaluation rests on their ability to articulate their assumptions (or to assent to someone else's formulation), and it is important to see how well this phase of the task can be done.

Then it will be useful to assemble the available evidence from prior evaluation and research studies. Perhaps, where the weight of the evidence casts doubt on the efficacy of particular strategies and lines of work, practitioners may feel impelled to find alternative ways to think and to act. Even before the evaluation gets under way, the process of subjecting assumptions to the test of available evidence can be a useful stimulus to re-thinking and re-tooling.

Another advantage of looking at past studies comes when an initiative has many ideas and assumptions that are worth studying and, because of inevitable limitations on resources, has to choose among them. Earlier studies can help narrow the choices. Where the overwhelming weight of existing evidence supports a theory and its associated activities, there may be less urgency to include that issue in the new evaluation. Other issues can receive priority. Similarly, it may be less important to evaluate issues where firm evidence already documents the causal chains that link interventions to early stages of progress or link early stages of progress to long-term outcomes. For example, in the evaluation of smoking-cessation programs, evaluators concentrate their efforts on studying the programs' effectiveness in getting people to give up cigarettes. They do not go on to study the health benefits of stopping smoking. Researchers have long since proved to everyone's satisfaction that giving up smoking yields significant decreases in morbidity and mortality. Analogously, if there is sufficient evidence that some indicator of intermediate progress is firmly linked to successful long-range outcomes, the evaluation need not proceed to verify the connection.

One significant point should be mentioned here. A program may operate with multiple theories. I do not mean that different actors each have their own theories, but that the program foresees several different routes by which the expected benefits of the program can materialize. To take a simple example, a counseling program may work because the counselor gives support and psychological insight that enables a young person to understand her situation and cope with it; it may work because the counselor serves as a role model for the young woman; it may work because the counselor provides practical information about jobs or money management; it may work because the counselor refers the client to other useful sources of help. All of those mechanisms are possible, and some or all of them may work simultaneously.

Similarly, a community initiative may work through a variety of different routes. There is no need to settle on one theory. In fact, until better evidence accumulates, it would probably be counterproductive to limit inquiry to a single set of assumptions. Evaluation should probably seek to follow the unfolding of several different theories about how the program leads to desired ends. It should collect data on the intermediate steps along the several chains of assumptions and abandon one route only when evidence indicates that effects along that chain have petered out.

OUTCOME INDICATORS FOR ACCOUNTABILITY

The aim of this paper has been to indicate a style of evaluation that comprehensive community initiatives might pursue. Evaluators could set forth a number of hypotheses that underlie the initiatives. After discussing relevant factors with program participants and reaching agreement on theories that represent the "sense of the meeting," the evaluators would select a few of the central hypotheses and ask: To what extent are these theories borne out in these cases? What actually happens? When things go wrong, where along the train of logic and chronology do they go wrong? Why do they go wrong? When things go right, what are the conditions associated with going right? Also, the evaluation could track the unfolding of *new* assumptions in the crucible of practice. The intent is not so much to render judgment on the particular initiative as to understand the viability of the theories on which the initiative is based. The evaluation provides a variegated and detailed accounting of the why's and how's of obtaining the outcomes that are observed.

But sponsors and participants may also want periodic soundings on how the local program is faring and how much it is accomplishing. For purposes of accountability, they may want quantitative reports on progress toward objectives. Theory-based evaluation does not preclude—in fact, is perfectly compatible with—the measurement of interim markers and long-term outcomes, such as high school graduation rates, employment rates, or crime rates. As a matter of fact, if wisely chosen, indicators of interim and long-term effects can be incorporated into theory-based evaluation.

Indicators can cover a gamut of community conditions before, during, and after the interventions. Evaluators can collect information on:

- school attendance rates, drop-out rates, graduation rates, scores on standardized tests;

- infant mortality and low birth-weight rates;

- unmarried childbearing rates;

- overall crime rates, auto theft rates, arrests of minors, and other crime statistics;

- numbers of families receiving Aid to Families with Dependent Children (AFDC);

- numbers of families moving off welfare in a twelve-month period;

- unemployment rates for teenagers and adults;

- numbers of clubs and associations active in the community and average attendance at meetings and events;

- attendance at religious services;

- registration and voting rates;

- numbers of books borrowed from local libraries;

- usage of hospital emergency rooms; and so on.

Such data can give some indication of the state of the community before the initiatives start up, and they can be periodically updated. However, they represent gross measures of the community, not of individuals in the community. To find out about individuals (by age, race/ethnicity, income level, gender, family status, and so on), indicator data can be supplemented by survey data on a random sample of *individuals* in the community. Periodic updates can show whether changes are taking place, in what domains, and of what magnitude, and they allow comparison of those who received direct help versus those who did not, two-parent versus one-parent families, and so forth.

The shortcomings of relying *only* on indicator data are several-fold:

1. Data on community-based rates reflect the condition of the entire population of the community, not just those who are affected by the initiative's work. Therefore, they are likely to be "sticky"— difficult to move. Lack of change in the indicators does not necessarily mean that nothing good is happening, but if good things are happening, they are affecting too small a fraction of the community's residents to make a dent in population-based indicators.

2. Any changes that show up in the data are not necessarily due to the initiative. (This is true not only in the case of community-based indicators, but of survey data on individuals.) Many things go on in communities other than the intervention. Economic changes, new government programs or cutbacks of programs, influx of new residents, outflow of jobs, changes in the birth rate— all manner of exogenous factors can have enormous consequences in this volatile time. It would be difficult to justify giving the credit (or blame) for changes (or no changes) on outcome indicators to the initiatives.

3. We do not know *when* expected results are apt to appear. Little experience has prepared us to understand how soon change will occur. All we know is that there will be a time lag of unknown duration before the effects of CCIs are manifested. This lack of knowledge makes interpretation of indicators chancy.

4. One of the key features of CCIs is their belief that it is vital not only to help individuals but also to strengthen the community, and that strengthening the community will reciprocally work to trigger, reinforce, and sustain individual progress. CCIs tend to believe in the significance of changes at the community level, both in and of themselves and as a necessary precondition for individual advancement, just as they believe that individual improvement will support a revitalized community. But few data are systematically and routinely collected at the level of the neighborhood, and those data that are available rarely fit the boundaries of the neighborhood as defined by the CCI. It is problematic how well available indicators can characterize community-level conditions.

For a variety of reasons, then, I would propose that even if outcome-oriented data are collected on the community (and a random sample of its residents), the items selected for study be carefully chosen on the basis of program theory. Only those indicators should be studied that can be linked, in a coherent and logical way, to the expected activities of the initiatives and to the intermediary outcomes anticipated from them on the basis of thoughtful and responsible analysis.

POSSIBLE PROBLEMS WITH IMPLEMENTING THEORY-BASED EVALUATION

Using theories of change as the basis for evaluation promises to help us avoid some of the most debilitating pitfalls of past evaluations of community-wide programs: (1) exclusive reliance on individual-level data, which evades questions about the role of "community" or "neighborhood" and casts no light on the effectiveness of directing program efforts at "refocusing the system," and (2) an inability to explain how and why effects (or no effects) come about in response to program interventions. Theory-based evaluation addresses such issues directly.

With all its appeal, however, the theories-of-change approach to evaluation no doubt faces serious problems in implementation. Let me mention four of them: problems of theorizing, measurement, testing, and interpretation.

Problems of Theorizing

A first problem is the inherent complexity of the effort. To surface underlying theories in as complex and multi-participative an environment as these communities represent will be a difficult task. At the first level, the level of the individual stakeholder, many program people will find the task uncongenial. It requires an analytical stance that is different from the empathetic, responsive, and intuitive stance of many practitioners. They may find it difficult to trace the mini-assumptions that underlie their practice, dislike the attempt to pull apart ideas rather than deal with them in *gestalts,* and question the utility of the approach.

The next level arrives when agreement is sought *among* participants about the theory of the whole CCI. There is likely to be a serious problem in gaining consensus among the many parties. The assumptions of different participants are likely to diverge. Unless they have had occasion before to discuss their different structures of belief, there will be a confrontation over what the real theory of the CCI is. When the confrontation surfaces widely discrepant views, it may prove to be unsettling, even threatening. I believe that in the end, the attempt to gain consensus about the theoretical assumptions will prove to have a beneficial effect on practice, because if practitioners hold different theories and aim to achieve different first- and second-order effects, they may actually be working at cross-purposes. Consensus on theories of change may in the long run be good not only for the evaluation but for the program as well. But getting to that consensus may well be painful.

There is a third level, which comes when a CCI goes public with its theoretical statement, whether formally or informally. A CCI may run political risks in making its assumptions explicit.[5] Canny community actors do not always want to put all their cards on the table. Such revelation may lay them open to criticism from a variety of quarters. Particularly when racial and ethnic sensitivities are volatile, even the best-meaning of assumptions may call forth heated attacks from those who feel slighted or disparaged as well as from those who dispute the analytical reasoning of the theories proposed.

Before we reach conclusions about adopting theory-based evaluation, it will be important to try it out with engaged actors in communities undergoing significant interventions. Their willingness and ability to work through the concept are necessary conditions for effective conduct of this kind of evaluation.

Politics can also inhibit theorizing. Observers of evaluation and other policy-oriented research have suggested that the urge to be "policy-relevant" impels evaluators to take their research questions and their measures of success from the political sphere and to concentrate on issues and options that fit the current political agenda. To the extent that evaluators focus narrowly on issues that are politically acceptable, they fail to articulate and test "alternative sets of assumptions—or alternative causal stories. . . . [This omission] effectively creates conditions in which we are likely to 'know' more but 'understand' less" (Brodkin, Hass, and Kaufman 1993, 25). Analysts like Brodkin suggest that evaluation of government policies is so embedded in politics that it is fruitless to hope for the necessary attention to causal theory.

Perhaps the same limitation would hold for evaluation of foundation-supported activities. Organizational politics may call for a blurring of outcomes and alternatives. On the other hand, foundation initiatives operate at some remove from the turbulent politics of Washington, and they may allow greater scope for rational evaluation.

Problems of Measurement

Once consensual theories of change are in place, evaluators have to develop techniques for measuring the extent to which each step has taken place. Have agencies adapted their procedures in ways that enable them to function in a multi-agency system? Have practitioners reinterpreted their roles to be advocates for clients rather than enforcers of agency rules? Some of the mini-steps in the theories of change will be easy to measure, but some—like these—are complicated and pose measurement problems. Whether they will all lend themselves to quantitative measurement is not clear. My hunch is that some will and some will not.

Whether exclusively quantitative measurement is desirable is also not clear. To the extent that theory-based evaluation represents a search "for precise and decomposable causal structures" (Rockman 1994, 148) through quantitative measurement and statistical analysis, it may be taking too positivistic a stance. The logic of qualitative analysis may be more compelling, since it allows not only for rich narrative but also for the modification of causal assumptions as things happen in the field. But since sponsors often find quantitative data more credible than narrative accounts, efforts should probably be made to construct measures of key items.

Problems of Testing Theories

Under the best conditions of theory, design, and measurement, will it be possible to *test* (that is, to support or disconfirm) theoretical assumptions? It is possible that statements of theories of change will be too general and loosely constructed to allow for clear-cut testing. Data collected may be susceptible to alternative interpretations. Unless statements about the theoretical assumptions of the CCI expressly articulate what is *not* meant, what is *not* assumed, as well as what is, it may be difficult to formulate decision rules about the conditions under which a phase of theory is supported or rejected.

Problems of Interpretation

Even if we should find theories that tend to explain the success of particular initiatives in particular places, it is uncertain how generalizable they will be. Will interventions in another community follow the same logic and bring about the same outcomes? On one level, this is a question of how sufficient the theories are. It is possible that even when available data seem to support a theory, unmeasured conditions and attributes in each local case actually were in part responsible for the success observed. Unless other CCIs reproduce the same (unmeasured and unknown) conditions, they will be unable to reproduce the success. Only with time will enough knowledge accrue to identify all the operative conditions.

On a deeper level, the question involves the generalizability of any theory in the social sciences. Postmodern critics have voiced disquieting doubts on this score. But this subject gets us into deeper waters than we can navigate here.

CONCLUSION

For all its potential problems, theory-based evaluation offers hope for greater knowledge than past evaluations have generally produced. I believe that the current comprehensive community initiatives should try out its possibilities. If we are to make progress in aiding children and families, the nation needs to know and understand the effects of major interventions. These initiatives represent a potent opportunity not only to *do* good but, perhaps more important, to *understand* how, when, and why the good is being done. Only with greater understanding of the processes of change will it be possible to build on successes in demonstration communities, to "go to scale" and bring benefits to children and families all over the country.

NOTES

1. I wish to thank Penny Feldman, Ron Register, Gary Walker, and Jo Birckmayer for their helpful comments on an earlier version of this paper, as well as the participants in the Evaluation Steering Committee Workshop in Aspen in August 1994. I'd also like to acknowledge the originator of the title; it was, of course, Kurt Lewin who said that there is nothing as practical as a good theory.

2. Some people are concerned that without experimental design (or some close approximation to), evaluations will not yield valid conclusions. Others worry that good data are not available at the community level to use as markers of success, and that evaluators will settle for small-area data of doubtful quality and unknown reliability. Another worry is that the selection of indicators can distort the work of CCIs. Just as teachers can "teach to the test," CCIs can work on those issues that will be measured, rather than on issues that would yield greater benefit to the community. Still other observers wonder whether local residents and service providers are having adequate say in the definition of the outcomes (and the measures) that will render judgment on their efforts. Some people recommend an emphasis on qualitative evaluation, which has the advantages of enabling the evaluator to follow the dynamics of program development and to understand the perspectives of the participants and the meanings they attach to events. However, qualitative evaluation of large-scale CCIs is time-consuming and expensive, and to be feasible, it would have to be highly selective in focus. Moreover, qualitative reports might not have the immediate credibility that quantitative reports command among decision-making audiences. The discussion about appropriate evaluation methods goes on.

3. From time to time in this inventory of assumptions, I interject a contrary note, as in the reference to conflicting pressures on service staff. This is not to express my own beliefs (heaven forfend) but to recognize the status of these assumptions as hypotheses. While I try to represent the beliefs of CCI advocates fairly as I read and heard them, caution seems to be in order before we let the beautiful rhetoric sweep aside our sense of reality.

4. I thank Ron Register for suggesting this point.
5. I thank Martin Gerry for reminding me of this point.

REFERENCES

Arizona Department of Economic Security. 1989. *Arizona Community Services Integration Project: Final Evaluation Report.* December. Phoenix, Ariz.: Arizona Department of Economic Security.

Bane, Mary Jo, and D. T. Ellwood. 1994. *Welfare Realities: From Rhetoric to Reform.* Cambridge: Harvard University Press.

Brodkin, Evelyn Z., Debra Hass, and Alexander Kaufman. 1993. "The Paradox of the Half-Empty Glass: Speaking Analysis to Poverty Politics." Paper prepared for annual meeting of Association for Public Policy and Management, Washington, DC, October 1993.

Chaskin, Robert J. 1992. *The Ford Foundation's Neighborhood and Family Initiative: Toward a Model of Comprehensive Neighborhood-Based Development.* April. Chicago: Chapin Hall Center for Children at the University of Chicago.

Chen, Huey-Tsyh. 1990. *Theory-Driven Evaluations.* Newbury Park, Calif.: Sage Publications.

Chen, Huey-Tsyh, and Peter H. Rossi. 1987. "The Theory-Driven Approach to Validity." *Evaluation and Program Planning* 10: 95–103.

Enterprise Foundation. 1993. *Community Building in Partnership: Neighborhood Transformation Demonstration, Sandtown-Winchester, Baltimore.* Progress Report, March 1993, typescript. Baltimore: Enterprise Foundation.

Friedlander, Daniel, and Gayle Hamilton. 1993. *The Saturation Work Initiative Model in San Diego: A Five-Year Follow-up Study.* July. New York: Manpower Demonstration Research Corporation.

Hamilton, Gayle, and Daniel Friedlander. 1989. *Final Report on the Saturation Work Initiative Model in San Diego.* New York: Manpower Demonstration Research Corporation.

Haveman, Robert H., ed. 1977. *A Decade of Federal Antipoverty Programs: Achievements, Failures, and Lessons.* New York: Academic Press.

Haveman, Robert, and Barbara Wolfe. 1994. *Succeeding Generations: On the Effects of Investments in Children.* New York: Russell Sage Foundation.

Jencks, Christopher. 1992. *Rethinking Social Policy: Race, Poverty, and the Underclass.* Cambridge: Harvard University Press.

Lipsey, Mark W. 1993. "Theory as Method: Small Theories of Treatments." In *Understanding Causes and Generalizing About Them,* ed. L. B. Sechrest and A. G. Scott. New Directions for Program Evaluation, No. 57, pp. 5–38.

Pew Charitable Trusts. n.d. *The Children's Initiative: Making Systems Work, A Program of The Pew Charitable Trusts.* Typescript. Philadelphia: Pew Charitable Trusts.

Rockman, Bert A. 1994. "The New Institutionalism and the Old Institutions." In *New Perspectives on American Politics,* ed. L. C. Dodd and C. Jillson, pp. 143–61. Washington, DC: CQ Press.

Rostow, W. W. 1993. "The Austin Project, 1989–1993: An Innovational Exercise in Comprehensive Urban Development." Paper prepared for Seminar on Inner City Poverty, Yale University Institution for Social and Policy Studies, October 1993.

Schorr, Lisbeth B. 1988. *Within Our Reach: Breaking the Cycle of Disadvantage.* New York: Anchor Press/Doubleday.

————. 1991. "Attributes of Effective Services for Young Children: A Brief Survey of Current Knowledge and its Implications for Program and Policy Development." In *Effective Services for Young Children,* ed. L. B. Schorr, D. Both, and C. Copple. Washington, DC: National Academy Press.

————. 1994. Personal communication, August 9.

Shadish, W. R., Jr. 1987. "Program Micro- and Macrotheories: A Guide for Social Change." In *Using Program Theory in Evaluation,* ed. Leonard Bickman. New Directions for Program Evaluation, No. 33, pp. 93–108.

State Reorganization Commission (South Carolina). 1989. *An Evaluation of the Human Service Integration Project, 1985–1988* December. Columbia, S.C.: State Reorganization Commission.

Stephens, S. A., S. A. Leiderman, W. C. Wolf, and P. T. McCarthy. 1994. *Building Capacity for System Reform.* October. Bala Cynwyd, Pa.: Center for Assessment and Policy Development.

Walker, Gary, and Frances Vilella-Velez. 1992. *Anatomy of a Demonstration: The Summer Training and Education Program (STEP) from Pilot through Replication and Postprogram Impacts.* Philadelphia, Pa.: Public/Private Ventures.

Weiss, Carol H. 1972. *Evaluation Research: Methods of Assessing Program Effectiveness.* Englewood Cliffs, N.J.: Prentice-Hall.

Wilner, Daniel, and others. 1962. *The Housing Environment and Family Life: A Longitudinal Study of the Effects of Housing on Morbidity and Mental Health.* Baltimore: Johns Hopkins Press.

Wilson, William Julius. 1987. *The Truly Disadvantaged: The Inner City, the Underclass, and Public Policy.* Chicago: University of Chicago Press.

How Do Urban Communities Affect Youth? Using Social Science Research to Inform the Design and Evaluation of Comprehensive Community Initiatives

James P. Connell and J. Lawrence Aber
with contributions by Gary Walker

The purpose of this paper is to explore one possible strategy for integrating social science research more fully into the design and evaluation of comprehensive community initiatives (CCIs) for children and families. It is our belief that social science researchers can play an important and useful part in these efforts. In this paper, we examine the social scientist's role in helping those who design, fund, implement, and evaluate CCIs to develop more specific and well-supported theories of what interventions are doing and how they might achieve their stated goals.

The paper presents a "framework" that we believe represents current social science thinking and research with regard to the major influences on key social outcomes that are of concern to policymakers and program designers in the youth field. We then suggest one set of urban intervention strategies that are consistent with the elements of this research-based framework. Finally, we draw out the implications of the framework for the evaluation of such initiatives. We recognize that, because it is restricted to urban youth (from early to late adolescence), the framework and its implications for program design are more limited in scope than the universe of initiatives represented by the Roundtable's participants. However, through the Social Science Research Council (SSRC) Working Group's ongoing collaboration with the Roundtable, we expect to broaden the work presented in this paper.

BACKGROUND

The immediate impetus for developing the framework presented in this paper was a project funded by the Annie E. Casey Foundation (James Hyman, Associate Director) and conducted by Public/Private Ventures under the directorship of James Connell, with Larry Aber as co-principal investigator. The title of the project was "Community Ecology and Youth Resilience." Out of that project came a report submitted to the Casey Foundation by Public/Private Ventures that was co-written by the two project directors and Gary Walker, president of Public/Private Ventures, with input from a number of Public/Private Ventures' staff members (Public/Private Ventures 1994). The framework, particularly its implications for the design of community-level initiatives focused on youth, was strongly influenced by the advisory committee to the Community Ecology and Youth Resilience Project.

The intellectual content of the framework has a longer history. It stems in part from an increasing awareness among social scientists of the limits of their individual disciplines to address complex social problems and promote healthy development of youth in urban communities, and from the increasing commitment of some social scientists to collaborative research efforts that try to untangle some of the complex cross-disciplinary issues that inhabit the world of policy and intervention design and evaluation.

The past and present work of the Social Science Research Council Working Group on Communities and Neighborhoods, Family Processes and Individual Development is one context in which these historical developments have taken form. The framework, while primarily representing the views of this paper's authors, has been germinating over the past three years in the interactions and writings of this group, and strongly reflects these inputs.

The paper is organized in three sections. First, the framework developed for the Casey-sponsored project is presented. The framework is based on the work conducted as part of the project, which included a series of meetings and interviews with an advisory group as well as literature reviews organized around the themes of youth resilience and community ecology, the authors' own work, and the work of the SSRC Working Group (whose members were heavily represented on the Casey project's advisory committee). The next section presents a set of intervention strategies for urban communities targeted at improving the life chances of youth in transition from late childhood to early adolescence (approximately ages 9 to 15). The final section discusses the utility of frameworks such as this one for evaluating comprehensive community initiatives.

A RESEARCH-BASED FRAMEWORK FOR THE ANALYSIS AND DESIGN OF INTERVENTIONS FOR YOUTH

The conceptual model presented in Figure 1 portrays a set of hypotheses about how communities affect our society's desired outcomes for youth, and the factors and processes that mediate that relationship. There are, no doubt, other ways to express these relationships and to define the key elements of such a framework—the research evidence is uneven and not always dispositive on these issues. However, we believe our framework accurately captures the *directions* now shaping social science theory and research.

Research literature suggests that the community dimensions identified in Figure 1 can directly and indirectly affect all three of the desired outcomes for young adults—economic self-sufficiency, citizenship, and healthy family and social relationships. The social mediators (family, peers, and other adults) and developmental processes (learning to be productive, to connect, and to navigate) are the factors that connect the community dimensions to the desired outcomes.

The framework is purposefully unidirectional, since the focus is on explaining the outcomes. However, we do want to note that in reality the various components exert influence in both directions—for example, the extent to which youth achieve the three outcomes affects community dimensions and social mediators. The influences and relationships involved in this "reverse" direction define a separate and even less well-researched set of issues.

In the remainder of this section we focus on the key components and subcomponents of the framework and their relationships with one another. As discussed above, we draw heavily on the literature review

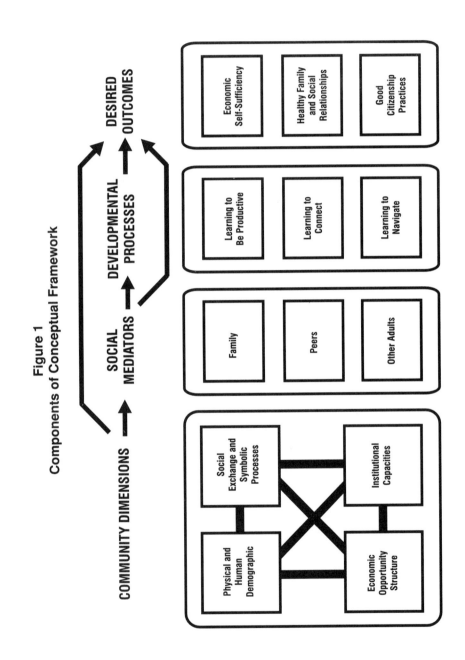

Figure 1
Components of Conceptual Framework

conducted as part of Public/Private Ventures' "Community Ecology and Youth Resilience" project, as well as from the insights of that project's advisory committee and the work of the SSRC Working Group.

Community Dimensions

Physical and Demographic Characteristics. The physical and demographic characteristics of neighborhoods include the economic, racial, educational, and social characteristics of the residents; the relative locations of the major subgroups of residents who differ in those respects; and the physical presentation, structure, safety, accessibility, and habitability of the neighborhood. A broad array of demographic characteristics—all of which are disproportionately prevalent in communities where high numbers of poor minority youth live—have been linked to problematic youth outcomes. In interpreting these findings, researchers have discussed the concentration of poor, female-headed families and the probable lack of adult supervision and monitoring (Brooks-Gunn et al. 1993); the absence of middle-class or high-status professionals and the probable lack of positive role models and institutional resources (Crane 1991); and male joblessness and its probable undermining of rational planning for families and youth (Wilson 1991). Researchers working in the tradition of social organization theory (for example, Sampson 1992) have also suggested that high degrees of ethnic heterogeneity and residential instability are associated with less cohesive adult friendship networks and less consensus on values. Coulton and Pandey (1992) have argued that population density and age and gender segregation in poor neighborhoods create extreme child-care burdens for some communities.

Recent research by the SSRC Working Group on these issues has expanded the age range and types of outcomes covered by previous work and has compiled more compelling evidence that neighborhoods with higher concentrations of middle-class residents confer benefits on youth. These researchers point out that more precise estimates of these effects await more sophisticated analyses and better measures of the community characteristics that accompany the presence of more middle-class neighbors (Duncan, Connell, and Klebanov 1994).

Economic Opportunity Structure. The economic opportunity structure affects community youth directly, and indirectly through its effect on the young and older adults of the community.

Important aspects of the economic opportunity structure are its industrial composition, the location of jobs, and the overall demand for labor. The deterioration of employment for inner-city residents has been linked to each characteristic. For example, the decline in the manufacturing sector in general and its relocation out of cities to industrial parks are often mentioned as important determinants of inner-city unemployment.

Minority employment, and especially minority youth employment, is very sensitive to the overall demand for labor. For example, Freedman estimates that for every 1 percent increase in the general unemployment rate, the unemployment rate for young men increases 2 to 5 percent (Freedman 1982).

Ellwood (1982) and Corcoran (1982) show, contrary to simple observation, that teenage labor market experience itself has little effect on future employment rates but does help youth accumulate work experience that employers later reward through higher wages. Thus, a lack of the opportunity to work does disadvantage youth in communities with poor economic opportunity structures.

There are several reasons why better economic opportunities may reduce the likelihood that youth get involved in antisocial behavior. First, youth who hold jobs are presumed to spend more time under adult supervision and less time with potentially subversive peers. Second, when youth have jobs or have the possibility of getting jobs easily, crime becomes a less attractive source of income (Fleisher 1966).

Institutional Capacities. Poor communities—communities with high concentrations of poor, single-parent families and jobless males, and low concentrations of well-educated, professional, and managerial workers— do not usually command the economic or political resources necessary to develop and sustain high-quality institutions and organizations that support healthy youth development. For example, funding of schools is in most states based primarily on local tax revenues, while funding of child care is a family responsibility. Thus, the basic educational and child care organizations in poor communities have relatively few resources. In addition, perceptions of neighborhood conditions by teachers and other adults from outside these communities may limit the pool of adults who are willing to work with these communities' youth. Because single-parent families and jobless males are cash poor, they are hard-pressed to support local commercial enterprises (stores, services), churches, and recreational and service organizations.

Likewise, the institutions that provide "primary services" to youth—Boys and Girls Clubs, Little Leagues, YMCAs, and so on—are typically scarce in poorer neighborhoods. This dearth of institutional capacity, along with that of the schools, means that youth often are without attractive, organized, and positive activities for most of their weekdays, evenings, and weekends.

To exacerbate matters, the greater educational and human services needs of the residents of poor neighborhoods place great demands on the community institutions and organizations that are present. Of course there are exceptions—a few poor communities have been able to make creative use of public subsidies and other resources to develop an array of high-quality institutions and organizations. But in general, the institutional infrastructure and capacity of poor communities are inadequate to provide the services and activities necessary for healthy youth development. Policy efforts to redistribute resources, and to initiate community and economic development strategies, have not been able to offset the more basic financial forces that depress institutional capacity in distressed neighborhoods.

It is precisely this community institutional capacity that, according to several research studies (for example, Coulton and Pandey 1992), appears to have the potential to ameliorate the debilitating effects of the two community dimensions previously discussed.

Social Exchange and Symbolic Processes. Research by Sampson and others suggests that neighborhood factors like high concentrations of poor families, high levels of ethnic diversity, and high population turnover directly affect community processes such as:

- the formation of dense friendship networks among adults;

- the articulation of and support for common values about child and youth development;

- the monitoring and supervision of youth, especially by nonparental adults; and

- mutual accountability among adults on behalf of youth.

These same community-level processes have been found to mediate the effects of neighborhood structure on such youth outcomes as delinquency rates (Sampson and Groves 1989) and educational attainment and economic mobility (Jarrett 1994). These same processes are implicated in explaining differences between communities on other key outcomes in childhood and adolescence, including rates of infant mortality, child abuse, and adolescent substance abuse.

Other research suggests that the presence of such factors may buffer the negative effects of different community dimensions (poverty, poor labor markets, and weak institutional capacity) on youth's peer groups (Sullivan 1989), families (Furstenberg 1990), and schools (Rutter et al. 1979).

The four community dimensions described above are major forces common to all communities, and have important effects, direct and indirect, on youth development. Research and observation also indicate that these processes interact, though we are on less firm ground in delineating the precise nature of those interactions and their effect on youth.

Social Mediators

Social mediators—or what Bronfenbrenner (1986) calls microsystems— are the conceptual linchpins between community dimensions, youth development processes, and, ultimately, socially desired outcomes. How well these mediators—family, peers, and other adults—function directly shapes the developmental processes that, in turn, determine whether individual youth achieve desired outcomes or not. Research has made considerable progress in the last two decades in showing how those social mediators affect outcomes and developmental processes. What is less well documented is how the major community dimensions shape the functioning of these mediators—for example, how the institutional capacities of schools and other organizations in the community affect the ability of adults in these institutions to support the community's youth. Some research demonstrates that these mediators make a difference in communities with problematic profiles on the major community dimensions, although the exact extent to which they can overcome those conditions is still largely unexplored.

What is clear is that social mediators, along with the major community dimensions, are vital parts of the overall ecology that influences youth development.

Family. Although youth become increasingly autonomous in relation to their families and increasingly engaged with peers over the second decade of life, our review of the resilience research indicates that families remain crucial contributors to youth development. The critical aspects of parents' and other care-givers' support appear to be a balance of nurturance and firm behavioral guidance and supervision. Our review of the literature suggests that this balanced style of parenting facilitates positive development in youth from diverse ethnic and socioeconomic backgrounds. Our review also reveals that a crucial factor in predicting positive youth outcomes in poor minority youth is the ability of caregivers to persist in their effective parenting in the face of worsening community conditions (Jarrett 1994).

But the research is sketchy and less directive about the exact relationships between community dimensions and specific aspects of care-givers' support for youth. Research does suggest that many care-givers' responsibilities are less consistently carried out in poor urban communities (Sampson 1992), but that denser social networks among adults who share values about youth can compensate for some individual deficiencies in care-giving competence (Furstenberg 1990).

Peers. The role of peers becomes increasingly important to development during adolescence. Peers include not only close friends, but classmates, neighborhood chums, and even members of the same age cohort who are not in direct contact with youth but with whom the youth competes for resources and the like. Our analysis of existing research suggests that peer culture in poor urban communities reflects in large part the community dimensions discussed earlier. More specifically, historical declines in those dimensions are associated with increasingly violent and virulent gang activity in urban areas, with youth remaining in gangs longer, and with increasingly negative effects on their life chances (Moore 1991).

Other research points to the ability of peers to provide positive support and to communicate prosocial and mainstream values. Some research indicates that such a social system appears to support youth development when there are opportunities for positive activities for youth and higher levels of social organization among adult community members (Sullivan 1989). For instance, whether a group of male friends becomes involved in prosocial or antisocial behavior appears to depend on factors such as the density of adult friendships in the neighborhood, the quality of adult monitoring of youth behavior, and youth's perceptions of whether there is a positive, productive niche they can fill.

Other Adults. The final mediator that exerts strong influence on youth developmental processes and outcomes is the network of nonparental adults relating to the lives of youth. In addition to teachers/mentors (especially early in adolescence) and trainers/employers (later in adolescence), many other adults play critical roles. These include coaches, club directors, community leaders, service providers, and ministers. Unfortunately, the adult composition and institutional capacities of many very poor communities in America restricts access to these other adults.

In addition, there are adults who are indirectly important to youth development, such as peers' parents, parents' friends, and employers. There is some evidence that peers' parents affect youth development independent of other influences. Werner's research suggests that the roles, activities, and values of other adults may prove to be one of the most important factors in distinguishing community ecologies that promote youth resilience from those that do not.

Family, peers, and other adults—these are the key mediums through which youth learn to experience and understand the world. As such, they are mediums through which community-level interventions must logically have their effects on youth. We will now turn to the developmental processes that these social networks shape across the life span of youth.

Developmental Processes

Research on child and adolescent development points to several critical processes that help children and youth beat the odds. These processes are many and varied, and the literature that describes their effects on youth development is rather technical. To facilitate discussion, we describe these processes as learning to be productive, learning to connect, and learning to navigate. Our review of the empirical and theoretical literature, and research in progress on poor urban children and adolescents, provide support for the importance of these processes as markers of progress. Empirical evidence of links between these processes and the desired outcomes is strong in some cases, inchoate in others; and much of the research reveals poor outcomes for youth who do *not* make progress in these three areas, not positive outcomes for those who do.

Learning to Be Productive. School achievement and, at later ages, work performance are the primary indicators of productivity. As numerous studies we reviewed indicate, school achievement in particular and cognitive and intellectual development more generally are consistent predictors of later employment and earnings. In addition to these "performance" factors, youth's beliefs in their own abilities and in the likely outcomes of their behavior, their engagement in productive activities, and their experience of support from care-givers and other adults, also affect their efforts to be productive in school (Connell, Spencer, and Aber 1994).

Research on youth in work settings implicates several other factors in learning to be productive: character (a sense of industry, initiative, reliability, and responsibility), self-regulatory abilities (both behavioral and emotional), and ability to cooperate with others.

Learning to Connect. A number of discrete (but related) factors are associated with youth's capacity to connect to others. Differences in childcare practices can affect individual differences in youth's "security of attachment" to their parents, their capacity to trust, and their sensitivity to and empathy with others, including friends, romantic partners, and, eventually, their children. These differences affect not only youth's capacity for healthy social and family relationships, but also the processes by which they appraise, select, and evaluate friends and partners.

The evidence we reviewed is strong that family cohesion and healthy care-giver–child relationships are associated with youth's ability to avoid later relationship problems. Evidence is also clear that peers strongly influence the likelihood of youth engaging in antisocial behavior.

In addition to learning to connect in friendships, romantic relationships, and parent–child relationships, youth also undergo processes that affect their identification with their own and other ethnic groups, communities, fellow human beings, and other less concrete, more abstract social groupings. The development of a sense of affiliation, belonging, community, and group identity are all part of the process of learning to connect.

Learning to Navigate. All youth must learn the rules and procedures that make up the socially accepted routines of daily life. These routines typically have no direct legal consequences if they are not adhered to. Rather, they influence others' perceptions of the individual's appropriateness and predictability in mainstream situations, and thus the options and opportunities that are made available. Going to the bank, eating out, attending public functions, using various forms of transportation, establishing credit and using it, dealing with a work supervisor or a customer—all these, and an increasing number of other rules and procedures that are generated by a complex and technically oriented modern world, are part of "learning to navigate."

Two other processes involved in learning to navigate are "coping" and "code switching." A growing literature in psychology demonstrates the benefits to children and youth under stress of coping strategies that include clear problem definition and subsequent fashioning of problem-oriented solutions. Unfortunately, most of this research has not been conducted with minority populations or with respect to the chronic stressors presented to poor urban youth. Studies of youth's reactions to violence are under way and may define more precisely successful coping strategies on the part of these youth.

"Code switching," another such process, is a term borrowed from psycholinguistics. In its broader use, it refers to the capacity to move among multiple worlds and switch codes accordingly—in terms of language, behavior, and expectations. The term has been applied to youth's capacity to make transitions between institutional settings (elementary to middle to high school); to adapt to minority status in majority-culture settings; to move effectively between the worlds of work or school and the streets; and, for youth from immigrant families, to navigate between their families' cultural norms and values and those of mainstream America. Research is just beginning on these issues, but qualitative evidence suggests that learning to code-switch is a key aspect of the navigation process for urban youth and may be associated with longer-term success and adjustment.

Learning to navigate is relatively easy for youth who grow up in advantaged neighborhoods, where they daily witness adults who practice these rules and procedures. But many poor youth do not grow up where adults practice these mainstream rules and procedures; instead, these youth learn different kinds of navigation skills, aimed at surviving on the streets. In some ways the skills they learn are similar to combat skills in their challenges and the seriousness of their consequences—and also in their low applicability and transferability to mainstream life. This inability to navigate in mainstream circumstances puts many poor youth at a serious disadvantage in joining mainstream life, even when they have the will and opportunity.

◊   ◊   ◊   ◊   ◊

These three processes are central during the late-childhood to late-adolescent period. For youth of different ages and life experiences, these processes will occur in different circumstances, and also shift in their relative importance. Researchers and practitioners have pointed out that the lives of many youth in poor urban communities do not follow a predictable or desirable developmental sequence—for example, some 10-year-olds are forced to become adults in terms of their economic productivity and caretaking responsibilities. Thus, community conditions may influence these processes in ways that defy or severely challenge conventional social interventions. But research also indicates that youth's experience of these learning processes is highly dependent on the quality and nature of their interactions with social mediators.

Desired Outcomes

Youth development comes to an end in early adulthood, when young men and women face a number of new expectations. Different communities, families, and ethnic and social groups have a variety of such expectations, but our society—as indeed most societies—has a core set of outcomes that it requires, in varying degrees of achievement, if an individual is to flourish. These outcomes are not defined by research, but rather by analysis of what it takes to secure a sense of achievement, freedom, and participation in mainstream adult life.

Economic Self-Sufficiency. The ability to sustain one's self and one's dependents is a hallmark of responsible adulthood in most societies. While enhanced economic well-being is highly desirable, many would define adult responsibility by the lower but more severely judged criterion of self-sufficiency—not requiring public assistance.

A growing literature is available on the determinants of economic self-sufficiency. They include the technical and employability skills, navigation skills, motivation, ability to work with others, and accessibility of decent jobs. For many youth, especially those living in poor communities, these pathways to economic self-sufficiency are severely constrained by the community dimensions and social mediators previously described (Connell 1994).

Healthy Family and Social Relationships. Another major feature of successful adulthood in most societies is the creation and maintenance of healthy relationships, both within and outside the family. A variety of factors index healthy relationships: marriage and divorce rates, child support and child abuse rates, presence of friendships and absence of social isolation, positive mental health and lack of depression, addictions, and so on.

Once again, research indicates that in distressed communities the development of healthy relationships is constrained by the influence of community dimensions and social mediators.

Good Citizenship Practices. It is possible to meet minimum expectations of citizenship through economic self-sufficiency (by paying taxes) and by obeying the law. Both of those practices are less prevalent in distressed communities. In addition, there are features of citizenship—contribution to the community and social responsibility, for instance—that are beyond the minimum, but that are at some threshold level indispensable to any civil society.

The pathways to full citizenship behavior are much less well understood than the pathways to economic self-sufficiency and family and social health. Nonetheless, our society expects and needs youth development to result in adult citizens who pay their taxes, vote, and obey the law, and who, in varying degrees, seek to contribute to the "common good" with actions beyond the minimum expectations.

Life in America's most distressed neighborhoods places constraints on youth's achievement of desired citizenship behavior by constraining their opportunities to achieve economic self-sufficiency and family and social health, two foundations of civil life. Youth in these neighborhoods must also overcome repeated exposure to racism, violence, and injustice and fight off the experiences of helplessness and hopelessness—experiences that can erode even the strongest civil instincts.

A Final Note. There is no absolute level of achievement on these desired outcomes that defines "successful" youth, because success is defined differently depending on the level of adversity faced. For some urban youth, just surviving—economically, socially, and politically—indicates success; for other youth, expectations are that they should be doing more than just surviving in order to be described as successful: they should be actively coping or even thriving. "Successful" is thus a dynamic and relative concept that will shift in definition depending on the context in which it is employed. However, setting minimal thresholds and optimal levels on these outcomes for individuals and groups of individuals will remain important tasks in the application of this framework to the design and evaluation of interventions.

Summary

We think that the conceptual model in Figure 1 accurately portrays basic connections between community dimensions, social mediators, developmental processes, and desired outcomes for youth. The evidence for the links in the model is not equivalent—for example, much stronger evidence exists for the links between the functioning of youth's social networks and youth developmental processes than exists for links between the community dimensions and these social networks. And, some elements in the model have been and will probably continue to be more susceptible to social intervention and, for that matter, to evaluation research as well. But the model reflects our best effort to represent the findings of research and the logic of current theorizing about how community ecologies shape the lives of their youth and yield differential success for these youth in young adulthood.

Our hope is that these efforts will provide a lens through which existing and planned interventions targeting youth outcomes can be analyzed and located. For example, an intervention could attend to its place in the framework's sequence; and could account for the supports and opposing forces that will likely arise from other key elements in the framework.

Analyses such as these need not conclude that all interventions should seek to change all aspects of the framework; they do imply that irrespective of the intervention's point or points of entry in the sequence—community dimensions, social mediators, developmental processes—the subsequent and preceding elements in the framework will affect the intervention's eventual payoff in terms of outcomes. Therefore, evaluations of initiatives that do not include those elements should still consider them as variables to be included in assessments of the payoffs.

The framework, in some respects, only codifies the judgments already formed by those experienced in the development, evaluation, and operation of social policy initiatives. But given the inconsistent, often politically derived nature of public policy—and relatively tight public budgets for new youth initiatives (or broader community-based initiatives)—we think codification such as that described in this paper, and the evidence behind these frameworks, will assist in deepening and widening the influence of those judgments.

In the next section of the paper we present one set of intervention strategies that we believe are consistent with the elements of the framework. By presenting these implications of the framework for the design of comprehensive community initiatives (in our case focusing on youth outcomes), we hope to provide the field with more concrete examples of how such a framework can be used.

IMPLICATIONS OF THE FRAMEWORK
FOR THE DESIGN OF COMMUNITY INTERVENTIONS
FOR YOUNG URBAN ADOLESCENTS

The purpose of this section is to draw on the framework to generate intervention strategies that we hypothesize would have positive and significant effects on the lives of young urban adolescents. At its most general level, the "theory of change" represented in this set of intervention strategies is that by strengthening particular community dimensions and social mediators, the three sets of developmental processes included in the framework will also improve and thereby increase youth's chances for achieving economic self-sufficiency, healthy family and social relationships, and good citizenship practices.

As stated earlier, the framework represents a set of hypotheses generated from existing research and theory. Up to this point, no specific tests of the efficacy of intervention strategies based on these hypotheses have been performed. So, while we do not intend to stray too far from the elements of the framework in suggesting intervention strategies and how to configure them, we recognize that other intervention strategies and configurations exist that would be consistent with the framework. We also recognize that we have moved beyond the framework and its research base in our presentation of these strategies and, certainly, in any suggestions for how they might be implemented.

Building Networks of Competent Adults
to Meet the Needs of Young Adolescents

It is clear from existing research that the lives of younger and older youth in urban communities differ markedly in where, how, and with whom time is spent. It is also clear that both groups of youth in these communities are adversely affected by less than optimal levels of the community dimensions and social mediators included in the framework. We have chosen to generate intervention strategies for younger adolescents—in school and between the ages of 9 and 15—in recognition both of developmental differences and shared contextual conditions between these youth and older youth. This age span encompasses the key developmental transition from childhood to adolescence, a fact that will be recognized in the intervention strategies we now discuss.

From the description of the framework provided earlier, it is clear that youth's relationships with adults in and outside their families are important predictors of their developmental trajectories in later life. From early in life through the teenage years, the quality of parent–child interactions affects the developmental processes included in the framework. Relationships with teachers and mentors have more specific but still important effects on this age group's capacities to build positive relationships and to participate successfully in educational and other socially valued endeavors. Thus, we are inferring from the framework's hypotheses regarding the effects of social mediators on youth's developmental processes that:

- the adults who either live or work with this age group of youth are the key "deliverers of the goods" in terms of supports for their development; and

- when these adults are vested with the competence, authority, and ultimate responsibility to create and manage their children's and young adolescents' daily activities and schedules, youth will become more productive and connected, and will navigate more effectively toward maturity and adult responsibility.

Research on youth crime and other youth outcomes argues for the importance of competent care-givers being available to meet the needs of youth, and also for these adults to be more connected to each other and to the youth in the community. Therefore, we are focusing on intervention strategies that can build shared values and norms that will energize and hold together these adult networks and reinforce their authority and legitimacy with their youth.

In addition, the research on peer influences that informed the framework points out that the coercive power and omnipresence of youth gangs in the lives of urban youth has filled a vacuum left by the absence of close ties to familial and non-familial adults—ties that can only be built through histories of shared activities. Therefore, we will need to include strategies that build adults' individual and collective competence and determination to reclaim authority from the peer culture, while respecting and harnessing its power to shape youth behavior.

Finally, a recurrent policy theme that has motivated many recent comprehensive community initiatives also appears as a hypothesis in our framework. That is, that society's goals for youth are undermined when educational, social, and other public services are fragmented, unresponsive to the needs of urban youth and their families, and isolated from their clients' associational networks. These defects in institutional capacity directly affect the ability of nonfamilial adults to effectively work with youth. Interventions are needed to support these adults' ability to deliver primary and secondary services and educational practices in more competent and coherent ways.

Building on two of the framework's social mediators—family and nonfamilial adults—we identify three sets of adults who are primarily involved with this age group of youth:

- adults living with the youth, including primary care-givers and other adult household residents;

- adults in the professional support network, including those working with youth in school and in primary and secondary service settings; and

- adults in the community-support network, including neighbors, local employers of youth, and adults who work in the community where youth live.

Building a network of adult support for young adolescents in these communities will involve all three of these sets of adults, but with different expectations for their responsibilities and involvement.

By suggesting that building competent adult networks is amenable to intervention, we also presuppose that what it takes to be a competent adult within a particular role and community setting is knowable and definable, and that, for example, the key elements of good teaching, parenting, social work, and health care can be communicated to adults. We also assume that existing groups of adults in these communities are ready and willing to engage in the community-level processes that will strengthen existing networks of adults and youth, and bring together different and even competing interests in the community around these common goals.

Based on existing research with this population and other populations of youth, and with input from experts in these areas, we have compiled a list of supports that youth this age need from adults. These are presented in Table 1 along with the three sets of adults who are candidates for carrying out these responsibilities. Some of these responsibilities clearly fall within the purview of one set of adults. For example, primary responsibility for transferring formal educational skills resides with teachers and within the professional network of adults; and providing emotional support to youth in this age group is mostly the responsibility of care-givers and family members. However, communities will vary in how, when, and which adults and youth interact. Recognizing and planning for this variation will require flexibility in clustering and allocating these responsibilities to adults in the community, but we hypothesize that the greater the number of adults in a community who are competent to carry out these responsibilities, the more adaptive and effective the community will be in supporting their youth.

We suggest three points of intervention for these three sets of adults:

- the adults' knowledge about the community's youth;

- their depth of experience with youth; and

- their level of competent support from other adults.

We expect that, with improvement along each of these dimensions, the effectiveness with which the adults carry out each responsibility should improve and, to the extent that these responsibilities are carried out more competently, youth should benefit. What constitutes sufficient improvement along these dimensions to improve youth outcomes remains an empirical question.

Table 1
Supports that Urban Youth Need from Adults

ADULT RESPONSIBILITIES	(1) FAMILY/HOUSEHOLD	
	Primary Care-giver	*Other Adult Care-givers*
Providing Incentives for Positive Behavior		
Setting and Delivering Consequences for Violating Community Norms		
Planning, Supervising, and Monitoring Individual Activities		
Monitoring Informal Group Activity		
Planning and Supervising Formal Group Activities		
Brokering Institutional Relationships		
Providing Positive Role Models		
Accessing Opportunity Structures: *Education*		
Recreation		
Cultural		
Employment		
Service		
Providing Personal Resources: *Emotional*		
Material		
Physical/Health		
Holding Other Adults Accountable: *Family*		
Non-Familial		
Professional		
Transfer of Formal Skills: *Education*		
Work		
Health		
Life		

Table 1
Supports that Urban Youth Need from Adults

(2) PROFESSIONAL SUPPORT NETWORKS			(3) COMMUNITY SUPPORT	
School	Primary Services	Secondary Services	Employers	Neighbors

Building the Knowledge Base. Adults who either live or work with youth in these communities will need to recognize the developmental needs and capacities of this community's youth in order to provide effective supports for them. They will also have to use effective strategies for meeting those needs in the different contexts in which they interact with the youth. To build this collective knowledge base among adults who live or work with these youth, we offer the following suggestions:

- Design community-level programs in which trained and experienced parents from the community are paid to work with and provide support for other, less experienced parents and care-givers.

- Involve the professional support network of adults—including school, social service, juvenile justice, and police personnel—in shared professional development programs to build their knowledge base and repertoire of effective practices with respect to this group of youth.

- Augment the training of adults working with youth in voluntary youth-serving organizations and other primary services such as churches, synagogues, parks, and recreation departments to include specific instruction and supervised experiences in these areas.

- Initiate community programs for all residents in the areas of conflict resolution and violence prevention, with particular emphasis on adult–youth relationships outside the home and school.

- Work with local employers to craft mutually beneficial strategies for creating more developmentally oriented workplaces for younger youth (Gambone 1993).

What is not elaborated but will be critical to the success of these knowledge-building efforts is the sharing of *specific* strategies for carrying out these responsibilities with individual adults within particular roles—for parents, how to discipline a ten-year old; for teachers, ways of teaching fractions to underachievers; for coaches, strategies for building teamwork among adolescents through sports activities. To validate the links in the framework between adult competence and youth's developmental processes, the intervention strategies will have to deliver specific, concrete, and, to some extent, prescriptive information to adults about what, when, and how to carry out the responsibilities presented in Table 1.

Knowledge-building activities such as those suggested above for caregivers, service providers, and community residents are hypothesized to increase community adults' knowledge about youth and what to do with them. But, key to the successful application and adaptation of this knowledge base will be the other two elements of the overall strategy—deeper understanding and experience of individual youth, and increasing levels of support among adults. Implementing these two elements will require additional efforts of a different but complementary sort. Specifically, interventions will have to be developed to promote connectedness between adults and youth in the community and among the adults themselves.

Promoting Connectedness between Adults and Youth. Research and experience working with youth in urban communities suggest that for many youth, mobility is the norm—in where they live, with whom they live, who their teachers are, and where they receive services. Research and experience also suggest that mobility is detrimental to these youth's school performance and adjustment and, by inference, to their longer-term success. Likewise, the amount of sustained adult contact that youth experience on a daily basis in these communities is arbitrarily constrained by school schedules demanding changes in classes every 45 minutes, and social service appointments of similar length. From year to year, the professional network of adults supporting youth changes without reference to effectiveness or to developmental principles such as the youth's need for stable adult relationships.

In attempting to extract the framework's implications for strengthening the social mediators involving adults, we suggest the following intervention strategies that involve all three sets of adults:

- changes in school catchment areas, schedules, and staffing patterns to promote continuity of adult support in school;

- case management approaches to social service provision that keep one adult or a small team of adults coordinated across specialties with the youth over time;

- planned and regular interactions between community residents
  and youth, and between parents and youth, that build collective
  traditions of shared activities;

- provision of high-quality day care for younger children that "frees
  up" parents to spend more time with their older children; and

- programs to improve employers' family support practices that
  encourage increased parent–youth contact.

Connecting Adults in Youth's Support Networks. According to existing
research on community social exchange processes, perhaps the most important result of efforts to build adult competencies and increase positive
contact between adults and youth would be the creation of a common,
consensually validated set of expectations and practices. For example:

- All adult care-givers are able to call on three other adults in the
  community who can provide competent care of their twelve-year-
  old for an evening.

- Adults living or working with this community's youth refrain
  from using violent and profane language in front of the youth.

- All adults with responsibilities for youth have effective techniques
  for discouraging the use of physical violence to solve conflicts.

- Adults working with youth in the community can legitimately
  and effectively "call each other on the carpet" for not following
  through with their commitments to their youth.

The framework includes hypotheses about the importance of social
exchange processes to the effectiveness both of family and nonfamilial
adults' support for youth development. One such process is the building
of adult networks, a process that we hypothesize will reinforce the adult
competencies and involvement with youth targeted by the first two sets of
intervention strategies. We also speculate that communities may go
through stages as they build these networks and that activities could be
planned and sequenced that encourage and support parents to form denser

and more mutually supportive networks. For example, a progressive series of activities could be planned that encourage parents in the community to:

- find out who their neighbors are and whether and how many children they have;

- make initial contact where appropriate and feasible, such as exchanging phone numbers;

- engage in some shared activity (for example, a block party, group dinner, or attendance at a cultural or recreational event);

- exchange information about themselves and their youth (such as daily schedules, areas of concern about the neighborhood, positive activities for youth);

- discuss their goals and values for youth, not seeking to achieve immediate consensus but looking for opportunities for shared action (for example, in getting rid of sleep-disrupting noise in the neighborhood);

- plan necessary actions and share responsibility for carrying them out (for example, evening neighborhood watches);

- develop ways to look out for and offer support to other care-givers and their youth; and

- recognize and accept that there are consequences when adults do not give what is deemed to be the minimum support for their own and each others' youth.

It is possible that these stages and their associated activities can be adapted to building supportive networks for youth within and among sets of other adults as well—for example, care-givers and police, the community's teachers in elementary and middle schools, or primary and secondary service providers. The starting points and the degree and kinds of external support required to move this process ahead will vary between and within communities, depending on which set or sets of adults are trying to build their networks. In some cases, once the process is under way it could move through the later stages without any external support; or the process could stall at some point and require external support to move it across a difficult transition.

Relevant examples exist in current "youth development" initiatives, such as school reforms that bring parents into school governance, and interventions that locate social services in residential housing units to promote more responsive practices and better communication between parents and service providers.

Facilitating Community Conditions. By drawing out the conceptual framework's implications for intervention strategies for this age group of youth, we are highlighting certain elements of the framework and not others. This was intentional—as stated earlier, the framework is not intended to encourage comprehensiveness for its own sake. It was intended to lay out the major influences—direct and indirect—that community factors can have on positive youth outcomes in young adulthood. However, we will now discuss *other* elements of the framework that could facilitate or undermine the effectiveness of the intervention strategies suggested above.

These elements are:

- improving the physical and human conditions of the community so that levels of safety increase;

- enhancing the economic opportunity structure in order to provide meaningful adult employment; and

- catalyzing the social exchange processes to build political capital in these communities.

We now discuss how each of these conditions could promote or undermine building networks of competent adults to support youth in urban communities.

Qualitative and quantitative studies of urban communities have revealed that safety is an overriding concern. It factors strongly into adults' decisions about the breadth and frequency of their own social interactions, about whether to permit youth to spend time in educational activities outside of school or during evening hours, and about their willingness to travel with their youth to cultural, educational, and recreational facilities within and outside their communities. Without safer conditions at home, in schools, and on the streets, adults who either live or work with youth will be stifled in their attempts to develop their social networks and plan activities with and for youth.

Increasing economic opportunities for adults in these urban communities should have beneficial effects on youth by encouraging them to have more positive and realistic expectations for their own employment futures and to participate in and learn about the regularities of work through observation of their working care-givers and other adults. Research undergirding the framework also documents that adults' ability to be involved in their children's lives in productive ways can be undermined by the effects of persistent economic distress. Given that one goal of this set of intervention strategies is to enhance the level and quality of adult care-givers' interactions with youth, increasing adult employment in meaningful jobs should help set the stage for intervention strategies focused on this goal.

Based on the framework, we have hypothesized that changes in the practices of youth-serving institutions that increase the competence, connectedness, and continuity of adults' interactions with youth will result in better developmental outcomes for youth. How will these institutions be encouraged to change and what forces will sustain these reforms? While those questions do not yet have any answers, we would hypothesize that when parents and other adults who work directly with youth have greater access to, and additional leverage on, the mainstream institutions affecting them and their youth, it will be easier to initiate and maintain reforms. Neighborhood schools, social services, and juvenile justice and health care systems are examples of such mainstream institutions. Without that leverage, the potential impact of this set of intervention strategies is compromised in several ways.

First, adult care-givers in the community will not be able to disturb the inertia of institutions that mitigate against the goals of competence, connectedness, and continuity of adult supports for these youth. Second, it will not be possible to reallocate existing resources controlled by these institutions—resources that will be necessary to initiate, implement, and institutionalize change in practices. Finally, the building of community-specific systems of collective accountability among adults who live or work with youth will be inhibited unless community residents and their advocates have some regulatory authority over activities involving their youth.

Neither existing evidence nor theory allows us to speculate *which* of these facilitating conditions is necessary or sufficient for urban communities to build strong adult networks to support their youth. However, the history of evaluation research and field experience suggest that current levels of safety, economic opportunity, and political capital in these communities will have profound dampening effects on their efforts to do so.

Summary

In order to demonstrate the utility of a research-based framework linking community and individual change as a basis for designing comprehensive community initiatives, we have offered a set of community-level intervention strategies that are consistent with the framework. This set of strategies focuses on strengthening the social mediators between community dimensions and developmental processes in the framework. The intervention strategies themselves are community-level efforts to increase the competence, connectedness, and continuity of adults' interactions that involve school-aged youth ages 9 to 15. Other intervention strategies for this age group of youth would also be consistent with the framework—for example, focusing on peer groups directly versus strengthening adult networks in order to offset negative peer influences; or offering discrete activities for youth specifically geared toward enhancing their productivity, connectedness, and ability to navigate.

The implications of the framework for program design will also be different as the framework is applied to different age groups and/or different community settings. The Evaluation Steering Committee of the Roundtable intends to develop a similar research-based framework for younger children and their families.

We were somewhat reluctant to extrapolate from the framework as far as we did in presenting these strategies. First, research on naturally occurring variation in these processes does not easily or even appropriately translate into what to do to change them. Second, although we were relatively confident about the research base undergirding our theory about what will produce change in youth, we are sorely lacking in theory or research on what brings about change in communities and institutions.

For example, we feel confident that if these strategies "took"—if more adults began to interact with youth on a day-to-day basis in these communities, and if these adults were more competent in their specific roles and responsibilities, more connected and mutually supportive and more intensively involved with youth over longer periods of time—there would be payoffs for these younger adolescents. They should be more productive, connected, and better able to navigate their way through the challenges they face as they make the transition to and from adolescence in these urban communities.

But, neither researchers nor practitioners have identified the appropriate incentives and supports that are necessary to instigate and maintain these changes in institutional practices, community norms, and adult behavioral patterns. And, even if we could achieve the interventions' short-term payoffs for youth, those payoffs would only lead to longer-term outcomes (1) if the intervention strategies "took" strongly and persistently enough so that individual change in the community's youth was widespread and deeply internalized, and (2) if there were future opportunities within and outside their communities for older youth to build on the developmental processes that were strengthened during their earlier years.

We recognize that CCIs will continue to be designed and implemented based on incomplete knowledge and with some skepticism about their ability to produce long-term outcomes. We also believe we can continue to build this knowledge base and bolster our confidence in the lasting impact of CCIs by:

- making explicit the theories of change that are guiding the initiatives;

- specifying the operational strategies that are being implemented to initiate and maintain these changes;

- identifying external conditions that facilitate or undermine the effectiveness of these operational strategies; and

- projecting the future supports that will permit short-term effects to lead to longer-term outcomes.

IMPLICATIONS OF THE FRAMEWORK
FOR EVALUATION OF
COMPREHENSIVE COMMUNITY INITIATIVES

We believe research-based frameworks such as the one described in this paper can benefit evaluations both of existing and future comprehensive community initiatives. For existing CCIs, evaluators can use a research-based framework as a lens to critically examine the elements of an initiative's "theory of change." For example, the evaluator can ask whether the community dimensions targeted for intervention and their putative outcomes match up in any way to existing knowledge about links between these dimensions and the outcomes. If either no evidence or, worse yet, contrarian evidence exists for the predicted effect of a targeted element on a particular outcome, the evaluator could recommend that funders' resources be redirected toward tracking more plausible effects of the initiative. In addition to focusing evaluation resources on "best bets," the power to detect these effects could be increased by reallocating resources to more precise and multi-method measurement of the inputs and outcomes that comprise them. Some of these more precise measurement strategies could be available from researchers studying these issues. Finally, if evaluators decide it is desirable and feasible to use these research measures, existing studies could potentially provide information on their psychometric properties in populations similar to those involved in the CCI.

In addition to their potential utility in evaluations of existing CCIs, research-based frameworks could make an important contribution to the design of future CCIs. As the example we provided shows, the links in the framework can generate fairly specific sets of community-level intervention strategies, which the framework suggests should affect interim and longer-term outcomes for the community's residents if the strategies change the community dimensions they target. The major benefit that evaluators derive from these framework-based designs is that it will be clearer what to evaluate and how to measure it: Which elements are the targets of the intervention? How is change in these elements expected to produce change in other elements? Which "downstream" outcomes can be expected to be affected earlier versus later in the life of the initiative? And where should we look for potential measures of the targeted elements and outcomes?

Caveats

What frameworks such as these will not do for evaluators is resolve the thorny issues raised in the Introduction to this volume and detailed in the paper by Rob Hollister and Jennifer Hill—specifically, the problems of attributing impact to CCIs through the creation of compelling counterfactuals. These issues await serious conceptual and methodological work outside the purview of this paper's contribution.

The empirical bases for the links hypothesized in these frameworks are from studies of "naturally occurring" covariation among the framework's elements—not from experimental evidence of cause and effect or, with a few exceptions, from studies providing evidence that change in one of these elements is associated with change in another element. Given these limits of the research data and the absence of data for some of these links, use of the framework as the sole or even primary criterion for important program design or evaluation decisions is not warranted.

Finally, as discussed earlier in this paper, the primary sources of research underlying these frameworks do not draw the distinction between variables that are subject to intervention and those that are not. In our review of the literature and the discussions among our advisors, we attempted to introduce susceptibility to intervention as an inclusion criterion for the elements of the framework. However, we recognize that there will be divergent views on whether some of our framework's elements meet this test.

◊   ◊   ◊   ◊   ◊

In conclusion, and on a more optimistic note, we predict that designers and evaluators of comprehensive community initiatives will find research-based frameworks to be useful. We hope this framework describing how communities affect urban youth, and our future efforts to develop similar frameworks for younger children and their families, will strengthen the ties between the designers and evaluators of CCIs and the basic research community. Increased use of research to inform the design and evaluation of CCIs could help catalyze the science research community to fill the gaps in these frameworks with more evidence, better measures, and clearer communications of their findings. Ultimately, these collaborative efforts can only serve to improve and enrich discussions of what should be done to support communities' efforts to improve the lives of their residents and how best to learn from these intervention efforts.

REFERENCES

Bronfenbrenner, U. 1986. "Ecology of the Family is a Context for Human Development: Research Perspectives." *Developmental Psychology* 22, No. 6: 723–42.

Brooks-Gunn, J., G. J. Duncan, P. Kato, and N. Sealand. 1993. "Do Neighborhoods Influence Child and Adolescent Behavior?" *American Journal of Sociology* 99, No. 2: 353–95.

Connell, J. P. 1994. "Applying a Youth Development Perspective to the Early Prediction of African-American Males' Labor Market Attachment." Working Paper. Philadelphia: Public/Private Ventures.

Connell, J. P., M. B. Spencer, and J. L. Aber. 1994. "Educational Risk and Resilience in African-American Youth: Context, Self, Action and Outcomes in School." *Child Development* 65.

Coulton, C.J., and S. Pandey. 1992. "Geographic Concentration of Poverty and Risk to Children in Urban Neighborhoods." *American Behavioral Scientist* 35, No. 3: 238–57.

Corcoran, M. 1982. "The Employment and Wage Consequences of Teenage Women's Nonemployment." In *The Youth Labor Market Problem: Its Nature, Causes, and Consequences,* ed. Richard Freeman and David Wise. Chicago: University of Chicago Press.

Crane, J. 1991. "The Epidemic Theory of Ghettos and Neighborhood Effects on Dropping Out and Teenage Childbearing." *American Journal of Sociology* 96, No. 5: 1926–59.

Duncan, G. J., J. P. Connell, and P. K. Klebanov. 1994. "Are Neighborhood Effects Really Causal?" SSRC Working Paper. New York: Social Science Research Council.

Ellwood, D. 1982. "Teenage Unemployment: Permanent Scars or Temporary Blemishes?" In *The Youth Labor Market Problem: Its Nature, Causes, and Consequences,* ed. Richard Freeman and David Wise. Chicago: University of Chicago Press.

Fleisher, B. 1966. *The Economics of Delinquency.* Chicago: Quadrangle Books.

Freedman, R. 1982. "Economic Determinants of Geographic and Individual Variation in the Labor Market Position of Young Persons." In *The Youth Labor Market Problem: Its Nature, Causes, and Consequences,* ed. Richard Freeman and David Wise. Chicago: University of Chicago Press.

Furstenburg, F. F. 1990. "How Families Manage Risk and Opportunity in Dangerous Neighborhoods." Paper presented at the 84th Annual Meeting of the American Sociological Association, Washington, DC, August 1990.

Gambone, M. A. 1993. *Strengthening Programs for Youth: Promoting Adolescent Development in the JTPA System.* Philadelphia: Public/Private Ventures.

Jarrett, R. L. 1994. "Community Context, Intrafamilial Processes, and Social Mobility Outcomes: Ethnographic Contributions to the Study of African-American Families and Children in Poverty." In *Ethnicity and Diversity,* ed. G. E. Brookings and M. B. Spencer. Hillsdale, N.J.: Erlbaum.

Moore, Joan W. 1991. *Going Down to the Barrio: Home Boys and Home Girls in Change.* Philadelphia: Temple University Press.

Public/Private Ventures. 1994. *Community Ecology and Youth Resilience: A Report to the Annie E. Casey Foundation.* Philadelphia: Public/Private Ventures.

Rutter, Michael, Barbara Maughan, Peter Mortimer, and Janet Ouston, with Alan Smith. 1979. *Fifteen Thousand Hours: Secondary Schools and their Effects on Children.* Cambridge, Mass.: Harvard University Press.

Sampson, R. J. 1992. "Family Management and Child Development: Insights from Social Disorganization Theory." In *Advances in Criminological Theory,* ed. J. McCord. New Brunswick: Transaction Books.

Sampson, R. J., and W. B. Groves. 1989. "Community Structure and Crime: Testing Social Disorganization Theory." *American Journal of Sociology* 94, No. 4: 774–802.

Sullivan, M. 1989. *Getting Paid: Youth and Work in the Inner City.* Ithaca: Cornell University Press.

Wilson, W. J. 1991. "Studying Inner City Dislocations: The Challenges of Public Agenda Research. *American Sociological Review* 56: 1–14.

Problems in the Evaluation of Community-Wide Initiatives

Robinson G. Hollister and Jennifer Hill

In this paper we outline the types of problems that can arise when an attempt is made to evaluate the effects of community-wide programs, or comprehensive community initiatives (CCIs). Our particular focus is on interventions that target all the individuals in a given geographic area or among a given class of people. We emphasize this feature at the outset because we make sharp distinctions between evaluations of those types of interventions and those in which it is possible to use random assignment methods to create control and treatment groups of individuals. We begin with a brief introduction of some key problems in the evaluation of community-wide initiatives: establishing a counterfactual (for determining what would have happened in the absence of the intervention), defining the unit of analysis, assigning community boundaries, and defining and measuring outcomes. The next section of the paper goes into some detail on the creation of a counterfactual and, specifically, the problems of establishing comparison groups against which to judge the effects of an intervention. We introduce random assignment as the preferred method for creating comparison groups but, given that random assignment is not possible in the evaluation of community-wide initiatives, we go on to review experience using alternative methods for establishing comparison groups of individuals, institutions, and communities. The third part of the paper discusses the types of research questions that could be addressed in community-wide initiatives *if* key methodological problems could be resolved.

The general conclusion from our review is that we find all of the alternative strategies for establishing counterfactuals problematic with respect to evaluations of community-wide initiatives. As a result, in the final section, we provide some suggestions for developing improved methods to use in these situations.

KEY PROBLEMS IN THE EVALUATION OF COMMUNITY-WIDE INITIATIVES

The Counterfactual

The basic question an evaluation seeks to address is whether the activities consciously undertaken in the community-wide initiative generated a change in the outcomes of interest. The problem in this case, as in virtually all evaluation cases, is to establish what would have happened in the absence of the program initiative. This is often referred to as the *counterfactual*. Indeed, most of our discussion turns around a review of alternative methods used to establish a counterfactual for a given type of program intervention.

To those who have not steeped themselves in this type of evaluation, it often appears that this is a trivial problem, and simple solutions are usually proposed. For example, we might look at the situation before and after the initiative is implemented in the given community. The counterfactual, in this case, would be the situation before the initiative. Or, we might find another community that initially looks very much like our target community, and then see how the two compare on desired outcome measures after the initiative is in place. In this case, the comparison community would provide the counterfactual—what would have happened in the absence of the program.

As we shall see, however, and as most of us know, these simple solutions are not adequate to the problem—primarily because individuals and communities are changing all the time with respect to the measured outcome even in the absence of any intentional intervention. Therefore, measures of the situation before the initiative or with comparison communities are not secure counterfactuals—they may not represent well what the community would have looked like in the absence of the program.

Let's turn to some concrete examples. In the late 1970s and early 1980s, the federal government funded the Youth Incentive Entitlement

Pilot Project (YIEPP) to encourage school continuation and employment among all low-income 16–19-year-olds in school catchment areas in several states. YIEPP pursued a strategy of pairing communities in order to develop the counterfactual. For example, the Baltimore school district was paired with Cleveland, the Cincinnati school district was paired with a school district in Louisville, and so forth. In making the pairs the researchers sought communities that had labor market conditions similar to those of the treatment community. Even though the initial match seemed to be quite good, circumstances evolved in ways that made the comparison areas doubtful counterfactuals. For example, Cleveland had unexpectedly favorable improvement in its labor market compared with Baltimore. Louisville had a disruption of its school system because of court-ordered school desegregation and busing. Those developments led the investigators to discount some of the results that came from using these comparison cities.

A similar procedure, with much more detailed analysis, was adopted as part of an ongoing study of school dropout programs being conducted by Mathematica Policy Research, Inc. The school districts with the drop-out program were matched in statistical detail with school districts in a neighborhood within the same city or standard metropolitan statistical area. Although these districts initially matched well in terms of detailed school and population demographics, when surveys were done of the students, teachers, and school processes, it was found that the match was often very bad indeed. The schools simply were operating quite differently in the pre-program period and that had different effects on students and teachers.

The Unit of Analysis

For most of the programs that have been rigorously analyzed by quantitative methods to date, the principal subject of program intervention has been the individual. When we turn to community-wide initiatives, however, the target of the program and the unit of analysis usually shift away from just individuals to one of several possible alternatives. In the first, with which we already have some experience, the target of the program is still the individual, but individuals within geographically bounded areas—a defining factor that remains important. It is expected that interactions among individuals or changes in the general context will generate different responses to the program intervention than would treatment of isolated individuals.

Another possible unit of analysis is the family. We have had some experience with programs in which families are the targets for intervention (for example, family support programs), where the proper unit of analysis is the family rather than sets of individuals analyzed independently of their family units. When the sets of families considered eligible for the program and therefore for the evaluation are defined as residing within geographically bounded areas, these family programs become community-wide initiatives. Many of the recent community-wide interventions seem to have this type of focus.

Another possibility for community initiatives is where the target and unit of analysis are institutions rather than individuals. Thus, within a geographically bounded area a program might target particular sets of institutions—the schools, the police, the voluntary agencies, or the health providers—to generate changes in the behavior of those institutions per se. In this case, the institutions become the relevant unit of analysis.

The unit of analysis becomes critical because, when using statistical theory, the ability to make statements about the effects of interventions will depend on the size of the samples. So if the community is the unit of analysis, then the number of communities will be our sample size. If we are asking about changes in incarceration rates generated by alternative court systems, the size of the sample would be the number of such court systems that are observed. Using a unit of analysis of this size might make it more difficult to reach a sample size adequate for effective statistical inference.

The Problem of Boundaries

In community-wide initiatives, we generally focus on cases where geographical boundaries define the unit or units of analysis. Of course, the term "community" need not imply specific geographic boundaries. Rather, it might have to do with, for example, social networks. What constitutes the community may vary depending upon the type of program process or the outcome that we are addressing. The community for commercial transactions may be quite different from the community for social transactions. The boundaries of impact for one set of institutions—let us say the police—may be quite different from the boundaries for impacts of another set of institutions—let us say schools or health-care networks. That might suggest particular problems for community-wide initiatives that have as one of their principal concerns the "integration of services": the catchment areas for various types of service units may intersect or fail to intersect in complicated ways in any given area. (For a thorough discussion of the problems of defining neighborhood or community, see Chaskin 1994.)

For the purposes of evaluation, these boundary problems introduce a number of complex issues. First, where the evaluation uses a before-and-after design—that is, a counterfactual based on measures of the outcome variables in a community *prior to* the intervention is compared with such measures in the same area *following* the intervention—the problem of changes in boundaries may arise. Such changes could occur either because some major change in the physical landscape takes place—for example, a new highway bisects the area or a major block of residences is torn down—or because the data collection method is based on boundaries that are shifted due to, say, redistricting of schools or changing of police districts. Similar problems would arise where a comparison community design is used for the evaluation, and boundary changes occur either in the treatment community or in the comparison community.

Second, an evaluation must account for inflow and outflow of people across the boundaries of the community. Some of the people who have been exposed to the treatment are likely to migrate out of the community and, unless follow-up data are collected on these migrants, some of the treatment effects may be misestimated. Similarly, in-migrants may enter the area during the treatment period and receive less exposure to the treatment, thereby "diluting" the treatment effects measured (either negatively or positively).

Finally, the limited availability of regularly collected small-area data causes serious problems for evaluations of community-wide initiatives. The decennial census is the only really complete data source that allows us to measure population characteristics at the level of geographically defined small areas. In the intercensal years, the best we can do in most cases is to extrapolate or interpolate. For the nation as a whole, regions, states, and standard metropolitan statistical areas, we can get some regularly reported data series on population and industry characteristics. For smaller areas, we cannot obtain reliable, regularly reported measures of this sort. We suggest below some steps that might be taken to try to improve our measurements in small geographic areas, but at present this remains one of the most serious handicaps faced in quantitative monitoring of the status of communities. (See the paper by Claudia Coulton in this volume for further discussion of these measurement dilemmas.)

Problems with Outcome Measures

In many past evaluations in the social policy arena, the major outcome variables have been relatively straightforward and agreed-upon—for example, the level of employment, the rate of earnings, the test scores of children, the incidence of marriage and divorce, birth outcomes, arrests and incarcerations, and school continuation rates or dropout rates. For community-wide initiatives, these traditional types of outcomes may not be the primary outcomes sought, or, even if they are, they may not show detectable effects in the short term. For example, in the famous Perry Pre-school study, the long-term outcomes are now often talked about—employment, earnings, and delinquency, among others—but during the early phases of the program's evaluation these outcomes could not, of course, be directly measured. This may be true for some of the community initiatives as well: during the period of the short-term evaluation, it may be unlikely that traditional outcome measures will show much change even though it is hypothesized that in the long run they will show change. For community initiatives, then, we need to distinguish intermediate outcomes and final outcomes.

In addition, in community initiatives there may be types of outcome measures that have not been used traditionally but are regarded as outcomes of sufficient interest in and of themselves, regardless of whether they eventually link to more traditional outcome measures. That might be particularly relevant where the object of the community initiative is a change in institutional behavior. For example, if an institution is open longer hours or disburses more funds or reduces its personnel turnover, these might be outcomes of interest in their own right rather than being viewed simply as intermediate outcomes.

Finally, we would want to make a careful distinction among input measures, process measures, and outcome measures. For instance, an input measure might be the number of people enrolled in a general educational development (GED) program, whereas the outcome measure might be the number of people who passed their GED exam or, even further down the road, the employment and earnings of those who passed. Process mea-sures might be changes in the organizational structure, such as providing more authority to classroom teachers in determining curriculum content rather than having it determined by superintendents or school boards. The ultimate outcome measure of interest for such a process measure would be the effect of the teachers' increased authority on student achievement.

For community-wide initiatives, the types of measurement questions that are likely to emerge are:

- First, starting from the initiative's statement of principles and development assumptions, could we define a set of final outcome variables by which the initiative's "success" or "failure" might be judged?

- Second, could we derive from those outcome variables a set of intermediate measures that we think would be related to the ultimate long-term outcomes but that would be more measurable in the short term?

- Third, could we distinguish from such principles those measures that would be input and process measures and those that would be outcome measures?

As one seeks to address these questions it becomes clear that it is important to try to determine as best as possible the likely audience for the evaluation results. The criteria for determining the important outcomes to be measured and evaluated are likely to vary with that audience. Will the audience in mind, for example, be satisfied if it can be shown that a community-wide initiative did indeed involve the residents in a process of identifying and prioritizing problems through a series of planning meetings, even if that process did not lead to changes in school outcomes or employment outcomes or changes in crime rates in the neighborhood? Academics, foundation staff, policymakers, and administrators are likely to differ greatly in their judgment of what outcomes provide the best indicators of success or failure.

Another dimension of this problem is the degree to which the audience is concerned with the outcomes for individuals versus the outcomes for place. This, of course, is an old dilemma in neighborhood change going back to the time of urban renewal programs. In those programs the geographical place may have been transformed by removing the poor people and replacing them through a gentrification process with a different population: place was perhaps improved but people were not. At the other extreme, experiments that move low-income people from the center city to the suburban fringe may improve the lives of the participants in the program, but the places that they leave may be in worse shape after their departure.

ESTABLISHING THE COUNTERFACTUAL USING COMPARISON GROUPS: SELECTION BIAS AND OTHER PROBLEMS

Many of the above problems associated with evaluations of CCIs are generic to the evaluation of any complex program. Most particular to CCIs is the degree of difficulty associated with creating a credible counterfactual for assessing impact. We now turn our attention to this issue.

Random Assignment as the Standard for Judgment

For quantitative evaluators random assignment designs are a bit like the nectar of the gods: once you've had a taste of the pure stuff it is hard to settle for the flawed alternatives. In random assignment design, individuals or units that are potential candidates for the intervention are randomly assigned to be in the treatment group, which is subject to the intervention, or to the control group, which is not subject to any special intervention. (Of course, random assignment does not have to be to a null treatment for the controls; there can be random assignment to different levels of treatment or to alternative modes of treatment.)

The key benefit of a random assignment design is that, as soon as the number of subjects gets reasonably large, there is a very low probability that any given characteristic of the subjects will be more concentrated in the treatment group than in the control group. Most important, this holds for *unmeasured characteristics* as well as measured characteristics.

Random assignment of individuals to treatment and control groups, therefore, allows us to be reasonably sure that no selection bias has occurred when we evaluate the intervention. This means that when we compare average outcomes for treatments and controls we can have a high degree of confidence that the difference is *not* due to some characteristics, which we may not even be aware of, that made the treatment group more or less likely to respond to the intervention. We can conclude instead that the difference is due to the treatment itself. The control group provides a secure counterfactual because, aside from the intervention itself, the control group members are subject to the same forces that might affect the outcome as are the treatment group members: they grow older just as treatment group members do, they face the same changes in the risks of unemployment or increases in returns to their skills, and they are subject to the same broad social forces that influence marriage and family practices.

We realize that this standard is very difficult, often impossible, for evaluations of community-wide initiatives to meet. Unfortunately, there appear to be no clear guidelines for selecting second-best approaches, but a recognition of the character of the problems may help set us on a path to developing such guidelines.

Experiences With Creating Comparison Groups

We now turn to assessing the utility of more feasible alternatives for establishing comparison groups. We compare impact results from studies in which random assignment of individuals was used to create comparison groups with impact results when alternative methods were used to create the comparison groups. In this case, we use the results from the randomly assigned treatment versus control groups as a standard against which to evaluate the types and magnitude of errors that can occur when this best design is not feasible.[1] Our hope is that if one or more of the alternatives looks promising in the evaluation of programs with individuals as the unit of analysis, then we would have a starting point for considering alternatives to random assignment in the evaluation of CCIs. Toward the end of this section we discuss experience with comparison institutions and comparison communities.

Constructed Groups of Individuals. Constructed comparison groups of individuals were the most-often-used method of evaluation prior to the use of random assignment in large-scale social policy studies and other programs in the 1970s and 1980s. The earliest type of constructed group was a before-and-after, or "pre–post," design. Measurements were made on the individuals before they entered the treatment, during the treatment, and following the conclusion of the treatment. Impacts were measured as the change from before program to after program.

This strategy for establishing counterfactuals is recognized as highly vulnerable to naturally occurring changes in individuals. For example, criminal behavior is known to decline with age regardless of treatment efforts, a phenomenon referred to as "aging out." With respect to employment and training programs, eligibility is often based on a period of unemployment prior to program entry. But, for any group of people currently unemployed, the process of job search goes on and often results in employment or re-employment. In those cases, it is difficult to untangle the program effects from those of normal job-finding processes.

Another strategy for constructing comparison groups is to compare non-participants with participants in a program. This strategy was used in early evaluations of the Job Corps and in evaluation of the special supplemental food program for women, infant, and children (WIC) (Devaney, Bilheimer, and Schore 1991), and the National School Lunch Program and School Breakfast Programs (Burghardt et al. 1993). This type of design is recognized as producing bias due to selection on unobserved variables. Usually there is a reason why an individual does participate or does not participate in the program—for example, an individual's motivation, or subtle selection procedures followed by the program administrators. If characteristics affecting the selection could also affect the final outcome, and if these characteristics are not measured, then the difference between the participant and the non-participant groups is a potentially biased estimate of program impact. This bias could either over- or under-estimate program effects.

A third strategy for creating comparison groups is to use existing survey data to sample individuals for the comparison group. The most commonly used source of information is the U.S. Census Bureau's Current Population Survey (CPS), which has large national samples of individuals. Comparison groups are usually constructed by matching the characteristics of the individuals in the treatment group to individuals in the CPS. This procedure was used in evaluations of employment training programs (Bloom 1987; Ashenfelter and Card 1985; Bassi 1983 and 1984; Bryant and Rupp 1987; Dickinson, Johnson, and West 1987), where program enrollment data were often used in combination with the CPS data or data from Social Security records. The Social Security data provide a long series of observations on individuals prior to the time of program eligibility as well as during program eligibility.

One important set of studies directly demonstrates the pitfalls of constructing comparison groups of individuals from data sources that differ from the source used for the treatment-group data. These studies were based on the National Supported Work Demonstration, which ran between 1975 and 1979 in eleven cities across the United States. This was a subsidized employment program for four target groups: ex-addicts, ex-offenders, high school dropouts, and women on Aid for Families with Dependent Children (AFDC). Two sets of investigators working independently used these experimental data and combined them with nonexperimental data to construct comparison groups (see Fraker and Maynard 1987; La Londe 1986; La Londe and Maynard 1987). Both studies used data generated from the random assignment experiment—differences between randomly assigned treatment and control groups—as the "true" estimates of program effects. Then, alternative comparison groups were constructed in a variety of other ways and estimates of the effects of the program on the outcome variable were made using the *constructed* comparison group in place of the randomly selected control group. These two estimates of effects—one based on the randomly selected controls and the other based on the constructed comparison groups—were then compared to determine how close the constructed comparison group estimates came to those provided by the randomly selected control groups. Both sets of investigators looked at various ways of matching the treatment subjects from the experiment with counterparts taken from other data sources—the CPS and Social Security data were used in combination in one study and the data from the Panel Study on Income Dynamics were used in the other.

The major conclusion from this set of important studies was that the constructed comparison groups provided unreliable estimates of the true program impacts on employment and earnings, and that none of the matching techniques used looked particularly superior one to the other—there was no clear second-best.

As part of their studies these investigators also tried to see if the bias resulting from constructed comparison groups could be corrected statistically. To try to address potential bias of this type, due to unobserved variables, analysts since the late 1970s have often relied on methods that attempt statistical correction for the bias. The methods used most often were developed by James Heckman (1979). Basically, these corrections try to "model" the selection process—that is, to develop a statistical equation that predicts the likelihood of being in the treatment group or in the comparison group. The results of this equation are then used to "adjust" the estimates of treatment versus control group differences. While the approach proposed could work in certain situations, experience has shown that it is not generally reliable for dealing with the problem of unobserved variables. Understanding the problem of unobserved variables and the weakness of any methodologies other than random assignment in dealing with this problem is central to appreciating the difficulties that are faced in the evaluation of community-wide initiatives. We will touch on this repeatedly in the following sections.

Constructed Comparison Groups of Institutions. In a few cases, where the primary unit of intervention and analysis has been an institution, attempts have been made to construct comparison groups of institutions. Those procedures come closer to the problems encountered in community-wide initiative evaluations.

For example, in parts of the school dropout studies that were introduced earlier in this paper (Dynarski et al. 1992), individuals were randomly assigned to a school dropout prevention program and to a control group. At other sites, however, the random assignment of individuals was not feasible, so an attempt was made to find other *schools* that could be used as a comparison group to judge the effectiveness of the dropout program. After the schools had been initially matched, survey data were collected from students, parents, and school administrators. As noted previously, comparison of these data showed that, in fact, the schools being "matched"— in spite of being demographically similar—were quite different in their operational aspects. Note that in this case even though the student outcomes are the ultimate subject of the study—that is, whether the students drop out or not—the institution was the unit of comparison selected in order to create a comparison group of "environments" similar to those in the treatment schools.

In one study, there was a large enough number of schools to attempt a quasi-random assignment of schools to treatment and control groups. Twenty-two schools were first matched on socioeconomic characteristics and then randomly assigned within matched pairs to treatment and control groups (Flay et al. 1985). It is doubtful that a sample size of twenty-two is adequate to assure that the random assignment has achieved balance on unmeasured characteristics.

Comparison Communities. There are several examples of attempts to use communities as the units for building the comparison group. At first blush, the idea is quite appealing: find a community that is much like the one in which the new treatment is being tested and then use this community to trace how the particular processes of interest or outcomes of interest evolve compared with those in the "treatment community." In most cases, the treatment site has been selected before the constructed comparison site is selected.

The most common method for selecting comparison communities is to attempt to match areas on the basis of selected characteristics that are believed, or have been shown, to affect the outcome variables of interest. Usually, a mixture of statistical weighting and judgmental elements enters into the selection.

Often a first criterion is geographic proximity—same city, same metropolitan area, same state, same region—on the grounds that this will minimize differences in economic or social structures and changes in area-wide exogenous forces. Sometimes an attempt is made to match communities based on service structure components in the pre-treatment period—for example, similarities in health service provision.

Most important, usually, is the statistical matching on demographic characteristics. In carrying out such matching the major data source is the decennial census, since this provides characteristic information even down to the block group level (a subdivision of census tracts). Of course, the further the time period of the intervention from the year in which the census was taken, the weaker this matching information will be. One study used 1970 census data to match sites when the program implementation occurred at the very end of the decade, and found later that the match was quite flawed.

Since there are many characteristics on which to match, some method must be found for weighting the various characteristics. If one had a strong statistical model of the process that generates the outcomes of interest, then this estimated model would provide the best way to weight together the various characteristics. We are not aware of any case in which this has been done. Different schemes for weighting various characteristics have been advocated and used.[2]

In a few cases, time-trend data are available on the outcome variable at the small-area level that cover the pre-intervention period. For example, in recent years, birth-record data have become more consistently recorded and made publicly available, at least to the zip-code level. In some areas, AFDC and Food Stamp receipt data aggregated to the census tract level are available. The evaluation of the Healthy Start program, a national demonstration to improve birth outcomes and promote the healthy development of young children, proposes to attempt to match sites on the basis of trends in birth data.

In the Youth Incentive Entitlement Pilot Project, which was described at the outset of this paper, four treatment sites were matched with sites in other communities in other cities, based on weighted characteristics such as the labor market, population characteristics, the high school dropout rate, socioeconomic conditions, and geographic proximity to the treatment site. Unforeseen changes in the comparison sites, however, reduced their validity as counterfactuals. The Employment Opportunity Pilot Project (EOPP), a very large-scale employment opportunity program that began in the late 1970s and continued into the early '80s, focused on chronically unemployed adults and families with children. It also used constructed comparison sites as part of its evaluation strategy. Once again there were problems with unexpected changes in comparison sites. For example, Toledo, which had major automobile supplies manufacturers, was subject to a downturn in that industry. Further, out of ten sites, one had a major hurricane, a second had a substantial flood, and a third had a huge unanticipated volcanic eruption.

Two projects under way may give us additional information about selecting comparison communities. For the Healthy Start evaluation, two comparison sites are being selected for each treatment site (Devaney and Morano 1994). In developing comparison sites, investigators have tried to add to the more formal statistical matching by asking local experts whether the proposed comparison sites make sense in terms of population and service environment. The evaluation of community development corporations (CDCs), being carried out by the New School for Social Research, has selected comparison neighborhoods within the same cities as the three CDC sites under evaluation.

Treatment and comparison sites randomly assigned. There are a couple of examples where the treatment sites were not predetermined but rather were selected simultaneously with the comparison sites. The largest such evaluation is that of the State of Washington's Family Independence Program (FIP), an evaluation of a major change in the welfare system of the state (Long and Wissoker 1993). The evaluators, having decided upon a comparison group strategy, created east/west and urban/rural stratifications within the state in order to obtain a geographically representative sample. Within five of these subgroups, pairs of welfare offices, matched on local labor market and welfare caseload characteristics, were chosen and randomly allocated to either treatment (FIP) or control (AFDC) status. This project's initial results surprised the researchers: utilization of welfare increased and employment decreased, whereas the intent of the reform was to reduce welfare use and increase employment. The researchers do not attribute these counterintuitive findings to flaws in the comparison site method, but that possibility exists. Again, it is doubtful that random assignment of just five matched pairs is sufficient to assure a balance between the treatment group office and comparison office in unmeasured variables affecting outcomes, even though the pairs were matched on several characteristics.

The Alabama Avenues to Self-Sufficiency through Employment and Training Services (ASSETS) Demonstration used a similar strategy for the selection of demonstration and comparison sites, except that only three pairs were chosen. The primary sampling unit was the county, and counties were matched on caseload characteristics and population size (Davis 1993). Results from that study did not match those of a similar study in San Diego in which random assignment of individuals was used to establish the counterfactual comparison group. For example, in the San Diego study, the estimated reduction in food consumption following Food Stamp cash-out was much less.

Pre–post design, using communities. As was noted with respect to individuals, contrasting measurements before and after exposure to the treatment is a method that has often been advocated. This procedure can also be applied with communities as the unit of analysis. The attraction of this approach is that the structural and historical conditions that might affect the outcome variables that are unique to this location are controlled for directly.

Often a pre–post design simply compares a single pre-period measurement with the post-treatment measure of the same variables. However, as in any longitudinal study, multiple measures of the outcome variable (especially in the pre-treatment period) allows for more reliable estimates of change in the variable. This procedure is often referred to as an "interrupted time-series," with the treatment taken to be the cause of the interruption (see, for example, McCleary and Riggs 1982).

The better the researcher's ability to model the process of change in a given community over time, the stronger is this approach. We discuss the evidence on ability to model community change below. Note also that this approach depends on having time-series measures of variables of interest at the community level and therefore runs into the problem, introduced above, of the limited availability of small-area data that measure variables consistently over many time periods. We are often limited to the decennial censuses for small-area measurements.

As with pre–post designs where individuals are the unit of analysis, events other than the treatment—for example, a plant closing, collapse of a transportation network, or reorganization of health care providers—can impinge on the community during the post-treatment period and affect the outcome variable. Those effects would be attributed to the treatment unless a strong theoretical and statistical model is available that can take such exogenous events into account.

We have been unable thus far to locate examples of community pre–post designs using time-series. The EOPP (Brown et al. 1983) used as one of its analysis models a mixture of time-series and comparison communities to estimate program impacts. The model had pre- and post-measures for both sets of communities. The impact of the intervention was estimated as the difference in percentage change (pre- to post-) between the treatment site and comparison site(s). Finally, the Youth Fair Chance demonstration (Dynarski and Corson 1994) has proposed an evaluation design that uses both pre- and post-measures and comparison sites.

Problems of spillovers, crossovers, and in- and out-migration. Where comparison communities are used, potential problems arise because of the community's geographic location relative to the treatment site and/or the movement of individuals in and out of the treatment and comparison sites.

Often investigators have chosen communities in close physical proximity to the treatment community on the grounds that it helps to equalize regional influences. However, proximity can cause problems. First, economic, political, and social forces often create specialized functions within a region. For example, one area might provide most of the manufacturing activities while the other provides the services; one area has mostly single-family dwellings while the other features multi-unit structures; one is dominated by Republicans, the other by Democrats; one captures the state's employment services office and the other gets the state's police barracks. These can be subtle differences that can generate different patterns of evolution of the two communities. Second, spillover of services and people can occur from the treatment community to the comparison community, so the comparison community is "contaminated"—either positively, by obtaining some of the services or governance structure changes generated in the treatment community, or negatively, by the draining away of human and physical resources into the now more attractive treatment community.

Two features of the New School's CDC study introduced above make it less susceptible to these types of problems. First, the services being examined relate to housing benefits, which are not easily transferable to nonresidents. Second, the CDCs in the study were not newly established, so to a large extent it can be assumed that people had already made their housing choices based on the available information (though even these prior choices could create a selection bias of unknown and unmeasured degree).

An example where this spillover effect was more troublesome was in the evaluation of The School/Community Program for Sexual Risk Reduction Among Teens (Vincent, Clearie, and Schluchter 1987). This was an education-oriented initiative targeted at reducing unwanted teen pregnancies. The demonstration area was designated as the western portion of a county in South Carolina, using school districts as its boundaries. Four comparison sites were selected, one of which was simply the eastern portion of the same county. Because the county is quite homogenous, the two halves were matched extremely well on factors that might influence the outcome measures (Vincent, Clearie, and Schluchter 1987, 3382). However, a good deal of the information in this initiative was to be disseminated through a media campaign, and the county shared one radio station and one newspaper. Moreover, some of the educational sites, such as certain churches and work places, served or employed individuals from both the western and eastern parts of the county (3386). Obviously, a comparison of the change in pregnancy rates between these two areas will not provide a pure estimate of program impact.

In-migration and out-migration of individuals occur constantly in communities. At the treatment site, these migrations might be considered "dilutions of the treatment." In-migration could be due to the increased attraction of services provided or it could just be a natural process that will diversify community values and experiences. Out-migration means loss of some of the persons subject to the treatment. Focusing data collection only on those who stay in the community creates a selection bias arising from both migration processes. Also, it is not clear whether the program treatment itself influenced the extent and character of in- and out-migration.

Dose-response models of treatment versus comparison communities. Sites can vary in the types and/or intensity of treatment, and this variation in dosage can be examined as part of the evaluation. For example, the South Carolina teen pregnancy prevention program, discussed above, could be viewed as having three different "treatment" groups: the western part of the county received full treatment, the eastern part of the county received moderate treatment, and the three noncontiguous comparison counties received little to no treatment.

The absolute changes in numbers in these three treatment groups seem to confirm the "dosage" effect. The noncontiguous comparison communities' estimated pregnancy rates stayed the same or increased, the rates in the eastern portion of the county were reduced slightly, and those in the western portion were more than halved (Vincent, Clearie, and Schluchter 1987). Of course, these estimates should be viewed with caution given the small sample size and failure to control statistically for even observed differences between communities other than dosage of treatment.

Another example of dose-response methodology is an evaluation of a demonstration targeted at the prevention of alcohol problems (Casswell and Gilmore 1989). Six cities were chosen and then split into two groups of three cities each, based on sociodemographic similarity. Within these groups, each city received a treatment of different intensity. One was exposed to both a media campaign and the services of a community organizer; the second had only the media campaign; and the third had no treatment. In this way researchers could examine the effect of varying levels of intervention intensity to determine, for instance, if there was an added benefit to having a community organizer available (in addition to the media campaign). It should be noted, however, that random assignment of cities within groups had to be sacrificed in order to avoid possible spillover effects from the media campaign. Results showed positive, though generally tiny, effects for many of the variables studied. As we would expect, the magnitude of the effects tended to grow with the intensity of the "dosage level." That is, the communities with the media campaign and a community organizer generally experienced stronger impacts than the communities with only a media campaign.

Most important, this procedure does not get around the underlying problem of comparison communities—the questionable validity of the assumption that once matched on a set of characteristics, the communities would have evolved over time in essentially the same fashion with respect to the outcome variables of interest. If this assumption does not hold, then the "dose of treatment" will be confounded in unknown ways with underlying differences among the communities, once again a type of selection bias.

The Magnitude of Problems with Comparison Communities Methods: A Case Study. A recent study allows us to get a fix on the magnitude of bias that can arise when comparison community designs of the several types just reviewed are used. This study used data from the Manpower Demonstration Research Corporation's (MDRC) Work/Welfare studies in several states (Friedlander and Robins 1994). Once again, as in the studies using National Supported Work Demonstration data, cited above (Fraker and Maynard 1987; La Londe 1986; La Londe and Maynard 1987), the basic data were generated by experiments using random assignment of individuals. In this case, the investigators used the treatment group from the Work/Welfare experiments and constructed comparison groups by using control groups *from other program locations* or *other time periods* to construct alternative comparison groups. For example, they used the treatment group from one state and the control group from another state. They also used a treatment group from one geographic location within the state or city and the control group from another geographic location within the state or city. Finally, they used the treatment group from one time period at a given site and the control group from another time period at the same site to get "across-cohort studies," similar to a pre–post study of a single community. In addition to trying these different strategies for constructing groups, the investigators also tried matching groups on different measured characteristics. And, they tried some sophisticated specification tests that had been suggested by Heckman and others to improve the match of the constructed comparison groups to the treatment groups. (See Heckman and Hotz 1989.)

This study is, in our view, so important that we have provided an appendix in which the results are discussed in detail and some of the estimates of magnitude of bias are summarized (Table A1). The study showed substantial differences between the estimated impacts from the true experimental results and the constructed comparison groups. In many cases, not only was the *magnitude* of the effect estimated from the constructed comparison group different from the "true effect" estimates provided by the random assignment control group, but the *direction* of the effect was different. Overall, the results from this study show substantial bias with all methods but that, at least for these data, comparison groups constructed from different cohorts in the same site perform somewhat better than the other types of comparison groups.[3]

The importance of this study is that it clarifies the problem of bias arising when comparison groups are constructed by methods other than random assignment, and it points to the severity of the problem. It shows that statistical controls using measured characteristics are in most cases inadequate to overcome this problem.

It has long been recognized that counterfactuals obtained by using constructed comparison groups (as opposed to control groups obtained by random assignment) may, in theory, yield biased estimates of the true impact of a program. What is important about this study is that it demonstrates, through the use of actual program data, that various types of constructed comparison groups yield substantially biased estimates. These real-life experiments demonstrate that *investigators could have been seriously misled in their conclusions about the effectiveness of these programs had they used methods other than random assignment to construct their comparison groups.* Moreover, we must keep in mind that these studies created comparison groups after the fact, with the luxury of making adjustments to potential comparison groups using all the data from the study. The problems described above are likely to be exacerbated when one is *developing* a design for an evaluation and must make *a priori* judgments about the extent of bias that might occur in the results.

Statistical Modeling of Community-Level Outcomes. Another approach to creating counterfactuals for the evaluation of community-level interventions is statistical modeling. This approach develops a statistical model of what would have happened to a particular outcome or set of outcomes at the community level had an intervention not been instituted. The predictions from the model are then used as the counterfactual and are compared with what happens in the community following the intervention. The difference is the estimated impact of the intervention.

Time-series modeling. Time-series models of community-level outcomes have long been advocated as a means of assessing the effects of program innovations or reforms (Campbell and Stanley 1966). In the simplest form, the time-series on the past values of the outcome variable for the community is linearly extrapolated to provide a predicted value for the outcome during and after the period of the program intervention. In a sense, the pre–post designs discussed above are a simple form of this type of procedure. It has been recognized for a long time that the simple extrapolation design is quite vulnerable to error because, even in the absence of any intervention, community variables rarely evolve in a simple linear fashion. An example of this procedure is a study assessing the impact of seat-belt legislation in Australia. The researchers used twenty years of fatality data to predict the number of deaths there would have been in the absence of the new legislation (Bhattacharyya and Layton 1979).

Some attempts have been made to improve on the simple linear form by introducing some of the more formal methods of time-series modeling.[4] Introducing non-linearities in the form can allow for more complex reactions to the program intervention (McCleary and Riggs 1982). One study had a series of cohorts enrolled in a program over time and used the pre-enrollment data for a later cohort (enrolled at time t) as the comparison with the in-program data of an earlier cohort (enrolled at time $t-1$) (McConnell 1982).

The problem with these methods is that they do not always explicitly control for variables, other than the program intervention, that may have influenced the outcome variable.

Multivariate statistical modeling. Some attempts have been made to estimate multivariate models of the community-level outcome variables in order to generate counterfactuals for program evaluation.[5] These multivariate models would attempt to specify, measure, and estimate the effects of the variables that determine the community-level outcome that are not themselves affected by the treatment. Then, with these variables "controlled," the effect of treatment would be estimated.

We have not been able to find examples of this approach at the community level, but there are several examples of attempts to estimate caseload models at the state or national level for programs such as AFDC and Food Stamps (Grossman 1985; Beebout and Grossman 1985; Garasky 1990; Garasky and Barnow 1992; Mathematica Policy Research 1985). Most analysts consider the results of these models to be unreliable for program evaluation purposes. For example, an attempt was made to model the AFDC caseload in New Jersey in order to assess the effect of a welfare reform. However, subsequent to the reform, the effects of changes in the low-wage labor market appeared to have swamped any changes in AFDC caseload predicted by the model, leading to implausible estimates of the impact of the welfare reform on AFDC levels. The model was unable to capture the way in which the low-wage labor markets operated to affect AFDC caseloads. Also recall, in the examples discussed above, how comparison communities in EOPP were affected by floods, hurricanes, and volcanic eruptions, or in YIEPP, where court-ordered school desegregation occurred in the comparison community. Adequate statistical modeling would have to attempt to incorporate such factors.

Statistical modeling at the community level also runs up against the persistent lack of small-area data, particularly data available on a consistent basis, over several periods of time or across different communities. Such data are necessary both to estimate the statistical model of the community-level outcome and to project the counterfactual value of the outcome for the program period. For example, if the model includes local employment levels as affecting the outcome, then data on local employment during the program period must be available to use in the model.

RESEARCH QUESTIONS TO ADDRESS
IN THE CONTEXT OF COMMUNITY-WIDE INITIATIVES

In this section we outline the types of research questions that are of particular relevance to community-wide initiatives and that, with the development of new evaluation strategies, might be investigated. This set of questions goes well beyond the simple models of a single treatment affecting a single outcome or even multiple treatments affecting multiple outcomes. Rather, we focus on several types of multivariate effects. These are effects that help explain how the participants' characteristics might influence treatment outcomes, how various dimensions of one treatment or multiple types of treatments may interactively affect treatment outcomes, and how different configurations of participant or institutional characteristics may produce different outcomes.

It seems evident that arguments for carrying out community-wide interventions are based on assumptions about the importance of several of these types of more complicated theories of how and for whom an intervention will work. Brown and Richman illustrate a key aspect of this multidimensional framework: "Too often in the past, narrowly defined interventions have not produced long-term change because they have failed to recognize the interaction among physical, economic and social factors that create the context in which the intervention may thrive or flounder" (Brown and Richman 1993, 8). Commentators have classified such interactions in a variety of ways: contagion or epidemic effects, social capital, neighborhood effects, externalities, and social comparison effects. We have not taken the time to carefully catalog and re-order these classifications (though such an analysis might help with an orderly development of evaluation research). We simply give examples of some broad categories that might be of concern to evaluators of community-wide initiatives.

It is important to be clear at the outset that credible estimation of these more complicated models of treatment-outcome linkages at the individual level depends on the presence of one or more "control" groups created by random assignment of individuals.[6] Given the apparent lack of feasibility of random assignment at the community level and the terribly flawed alternatives to it, answers to these research questions with respect to communities await further methodological work.

Networks and Group Learning

The importance of associational networks has been increasingly emphasized in the literature on communities and families. Some interventions may seek to operate directly on networks, having social network change as either an intermediate or final outcome of interest. These networks can also affect the way in which information about the form of the intervention and its treatment of individuals in various circumstances are likely to be passed from individual to individual. As a result, the group learning about the intervention is likely to be faster and greater than the learning of the isolated individual. This faster, deeper, and perhaps different communication of information could, in turn, change the ways individuals in different associational networks respond to the intervention.

Stronger forms of interaction within networks are what some have called "norm formation" (see Garfinkel, Manski, and Michalopoulous 1992). Network norms are potentially important in this context in two ways: pre-existing norms could either impede or facilitate response to the intervention, and new norm formation in response to the intervention could reshape pre-existing norms. For example, the existence of "gang cultures" may impede interventions, or some interventions may seek to use norm formation processes within gang cultures to reshape the norms of the gang and enlist it in promoting the goals of the intervention.

The evaluation problems will differ depending on how these associational networks are considered. For example, suppose the objective is to test how different associational networks affect response to a given intervention. If networks are measured and classified *prior* to the intervention, then individuals could be broken into different subgroups according to network type, and subgroup effects could be analyzed in the usual manner.

To the extent that the network characteristics are outcome variables (intermediate or final), they can be measured and the impact of the intervention upon them analyzed in the same fashion as for other outcome variables. However, the reliability and consistency of measures of associational networks may be problematic, as may be the determination of other relevant properties such as their normal variance or their likely sensitivity to intervention impacts.

Notice that the previous paragraphs take the network to be something that can be treated as a characteristic of the individual and the individual as the unit of analysis. These analyses could be carried out even without a community-wide intervention. Most would argue, however, that the group learning effects are really most important when groups of people, all subject to the intervention, interact. In such cases, we are immediately faced with the problems covered earlier in the discussion of using communities for constructed comparison groups: since random assignment of individuals to the treatment or control group is precluded when one wishes to treat groups of individuals who are potentially in the same network, testing for this form of interaction effect will be subject to the same problems of selection bias outlined above.

Effects of Formal and Informal Institutions

Most interventions take the form of an attempt to alter some type of formal institution that affects individuals: a day care center, a welfare payment, an education course. The interactions of formal institutions with treatments have been evaluated, for example, in studies of food-stamp cashouts. In this case, we would ask, "Is the impact of the treatment affected by the way in which it is delivered to participants—as a food stamp versus as a cash payment?"

However, most of those concerned with community-wide initiatives appear to be more interested in either the way the formal institutional structure in a given community conditions the individuals' responses or with the behavior of the formal institutions themselves as outcomes of the intervention.

With respect to the former concern, some studies seek to have the formal institutional structure as one of the criterion variables by which communities are matched and thus seek to neutralize the impact of interactions of formal institutions and the treatment. Both the Healthy Start and the school dropout studies have already been mentioned as examples in which matching formal institutional structures is a concern in selection of comparison sites, and we have already mentioned the problems of measurement and the limits of statistical gains from such attempted matches.

Access to a formal institution is sometimes regarded as an outcome, and it may be easy to measure—for example, the number of doctors visits by pregnant women or participation in bilingual education programs. The behavior of the institution may be the outcome variable of interest. For example, do schools change their tracking behavior? Are police procedures for intervention in domestic violence altered? In these cases, the institution itself, rather than individuals, may be the primary unit of analysis. Then we must face all the aspects of sample design for institutions as a unit of analysis if we wish to use formal statistical inference to estimate intervention effects on institutional behavior.

Informal institutions are also subjects of interest. The associational networks discussed above are surely examples, as are gangs. But there are informal economic structures that also fall into this category. The labor market is an informal institution whose operations interact with the intervention and condition its impact. This can be most concretely illustrated by reference to the problem of "displacement," sometimes discussed in the literature on employment and training programs. The basic idea is that workers trained by a program may enter the labor market and become employed, but if involuntary unemployment already exists in the relevant labor market, total employment may not be increased because that worker simply "displaces" a worker who would have been employed in that job had the newly trained worker not shown up.[7] An evaluation with a number of randomly assigned treatment and control group members that is small relative to the size of the relevant labor market would be unable to detect such displacement effects because their numbers are too small relative to the size of the market; the trained treatment group member is not likely to show up at exactly the same employer as the control group member would have. It has been argued by some that use of community-wide interventions in employment and training would provide an opportunity to measure the extent of such displacement effects because the size of the intervention would be large relative to the size of the local labor market. Indeed, one of the hopes for YIEPP was that it would provide such an opportunity. But, as the experience with YIEPP, described above, illustrates, the use of comparison communities called for in this approach is subject to a number of serious pitfalls.[8]

Interactions with External Conditions

Some attempts have been made to see how changes in conditions external to an intervention—experienced by both the treatment and control group members—have conditioned the response to the treatment. Here, the objective is to try to determine whether the impact of the program treatment changes when the external condition changes. For example, suppose a program sought to increase the employment of low-wage workers, and then the minimum-wage law changed. One could seek to determine whether the effect of the program was the same before the change in the minimum-wage law as it was after the change. Note that one would not be estimating how the minimum-wage law affects employment in general, but rather how it alters the estimated impact of the program. Consider another example: a program that seeks to reduce violent crime is in the middle of its evaluation period when a "three-strikes-and-you're-out" sentencing law is passed. Did the program have the same effects before the law passed as after it passed? An example of this sort of analysis was that carried out in the National Supported Work Demonstration. There, attempts were made to see if the response to the treatment (supported work) varied systematically with the level of local unemployment. In that case there were no statistically significant differences in response, but researchers felt it may well have been due to the weakness of statistics on the city-by-city unemployment rate.

Dynamics

An intriguing and largely unaddressed question for evaluation of community-wide initiatives is how to represent the dynamics of interventions as they change over time—in response to lessons learned from implementation and where the alterations are largely idiosyncratic. Although some evaluators of programs might prefer to delay their initial measures of outcomes until the program has stabilized and matured, many community-level initiatives are not expected to achieve a "steady state" but rather to evolve constantly in response to incoming results.[9]

Similarly, few attempts have been made to measure changes in the *response* of communities and their residents to treatments over time. Evaluations of employment and training programs have carried out post-program measurements at several points in time in an attempt to measure the time path of treatment effects. These time paths are important for the overall cost-benefit analyses of these programs because the length of time over which benefits are in fact realized can greatly influence the balance of benefits and costs. For example, studies have shown cases in which impacts appear in the early post-program period and then fade out quickly thereafter (as is often claimed about the effects of Headstart) and cases in which no impacts are found immediately post-program but emerge many months later (for example, in the evaluation of the Job Corps). Similar issues will arise in the evaluation of community-based initiatives, and the tracking of outcomes over longer periods of time would appear to be a sensible step in addressing this issue.

STEPS IN THE DEVELOPMENT
OF BETTER METHODS

We can make no strong recommendations on how best to approach the problem of evaluating community-wide initiatives. When the random assignment of individuals to treatment and control groups is precluded, no sure-fire method exists for assuring that the evaluation will avoid problems of selection bias. Constructed comparison groups—whether of individuals or communities—are problematic, and pre–post designs remain vulnerable to exogenous shifts in the context that may affect outcome variables in unpredictable (and often undetectable) directions. As of now, we do not see clear indications of what second-best methods might be recommended, nor have we identified what situations make a given method particularly vulnerable.

It is important to stress, once again, that the vulnerability to bias in estimating the impacts of interventions should not be taken lightly. First, the few existing studies of the problem show that the magnitude of errors in inference can be quite substantial even when the most sophisticated methods are used. Second, the bias can be in either direction: we may not only be led to conclude that an intervention has had what we consider to be positive impacts when in fact it had none; we may also find ourselves confronted with biased impact estimates indicating that an innocuous—or perhaps even valuable—intervention was actually harmful. As a result, we may end up promoting policies that use up resources and provide few benefits or we may recommend discarding interventions that actually have merit. Once these biased findings are in the public domain, it is very hard to get them dismissed or revisited and to prevent them from influencing policy decisions.

Beyond these rather dismal conclusions and admonitions, the best we can suggest at this time are some steps that might improve our understanding of how communities evolve over time and thereby help us create methods of evaluation that are less vulnerable to the types of bias we have pointed out.

1. *Improve small-area data.* We have stressed at several points that detailed small-area demographic data are very hard to come by except at the time of the decennial census. The paper by Claudia Coulton in this volume provides further confirmation of this problem and some suggestions for remedying it. Increasingly, however, records data are being developed by a wide variety of entities that can be tied to specific geographic areas (geocoded data). One type of work that might be fruitfully pursued would combine various types of records data with data taken from two or more censuses.[10] At the base period, correlations of the records data with census variables would be established. Then the time-series of the records data would be used along with the baseline correlations to predict the end-period values for the census variables. If the predictions were reasonably close, then the records data would provide a basis for tracking small-geographic-area variables in the intercensal period.

Our experience with availability of records data at the state level has convinced us that there are far more systems-wide records being collected—in many cases with individual and geographic area–level information—than we would have thought. Much of the impetus for the development of these data systems comes from the federal government in the form of program requirements (both for delivery of services and for accountability) and, more importantly, from the federal financial support for systems development.

Evaluations of employment and training programs have already made wide use of Unemployment Insurance records and these records have broad coverage of the working population. More limited use has been made of Social Security records. In a few cases, it has been possible to merge Social Security and Internal Revenue Service records. Birth records collection has been increasingly standardized and some investigators have been able to use time-series of these records tied to geographic location. The systems records, beyond these four, cover much more restricted populations—for example, Welfare and Food Stamps, Medicaid and Medicare, and WIC.

More localized record systems include education and criminal justice records but they present greater problems of developing comparability. In some states, however, statewide systems have been, or are being, developed to draw together the local records.

We are currently investigating other types of geo-coded data that might be relevant to community-wide measures. Data from the banking systems have become increasingly available as a result of the Community Reinvestment Act (Housing Mortgage Disclosure Act [HMDA] data). Local real estate transaction data can sometimes be obtained but information from tax assessments seems harder to come by.

In all of these cases, whenever individualized data are needed, problems of confidentiality present substantial barriers to general data acquisition by anyone other than public authorities. Even with the census data, there are many variables for which one cannot get data at a level of aggregation below block group level.

2. *Enhance community capability to do systematic data collection.* We believe that it is possible to pull together records data of the types just outlined to create community data bases that could be continuously maintained and updated. These data would provide communities with some means to keep monitoring, in a relatively comprehensive way, what is happening in their areas. This would make it possible to get better time-series data with which to look at the evolution of communities. To the degree that communities could be convinced to maintain their records within relatively common formats, an effort could be made to pull together many different communities to create a larger data base that would have a time-series, cross-section structure and would provide a basis for understanding community processes.

Going a step beyond this aggregation of records, attempts could be made to enhance the capability of communities to gather new data of their own. These could be anything from simple surveys of physical structures based on externally observed characteristics (type of structure, occupied, business or organization, public facility, and the like), carried out by volunteers within a framework provided by the community organization, to full-scale household surveys on a sample or on a census basis.

3. *Create a panel study of communities.* As already noted above, if many communities used common formats to put together local records data one

would have the potential for a time-series, cross-section data base. In the absence of that, admittedly unlikely, development, it might be possible to imitate the several nationally representative panel studies of individuals (*The Panel Study on Income Dynamics, The National Longitudinal Study of Youth*, or *High School and Beyond*, to name the most prominent), which have been created and maintained in some cases since the late 1960s. Here the unit of analysis would be communities—somehow defined. The objective would be to provide the means to study the dynamics of communities. They would provide us with important information on what the cross-section and time-series frequency distributions of community-level variables look like—important ingredients, we have argued above, for an evaluation sample design effort with communities as units of observation. That would provide the best basis for our next suggestion, work on modeling community-level variables.

Short of creating such a panel study, some steps might be taken to at least get federally funded research to try to pull together across projects information developed on various community-level measures. In an increasing number of studies, community-level data are gathered for evaluating or monitoring programs or for comparison communities. We noted above several national studies that were using a comparison-site methodology (Healthy Start, Youth Fair Chance, the School Dropout Study), and some gains might be made if some efforts of coordination resulted in pooling some of these data.

4. *Model community-level variables.* As we mentioned above, statistical modeling might provide the basis for generating more reliable counterfactuals for community initiatives. A good model would generate predicted values for endogenous outcome variables for a given community in the absence of the intervention by using an historical time-series for that community and such contemporaneous variables as are judged to be exogenous to the intervention. At least such models would provide a better basis for attempting to match communities if a comparison-community strategy is attempted.

5. *Develop better measures of social networks and formal and informal community institutions.* We have not studied the literature on associational networks in any depth, so our characterization of the state of knowledge in this area may be incorrect. However, it seems to us that considerably more

information on and experience with various measures of associational networks are needed, given their central role in most theories relating to community-wide processes.

Measures of the density and character of formal institutions appear to us to have been little developed—though, again, we have not searched the literature in any depth. There are industrial censuses for some subsectors. We know of private-sector sources that purport to provide reasonably comprehensive listings of employers. Some Child Care Resource and Referral Networks have tried to create and maintain comprehensive listings of child-care facilities. There must be comprehensive listings of licensed health-care providers. Public schools should be comprehensively listed. However, when (for recent projects) we have talked about how one would survey comprehensively formal institutions, the choice of a potential sampling frame was not at all clear.

Informal institutions present even greater problems. Clubs, leagues, volunteer groups, and so forth are what we have in mind. Strategies for measuring such phenomena on a basis that would provide consistent measures over time and across sites need to be developed.

6. *Tighten relationships between short-term (intermediate) outcome measures and long-term outcome measures.* The inability or unwillingness to wait for the measurement of long-term outcomes is a problem that many studies of children and youth, in particular, face. Increasingly we talk about "youth trajectories." Again, perhaps good comprehensive information— of which we are unaware—exists, linking many short-term, often softer measures of outcomes to the long-term outcomes further along the trajectory. We find ourselves time and again asking, for example, "What do we know about how that short-term measure—participation in some activity (say, Boy Scouts)—correlates with a long-term outcome (say, employment and earnings)?" Even more rare is information on how *program-induced changes* in the short-term outcome are related to changes in long-term outcomes. We may know that the *level* of a short-term variable is highly correlated with a long-term variable, but we do not know to what extent a *change* in that short-term variable correlates with a *change* in the long-term variable. Thus, we believe systematic compilations of information about short-term and long-term correlations for outcome variables would be very helpful and could set an agenda for more data-gathering on these relationships where necessary.

7. Conduct more studies to determine the reliability of constructed comparison group designs. We have stressed the importance of information provided by the two sets of studies (reported in Fraker and Maynard 1987; LaLonde 1986; and Friedlander and Robins 1994) that used random assignment data as a base and then constructed comparison groups to test the degree of error in the comparison group estimates. It should be possible to find more situations in which this type of study could be carried out. First, the replication of such studies should look at variables other than employment or earnings as outcomes to determine whether any difference in degrees of vulnerability exist according to the type of outcome variable and/or a different type of intervention. Second, more studies of this type would give us a far better sense of whether, indeed, the degree of vulnerability of the nonexperimental methods is persistent and widely found in a variety of data sets and settings.

◊   ◊   ◊   ◊   ◊

Community-wide programs present special problems for evaluators because the "nectar of the gods"—random assignment of individuals to program treatment and to a control group—is beyond their reach. The central problem of impact evaluations, creating a reasonable and convincing counterfactual (what would have happened in the absence of the program intervention), remains a major challenge. Our review of the experience to date with alternative methods is generally discouraging; no clear second-best method emerges from the review.

Nonetheless, we feel that it is very important for evaluators to understand this message and to convey it clearly to those who look to them for evidence of program effectiveness. In addition, we feel it is important to push forward in the effort to build a stronger foundation for understanding how communities evolve over time. That understanding should enhance the ability of evaluators to determine how community-wide program interventions alter the course of a community's evolution.

APPENDIX:
SOME DETAILS ON THE FRIEDLANDER-ROBINS STUDY

In this appendix we discuss in detail some of the major findings of the study by Friedlander and Robins (1994). These details indicate the possible relative magnitude of problems with several of the alternative methods for constructing comparison groups.

Recall that this study used data from a group of Work/Welfare studies. In the base studies themselves random assignment of individuals was used to create control groups but Friedlander and Robins used data drawing the treatment group from one segment and the control group from a different segment (thereby "undoing" the random assignment). It was then possible to compare the effects estimated by the treatment-comparison group combination with the "true effects" estimated from the random assignment estimates of treatment-control group differences (the same treatment group outcome is used in each difference estimate).

Even more salient for the purposes of this paper, Friedlander and Robins were able to generate types of comparison groups that have often been suggested for community-wide program evaluation. In one type of constructed comparison, they were able to use the treatment group from communities in one state and a comparison group made up from the control group in a community in another state. In a second type, they used the treatment group entering the program from one office within a city, with the control group drawn from a different office within the city—a procedure that would be quite similar to a comparison neighborhood strategy. In a third type of comparison they used the treatment group from one period of time and a control group in the same site from another period of time, which would be like a pre- and post-treatment comparison in a single community.

Recall that this study is able to establish the degree of bias because the estimated impact results of the constructed comparison group are compared with the "true" impact results obtained from the randomly assigned treatment and control groups. With all three of the types of comparisons just described—comparison across state, comparison within state but across offices, and comparison of before-and-after cohorts in the same site—the average amount of bias was substantial.

The bias in using the constructed comparison groups occurred not just in differences in the order of magnitude of the estimated impact but also in the nature of the inference. A different statistical inference occurs when only one of the two impact estimates is statistically significant—for example, the random assignment estimates showed the program had a statistically significant positive impact and the constructed comparison group estimates indicated no statistically significant impact, or both random and constructed comparison estimates are statistically significant but have opposite signs, such as the random assignment showed a statistically significant positive impact and the constructed comparison indicated a statistically significant negative impact. For most of the methods of comparison, over 30 percent of the cases had such a conflict in statistical inference, and even in the best example, 13 percent of the cases had such conflicts. The point here is that when constructed comparison groups are used there is a substantial risk, not only of getting the order of magnitude of the impact wrong, but also of drawing the wrong conclusion about whether any impact exists or whether the direction of the impact is positive or negative.

It has long been recognized that counterfactuals obtained by using constructed comparison groups (as opposed to control groups obtained by random assignment) may, in theory, yield biased estimates of the true impact of a program. What is important about the Friedlander-Robins study is that it demonstrates through the use of actual program data that various types of constructed comparison groups yield very substantially biased estimates; *it is not just a theoretical possibility but it would actually have given very biased results if the comparison group methods had been used rather than random assignment in evaluating these Work/Welfare programs.* We reproduce here part of one table from their study (Table A1).

The data are drawn from four experiments carried out in the 1980s (in Arkansas, Baltimore, San Diego, and Virginia). The outcome variable is employment (the employment rate ranged from a low of .265 in Arkansas to a high of .517 in Baltimore). Across the top of the table there is a brief description of how the comparison group was constructed, using four different schemes for construction.

In columns 1 and 2, the two across-site methods use the treatment group from one site—for example, Baltimore—with the control group from another site—say, San Diego—used as the comparison group. In the second column the term "matched" indicates that each member of the treatment group was matched with a member of the comparison group using the Mahalanobis "nearest neighbor" method, and then the estimates of the impact were measured as the difference between the treatment group and the matched comparison group. In the first column no such member-by-member match was done; however, in the regression equation in which the estimate of the impact is made, variables for characteristics are included and this controls for measured differences in characteristics between the two groups.

The within-site/across-cohort category in column 3 builds on the fact that the samples at each site were enrolled over a fairly long time period, and it was, therefore, possible to split the sample in two parts—those enrolled before a given date, called the "early cohort," and those enrolled after that date, called the "late cohort." The treatment group from the "late cohort" is used with the control group from the "early cohort" as their comparison group. This approximates a pre–post design for a study.

Finally, in column 4, for two of the sites the Work/Welfare program was implemented through several local offices. It was possible, therefore, to use the treatment group from one office with the control group from the other office as

Table A1
Comparison of Experimental and Nonexperimental Estimates
of the Effects of Employment and Training Programs
on Employment Status

All Pairs of Experimental and Non-experimental Estimates	Comparison Group Specification			
	(1) Across-Site/ Unmatched	(2) Across-Site/ Matched	(3) Within-Site/ Across-Cohort	(4) Within-Site/ Across-Office
(1) Number of pairs	96	24	24	16
(2) Mean experimental estimate	.056	.056	.045	.069
(3) Mean absolute experimental-nonexperimental difference	.090	.076	.034	.044
(4) Percent with different inference	47%	38%	29%	13%
(5) Percent with statistically significant difference	70%	58%	4%	31%

Source: Daniel Friedlander and Philip K. Robins, "Estimating the Effect of Employment and Training Programs: An Assessment of Some Nonexperimental Techniques," *Manpower Demonstration Research Corporation Working Paper* (February 1994): Table 13.

a comparison group. This procedure approximates a matching of communities in near proximity to each other.

The first row of the table gives the number of pairs tested. This is determined by the number of sites, the number of outcomes (the employment outcomes at two different post-enrollment dates were used), and the number of subgroups (broken down by AFDC applicants and AFDC current recipients). The number of pairs gets large because each site can be paired with each of the three other sites. The smaller number of pairs in the within-site/across-office category (column 4) occurs because there were only two sites with multiple offices.

The second row gives the means of the experimental estimates—that is, the "true impact estimates" from the original study of randomly assigned treatment-control differentials. Thus for example, the experimental estimates of treatment-control differences in employment rates across all four sites was a 5.6 percent difference in the employment rate of treatments and controls.

The third row compares the results of the estimates using the constructed comparison groups with the "true impact" experimental estimates, averaged across all pairs. For example, the mean absolute difference between the "true impact" estimate and those obtained by the constructed comparison groups across-site/unmatched was .09; that is, the *difference* between the two sets of estimates was, on average, more than 1.5 times the *size* of the "true impact"!

The fourth row tells the percentage of the pairs in which the constructed comparison group estimates yielded a different statistical inference from the "true impact" estimates. A different statistical inference occurs when only one of the two impact estimates is statistically significant or both are statistically significant but have opposite signs. A 10 percent level of statistical significance was used.

The fifth row indicates the percent of the pairs in which the estimated impacts are statistically significantly different from each other.

For our purposes, we focus on rows 3 and 4. Row 3 tells us that under every method of constructing comparison groups the constructed comparison group estimates (called "nonexperimental" in the table) differ from the "true impact" estimates by a magnitude of over 50 percent of the magnitude of the "true impact."

Row 4 tells us that in a substantial number of cases the constructed comparison group results led to a different inference; that is, the "true impact" estimates indicated that the program had a statistically significant effect on the employment rate, and the constructed comparison group estimates indicated that it had no impact or vice versa, or that one said the impact was to increase the employment rates at a statistically significant level and the other said that it decreased the employment rate at a statistically significant level.

Now we focus more closely on columns 3 and 4 because these are the types of comparisons that are likely to be more relevant for community-wide initiatives. As already noted, the within-site/across-cohort category approximates a pre–post design in a single community, and the within-site/across-office designation approximates a close-neighborhood-as-a-comparison-group design.

It appears that these designs are better than the across-site designs in that, as indicated in row 3, the size of the absolute difference between the "true impact" and the constructed comparison group estimates is much smaller and is smaller than the size of the true impact. However, the difference is still over 50 percent the size of the "true impact." The magnitude of the difference is important if one is carrying out a benefit-cost analysis of the program. A 4.5 percent difference in employment rates might not be sufficiently large to justify the costs of the program but a 7.9 percent difference might make the benefit-cost ratio look very favorable; a benefit-cost analysis with the average "true impact" would have led to the conclusion that the social benefits of the program do not justify the costs, whereas the average constructed comparison group impact (assuming that it was a positive .034 or greater) would have led to the erroneous conclusion that the program did provide social benefits that justify its costs.

When we move to row 4 we have to be a bit more careful in interpreting the results because the sample sizes for the column 3 and 4 estimates are considerably smaller than those for the column 1 and 2 cases. For example, the entire treatment group is used in each pair in columns 1 and 2, but only half the treatment group is used in columns 3 and 4. Small sample size makes it more likely that both the random assignment estimates and the constructed comparison group estimates will be found to be statistically insignificant. Thus, inherently the percent with a different statistical inference should be smaller in columns 3 and 4. Even so, for the within-site/across-cohort category, nearly 30 percent of the pairs in the constructed comparison group estimates would lead to a different—and therefore erroneous—inference about the impact of the program. For the within-site/across-office estimates, 13 percent led to a different statistical inference. Is this a tolerable risk of erroneous inference? We would not think so, but others may feel otherwise.

A couple of additional points about the data from this study should be borne in mind. First, this is just one set of data analyzed for a single, relatively well-understood outcome measure, whether employed or not. There is no guarantee that the conclusions about relative strength of alternative methods of constructing comparison groups found with these data would hold up for other outcome measures. Second, in the underlying Work/Welfare studies, the populations from which both treatment group members and control group members were drawn were very much the same—that is, applicants or recipients of AFDC. Therefore, even when constructing comparison groups across sites, one is assured that one has already selected persons whose employment situation is so poor they need to apply for welfare. In community-wide initiatives, the population involved would be far more heterogenous. There would be a far wider range of unmeasured characteristics that could affect the outcomes; therefore, the adequacy of statistical controls (matching or modeling) in assuring comparability of the treatment and constructed comparison groups could be much less.

NOTES

A fuller version of this paper, including an annotated bibliography, is available as a working paper on request from the Russell Sage Foundation, 112 East 64th Street, New York, NY 10021.

1. We recognize that even with random assignment problems remain that we can only address with nonexperimental methods—in particular, attrition from the research measurement in follow-up periods.
2. The Friedlander and Robins (1994) study found little difference between controlling for measured differences in characteristics through a common linear regression model and using pairs matched on the Mahalanobis measure. Fraker and Maynard (1987) also compare Mahalanobis matches with other matching methods and find no clear indication of superiority.

3. It should be recognized that this is a study using data on Work/Welfare programs, looking at effects on employment, and we cannot be sure that the conclusions drawn about the risks of bias with constructed comparison groups that appear in these data would hold for other types of outcomes or for other types of program interventions. However, it seems to us to provide a very strong signal that the potential risks in the use of some of these comparison group strategies are very high.

4. For a classic reference on these methods, see Box and Jenkins (1976). Several applications of time-series modeling to program evaluation are presented in Forehand (1982).

5. There is a rich literature on the closely related development of simulation models used to estimate the likely effects of proposed program reforms in taxes and expenditures. See, for example, Citro and Hanushek (1991).

6. Many of these remarks would apply equally to situations in which constructed comparison groups are used, in the sense that the interaction effects themselves do not add further problems of bias beyond those associated with constructed comparison groups.

7. See Hollister and Haveman (1991) for a full discussion of the problems of displacement and attempts to measure it.

8. The best attempt of which we are aware to measure displacement is Crane and Ellwood (1984), but even it has serious problems. It used not comparison sites but data on national enrollments in the Summer Youth Employment Program and data on standard metropolitan statistical area (SMSA) labor markets from the Current Population Survey (CPS). The national program was large enough to have impacts on local youth labor markets, and the time-series data from the CPS made it possible to attempt to create a counterfactual with an elaborate statistical model.

9. In the medical experimentation literature, there is also some discussion about optimal stopping rules that introduce time considerations into decisions about when to terminate clinical trials as information accumulates.

Some work has been done on dynamic sample allocation. Here, learning effects are introduced sequentially as information flows back about the size of variances of outcome variables, and to some degree initial estimates of response. In light of this information, sequentially enrolled sample can be reallocated among treatments—that is, shift more sample into groups with the largest variance—so as to reduce the uncertainty of estimates. The National Supported Work Demonstration used such a sequential design to a limited degree.

10. Michael Wiseman of the University of Wisconsin made some partial steps in this direction in the work he did for Urban Strategies in Oakland.

REFERENCES

Ashenfelter, Orley, and David Card. 1985. "Using the Longitudinal Structure of Earnings to Estimate the Effect of Training Programs." *Review of Economics and Statistics* 67: 648–60.

Bassi, Laurie. 1983. "The Effect of CETA on the Post-Program Earnings of Participants." *The Journal of Human Resources* 18: 539–56.

_____. 1984. "Estimating the Effect of Training Programs with Nonrandom Selection." *Review of Economics and Statistics* 66: 36–43.

Beebout, Harold, and Jean Baldwin Grossman. 1985. "A Forecasting System for AFDC Caseloads and Costs: Executive Summary." Mimeographed. Princeton: Mathematica Policy Research.

Bhattacharyya, M. N., and Allan P. Layton. 1979. "Effectiveness of Seat Belt Legislation on the Queensland Road Toll—An Australian Case Study in Intervention Analysis." *Journal of the American Statistical Association* 74: 596–603.

Bloom, Howard S. 1987. "What Works for Whom? CETA Impacts for Adult Participants." *Evaluation Review* 11: 510–27.

Box, G. E. P., and G. M. Jenkins. 1976. *Time-Series Analysis: Forecasting and Control.* San Francisco: Holden-Day.

Brown, Prudence, and Harold A. Richman. 1993. "Communities and Neighborhoods: How Can Existing Research Inform and Shape Current Urban Change Initiatives?" Background memorandum prepared for the Social Science Research Council Policy Conference on Persistent Poverty, Washington, D.C., November 9–10. Chapin Hall Center for Children at the University of Chicago.

Brown, Randall, John Burghardt, Edward Cavin, David Long, Charles Mallar, Rebecca Maynard, Charles Metcalf, Craig Thornton, and Christine Whitebread. 1983. "The Employment Opportunity Pilot Projects: Analysis of Program Impacts." Mimeographed. Princeton: Mathematica Policy Research.

Bryant, Edward C., and Kalman Rupp. 1987. "Evaluating the Impact of CETA on Participant Earnings." *Evaluation Review* 11: 473–92.

Burghardt, John, Anne Gordon, Nancy Chapman, Philip Gleason, and Thomas Fraker. 1993. "The School Nutrition Dietary Assessment Study: Dietary Intakes of Program Participants and Nonparticipants." Mimeographed (October). Princeton: Mathematica Policy Research.

Campbell, D. T., and J. C. Stanley. 1966. *Experimental and Quasi-Experimental Designs for Research.* Chicago: Rand McNally.

Caswell, Sally, and Lynnette Gilmore. 1989. "An Evaluated Community Action Project on Alcohol." *Journal of Studies on Alcohol* 50: 339–46.

Chaskin, Robert J. 1994. "Defining Neighborhood." Background paper prepared for the Neighborhood Mapping Project of the Annie E. Casey Foundation. The Chapin Hall Center for Children at the University of Chicago.

Citro, Constance, and E. A. Hanushek, eds. 1991. *Improving Information for Social Policy Decisions: The Uses of Microsimulation Modeling* vol. 1. Washington, D.C.: National Academy Press.

Crane, J., and D. Ellwood. 1984. "The Summer Youth Employment Program: Private Job Supplement or Substitute." Harvard Working Paper.

Davis, Elizabeth. 1993. "The Impact of Food Stamp Cashout on Household Expenditures: The Alabama ASSETS Demonstration." In*New Directions in Food Stamp Policy Research*, ed. Nancy Fasciano, Daryl Hall, and Harold Beebout. Draft Copy. Princeton: Mathematica Policy Research.

Devaney, Barbara, Linda Bilheimer, and Jennifer Schore. 1991. *The Savings in Medicaid Costs for Newborns and their Mothers from Prenatal Participation in the WIC Program.* Vols. 1 and 2. Princeton: Mathematica Policy Research.

Devaney, Barbara, and Lorenzo Morano. 1994. "Comparison Site Selection Criteria." Princeton: Mathematica Policy Research.

Dickinson, Katherine P., Terry R. Johnson, and Richard W. West. 1987. "An Analysis of the Sensitivity of Quasi-Experimental Net Impact Estimates of CETA Programs." *Evaluation Review* 11: 452–72.

Dynarski, Mark, Alan Hershey, Rebecca Maynard, and Nancy Adelman. 1992. "The Evaluation of the School Dropout Demonstration Assistance Program—Design Report: Volume I." Mimeographed (October 12). Princeton: Mathematica Policy Research.

Dynarski, Mark, and Walter Corson. 1994. "Technical Approach for the Evaluation of Youth Fair Chance." Proposal accepted by the Department of Labor (June 1994). Princeton: Mathematica Policy Research.

Flay, Brian, Katherine B. Ryan, J. Allen Best, K. Stephen Brown, Mary W. Kersell, Josie R. d'Avernas, and Mark P. Zanna. 1985. "Are Social-Psychological Smoking Prevention Programs Effective? The Waterloo Study." *Journal of Behavioral Medicine* 8: 3759.

Forehand, Garlie A. 1982. *New Directions for Program Evaluation*, No. 16. A publication of the Evaluation Research Society, Scarvia B. Anderson, Editor-in-Chief. San Francisco: Jossey-Bass, Inc.

Fraker, Thomas, and Rebecca Maynard. 1987. "The Adequacy of Comparison Group Designs for Evaluations of Employment-Related Programs." *The Journal of Human Resources* 22: 194–297.

Friedlander, D., and P. Robins. 1994. "Estimating the Effect of Employment and Training Programs: An Assessment of Some Nonexperimental Techniques." Manpower Demonstration Research Corporation Working Paper (February). New York: Manpower Demonstration Research Corporation.

Garfinkel, Irwin, C. Manski, and C. Michalopoulous. 1992. "Micro Experiments and Macro Effects." In *Evaluating Welfare and Training Programs*, ed. Charles Manski and Irwin Garfinkel. Cambridge, Mass.: Harvard University Press.

Garasky, Steven. 1990. "Analyzing the Effect of Massachusetts's ET Choices Program on the State's AFDC-Based Caseload." *Evaluation Review* 14: 701–10.

Garasky, Steven, and Burt S. Barnow. 1992. "Demonstration Evaluations and Cost Neutrality: Using Caseload Models to Determine the Federal Cost Neutrality of New Jersey's REACH Demonstration." *Journal of Policy Analysis and Management* 11: 624–36.

Grossman, Jean Baldwin. 1985. "The Technical Report for the AFDC Forecasting Project for the Social Security Administration/Office of Family Assistance." Mimeographed (February). Princeton: Mathematica Policy Research.

Heckman, J. 1979. "Sample Bias as a Specification Error." *Econometrica* 47: 153–62.

Heckman, J., and J. Hotz. 1989. "Choosing Among Alternative Nonexperimental Methods for Estimating the Impact of Social Programs: The Case of Manpower Training." *Journal of the American Statistical Association* 84, no. 408 (December): 862–80.

Hollister, Robinson, and Robert Haveman. 1991. "Direct Job Creation." In *Labour Market Policy and Unemployment Insurance,* ed. A. Bjorklund, R. Haveman, R. Hollister, and B. Holmlund. Oxford: Clarendon Press.

La Londe, R. 1986. "Evaluating the Econometric Evaluations of Training Programs with Experimental Data." *American Economic Review* (September).

LaLonde, R., and R. Maynard. 1987. "How Precise are Evaluations of Employment and Training Programs: Evidence from a Field Experiment." *Evaluation Review* 11, No. 4 (August): 428–51.

Long, Sharon K., and Douglas A. Wissoker. 1993. "Final Impact Analysis Report: The Washington State Family Independence Program." Draft (April). Washington, D.C.: Urban Institute.

Mathematica Policy Research. 1985. "Evaluation of the Nutrition Assistance Program in Puerto Rico: Volume II, Effects on Food Expenditures and Diet Quality." Mimeographed. Princeton: Mathematica Policy Research.

McCleary, Richard, and James E. Riggs. 1982. "The 1975 Australian Family Law Act: A Model for Assessing Legal Impacts." In *New Directions for Program Analysis: Applications of Time-Series Analysis to Evaluation,* ed. Garlie A. Forehand. *New Directions for Program Evaluation,* No. 16 (December). San Francisco: Jossey-Bass, Inc.

McConnell, Beverly B. 1982. "Evaluating Bilingual Education Using a Time-Series Design." In *Applications of Time-Series Analysis to Evaluation,* ed. Garlie A. Forehand. *New Directions for Program Evaluation,* No. 16 (December). San Francisco: Jossey-Bass, Inc.

Vincent, Murray L., Andrew F. Clearie, and Mark D. Schluchter. 1987. "Reducing Adolescent Pregnancy Through School and Community-Based Education." *Journal of the American Medical Association* 257: 3382–86.

SELECT BIBLIOGRAPHY:
EXAMPLES OF STUDIES USING
VARIOUS EVALUATION STRATEGIES

Counterfactual from Statistical Modeling

Bhattacharyya, M.N., and Allan P. Layton. 1979. "Effectiveness of Seat Belt Legislation on the Queensland Road Toll—An Australian Case Study in Intervention Analysis." *Journal of the American Statistical Association* 74: 596–603.

Fraker, Thomas, Barbara Devaney, and Edward Cavin. 1986. "An Evaluation of the Effect of Cashing Out Food Stamps on Food Expenditures." *American Economic Review* 76: 230–39.

Garasky, Steven. 1990. "Analyzing the Effect of Massachusetts's ET Choices Program on the State's AFDC-Based Caseload." *Evaluation Review* 14: 701–10.

Garasky, Steven, and Burt S. Barnow. 1992. "Demonstration Evaluations and Cost Neutrality: Using Caseload Models to Determine the Federal Cost Neutrality of New Jersey's REACH Demonstration." *Journal of Policy Analysis and Management* 11: 624–36.

Grossman, Jean Baldwin. 1985. "The Technical Report for the AFDC Forecasting Project for the Social Security Administration/Office of Family Assistance." Mimeographed (February). Princeton: Mathematica Policy Research.

Kaitz, Hyman B. 1979. "Potential Use of Markov Process Models to Determine Program Impact." In *Research in Labor Economics,* ed. Farrell E. Bloch, 259–83. Greenwich: JAI Press.

Mathematica Policy Research. 1985. "Evaluation of the Nutrition Assistance Program in Puerto Rico: Volume II, Effects on Food Expenditures and Diet Quality." Mimeographed. Princeton: Mathematica Policy Research.

McCleary, Richard, and James E. Riggs. 1982. "The 1975 Australian Family Law Act: A Model for Assessing Legal Impacts." In *New Directions for Program Analysis: Applications of Time-Series Analysis to Evaluation,* ed. Garlie A. Forehand. *New Directions for Program Evaluation,* No. 16 (December). San Francisco: Jossey-Bass, Inc.

McConnell, Beverly B. 1982. "Evaluating Bilingual Education Using a Time-Series Design." In *New Directions for Program Analysis: Applications of Time-Series Analysis to Evaluation,* ed. Garlie A. Forehand. *New Directions for Program Evaluation,* No. 16 (December). San Francisco: Jossey-Bass, Inc.

Comparison Group Derived from Survey Data

Ashenfelter, Orley. 1978. "Estimating the Effect of Training Programs on Earnings." *Review of Economics and Statistics* 60: 47–57.

Ashenfelter, Orley, and David Card. 1985. "Using the Longitudinal Structure of Earnings to Estimate the Effect of Training Programs." *Review of Economics and Statistics* 67: 648–60.

Barnow, Burt S. 1987. "The Impact of CETA Programs on Earnings." *The Journal of Human Resources* 22: 157–93

Bassi, Laurie. 1983. "The Effect of CETA on the Post-Program Earnings of Participants." *The Journal of Human Resources* 18: 539–56.

_____. 1984. "Estimating the Effect of Training Programs with Nonrandom Selection." *Review of Economics and Statistics* 66: 36–43.

Bloom, Howard S. 1987. "What Works for Whom? CETA Impacts for Adult Participants." *Evaluation Review* 11: 510–27.

Bryant, Edward C., and Kalman Rupp. 1987. "Evaluating the Impact of CETA on Participant Earnings." *Evaluation Review* 11: 473–92.

Dickinson, Katherine P., Terry R. Johnson, and Richard W. West. 1987. "An Analysis of the Sensitivity of Quasi-Experimental Net Impact Estimates of CETA Programs." *Evaluation Review* 11: 452–72.

Finifter, David H. 1987. "An Approach to Estimating Net Earnings Impact of Federally Subsidized Employment and Training Programs." *Evaluation Review* 11: 528–47.

Within-Site Comparison Groups

Burghardt, John, Anne Gordon, Nancy Chapman, Philip Gleason, and Thomas Fraker. 1993. "The School Nutrition Dietary Assessment Study: Dietary Intakes of Program Participants and Nonparticipants." Mimeographed (October). Princeton: Mathematica Policy Research. (See also the other reports from this study, including "Data Collection and Sampling"; "School Food Service, Meals Offered, and Dietary Intakes"; and "Summary of Findings.")

Cooley, Thomas M., Timothy W. McGuire, and Edward C. Prescott. 1979. "Earnings and Employment Dynamics of Manpower Trainees: An Exploratory Econometric Analysis." *Research in Labor Economics*, ed. Farrell E. Bloch, 119–48. Greenwich: JAI Press.

Devaney, Barbara, Linda Bilheimer, and Jennifer Schore. 1991. *The Savings in Medicaid Costs for Newborns and their Mothers from Prenatal Participation in the WIC Program.* Vols. 1 and 2. Mimeographed (April). Princeton: Mathematica Policy Research.

Jiminez, Emmanuel, and Bernardo Kugler. 1987. "The Earnings Impact of Training Duration in a Developing Country: An Ordered Probit Selection Model of Columbia's Servicio Nacional de Aprendizaje (SENA)." *The Journal of Human Resources* 22: 228–47.

Kiefer, Nicholas M. 1978. "Federally Subsidized Occupational Training and the Employment and Earnings of Male Trainees." *Journal of Econometrics* 8: 111–25.

_____. 1979. "Population Heterogeneity and Inference from Panel Data on the Effects of Vocational Training." *Journal of Political Economy* 87: 213–26.

Matched-Site Comparison Groups—No Modeling

Buckner, John C., and Meda Chesney-Lind. 1983. "Dramatic Cures for Juvenile Crime: An Evaluation of a Prisoner-Run Delinquency Prevention Program." *Criminal Justice and Behavior* 10: 227–47.

Duncan, Burris, W. Thomas Boyce, Robert Itami, and Nancy Puffenbarger. 1983. "A Controlled Trial of a Physical Fitness Program for Fifth Grade Students." *Journal of School Health* 53: 467–71.

Evans, Richard, Richard Rozelle, Maurice Mittelmark, William Hansen, Alice Bane, and Janet Havis. 1978. "Deterring the Onset of Smoking in Children: Knowledge of Immediate Physiological Effects and Coping with Peer Pressure, Media Pressure, and Parent Modeling." *Journal of Applied Social Psychology* 8, no. 2: 126–35.

Flay, Brian, Katherine B. Ryan, Allen J. Best, K. Stephen Brown, Mary W. Kersell, Josie R. d'Avernas, and Mark P. Zanna. 1985. "Are Social-Psychological Smoking Prevention Programs Effective? The Waterloo Study." *Journal of Behavioral Medicine* 8: 3759.

Freda, Margaret Comerford, Karla Damus, and Irwin R. Merkatz. 1988. "The Urban Community as the Client in Preterm Birth Prevention: Evaluation of a Program Component." *Social Science and Medicine* 27: 1439–46.

Hurd, Peter D., C. Anderson Johnson, Terry Pechacek, L. Peter Bast, David R. Jacobs, and Russel V. Luepker. 1980. "Prevention of Cigarette Smoking in Seventh Grade Students." *Journal of Behavioral Medicine* 3: 15–28.

McAlister, Alfred, Cheryl Perry, Joel Killen, Lee Ann Slinkard, and Nathan Maccoby. 1980. "Pilot Study of Smoking, Alcohol and Drug Abuse Prevention." *American Journal of Public Health* 70: 719–21.

Perry, Cheryl L., Joel Killen, and Lee Ann Slinkard. 1980. "Peer Teaching and Smoking Prevention Among Junior High Students." *Adolescence* 15: 277–81.

Perry, Cheryl L., Rebecca M. Mullis, and Marla C. Maile. 1985. "Modifying the Eating Behavior of Young Children." *Journal of School Health* 55: 399–402.

Perry, Cheryl L., Michael J. Telch, Joel Killen, Adam Burke, and Nathan Maccoby. 1983. "High School Smoking Prevention: The Relative Efficacy of Varied Treatments and Instructors." *Adolescence* 18: 561–66.

Vincent, Murray L., Andrew F. Clearie, and Mark D. Schluchter. 1987. "Reducing Adolescent Pregnancy Through School and Community-Based Education." *Journal of the American Medical Association* 257: 3382–86.

Zabin, Laurie S., Marilyn Hirsch, Edward A. Smith, Rosalie Streett, and Janet B. Hardy. 1986. "Evaluation of a Pregnancy Prevention Program for Urban Teenagers." *Family Planning Perspectives* 18: 119–23.

Matched-Site Comparison Groups—With Modeling

Brown, Randall, John Burghardt, Edward Cavin, David Long, Charles Mallar, Rebecca Maynard, Charles Metcalf, Craig Thornton, and Christine Whitebread. 1983. "The Employment Opportunity Pilot Projects: Analysis of Program Impacts." Mimeographed (February). Princeton: MathematicaPolicy Research.

Casswell, Sally, and Lynette Gilmore. 1989. "Evaluated Community Action Project on Alcohol." *Journal of Studies on Alcohol* 50: 339–46.

Devaney, Barbara, Marie McCormick, and Embry Howell. 1993. "Design Reports for Healthy Start Evaluation: Evaluation Design, Comparison Site Selection Criteria, Site Visit Protocol, Interview Guides." Mimeographed. Princeton: Mathematica Policy Research.

Dynarski, Mark, and Walter Corson. 1994. "Technical Approach for the Evaluation of Youth Fair Chance." Proposal accepted by the Department of Labor (June 1994). Princeton: Mathematica Policy Research.

Farkas, George, Randall Olsen, Ernst W. Stromsdorfer, Linda C. Sharpe, Felicity Skidmore, D. Alton Smith, and Sally Merrilly (Abt Associates). 1984. *Post-Program Impacts of the Youth Incentive Entitlement Pilot Projects* New York: Manpower Demonstration Research Corporation.

Farkas, George, D. Alton Smith, and Ernst W. Stromsdorfer. 1983. "The Youth Entitlement Demonstration: Subsidized Employment with a Schooling Requirement." *The Journal of Human Resources* 18: 557–73.

Gueron, Judith. 1984. *Lessons from a Job Guarantee: The Youth Incentive Entitlement Pilot Projects* New York: Manpower Demonstration Research Corporation.

Guyer, Bernard, Susan S. Gallagher, Bei-Hung Chang, Carey V. Azzara, L. Adrienne Cupples, and Theodore Colton. 1989. "Prevention of Childhood Injuries: Evaluation of the Statewide Childhood Injury Prevention Program (SCIPP)." *American Journal of Public Health* 79: 1521–27.

Ketron. 1987. "Final Report of the Second Set of Food Stamp Workfare Demonstration Projects." Mimeographed (September). Wayne, Pa.: Ketron.

Long, David A., Charles D. Malla, and Craig V. D. Thornton. 1981. "Evaluating the Benefits and Costs of the Job Corps." *Journal of Policy Analysis and Management* 1: 55–76.

Mallar, Charles, Stuart Kerachsky, Craig Thornton, and David Long. 1982. "Evaluation of the Economic Impact of the Job Corps Program: Third Follow-Up Report." Mimeographed (September). Princeton: Mathematica Policy Research.

Polit, Denise, Janet Kahn, and David Stevens. 1985. "Final Impacts from Project Redirection." Mimeographed (April). New York: Manpower Demonstration Research Corporation.

Steinberg, Dan. 1989. "Induced Work Participation and the Returns to Experience for Welfare Women: Evidence from a Social Experiment." *Journal of Econometrics* 41: 321–40.

Matched-Pair Comparison Sites

Davis, Elizabeth. 1993. "The Impact of Food Stamp Cashout on Household Expenditures: The Alabama ASSETS Demonstration." In *New Directions in Food Stamp Policy Research*, ed. Nancy Fasciano, Daryl Hall, and Harold Beebout. Draft Copy. Princeton: Mathematica Policy Research.

Long, Sharon K., and Douglas A. Wissoker. 1993. "Final Impact Analysis Report: The Washington State Family Independence Program." Draft (April). Washington, D.C.: Urban Institute.

Institutional Comparison

Dynarski, Mark, Alan Hershey, Rebecca Maynard, and Nancy Adelman. 1992. "The Evaluation of the School Dropout Demonstration Assistance Program—Design Report: Volume I." Mimeographed (October 12). Princeton: Mathematica Policy Research.

Using Community-Level Indicators of Children's Well-Being in Comprehensive Community Initiatives

Claudia J. Coulton

Children and their families live within local communities, which are often explicit targets of change in comprehensive community initiatives. It is indeed at the level of the local community that many of the processes that affect children transpire. Children interact with neighbors; participate in local institutions; receive social, health, and educational services; develop a sense of safety and belonging; form a vision of their opportunities; know what is expected of them and what they can expect from others. Parents' implicit understanding of the importance of local community is reflected in the serious thought that many of them give to their residential choices. Yet the locational options of a significant number of families are constrained by racism, low income, insufficient information, or public policy. Describing the variation in child well-being across local communities is, thus, a crucial task for comprehensive community initiatives.

Developing relevant and sensitive indicators of child well-being at the local community level, however, poses numerous conceptual, methodological, and practical challenges. Those challenges, as well as the important benefits of undertaking this level of measurement, are the focus of this paper.

173

LOCAL COMMUNITIES
AS UNITS OF ANALYSIS

Although the term "community" is a social rather than a geographic unit, this paper focuses on local communities that are bounded spatially. Such communities can serve as units for the measurement of child and family well-being. The local community of interest is typically the neighborhood, although for some purposes it is a political jurisdiction such as a ward or town, or a service delivery zone such as a school or health district.

Neighborhood boundaries are often difficult to draw because there is little consensus about what constitutes a neighborhood. Social scientists hold varying perspectives on the degree to which the term implies homogeneity, social interaction, and place identity on the part of the residents (White 1987). Most definitions of neighborhood imply a degree of social cohesion that results from shared institutions and space, but it is also widely accepted that neighborhoods differ in their levels of community social organization and integration (Lyon 1987). Further, it seems that neighborhoods that are least cohesive and organized may be the poorest community environments for rearing children (Coulton et al., forthcoming; Garbarino and Sherman 1980; Sampson 1992).

Despite the definitional ambiguities of neighborhood or other meaningful localities, local community indicators typically require geographic boundaries. These boundaries may be phenomenological, interactional, statistical, or political.

At the phenomenological level, each resident has a sense of the boundaries that are personally meaningful. These vary even for the same individual depending upon the context (Galster 1986). However, under some circumstances it is possible to use the consensus of residents as the basis for drawing geographic boundaries for neighborhoods. In our research on Cleveland's neighborhoods we have found some areas where there is considerable agreement among neighbors on the boundaries of their neighborhood while in other locales neighborhood boundaries seem virtually idiosyncratic. Consensus seems to be greater in areas with higher levels of community identity and attachment (Korbin and Coulton 1994). Where adequate consensus exists, the residents' perceived boundaries can be used to form units for the development of indicators. However, this consensus may change over time, making consensual boundaries problematic for tracking changes in communities over time.

A second approach to generating community-area boundaries is to use the patterns of social interaction of residents. This involves a process of "mapping locally-based social interaction onto a spatial grid" (Entwisle 1991). Friendship patterns and daily activities have both been used as methods of tying interaction patterns to spatial locations.

Statistical definitions of local community areas are a third approach. Census tracts have been most widely used to date in local indicator development even though concerns have been raised about the degree to which these units resemble the space that is meaningful to residents (Tienda 1991). Nevertheless, census tracts have proven quite useful for local planning and research on neighborhoods (White 1987; Kasarda 1993; Galster and Mincey 1993; Pandey and Coulton 1994). Block groups have also served as proxies for neighborhoods in some studies (Taylor, Gottfredson, and Brower 1984).

In cities such as Chicago, Cleveland, Philadelphia, and elsewhere, designated neighborhoods traditionally are used for planning purposes, and the Census Bureau has supported such local designations as well. Unlike census tracts, these designated neighborhoods can vary considerably in size but take into account local sentiments on natural boundaries. Although designated neighborhoods do not always match resident perceptions, they have been used successfully in research (for example, Galster and Hesser 1982).

Political units such as wards, districts, and towns are a fourth approach to defining community areas but they can seldom be equated with neighborhoods and they lack a social meaning. Nevertheless, when community indicators are used for planning or evaluation, political units may be appropriate for analysis.

Choosing a set of geographic boundaries for community indicators depends upon several considerations. First, it is important that the unit be constant over time so that trends can be tracked. Second, it must be possible to allocate available data to the unit of analysis that is chosen. Third, the choice of units should be appropriate given the assumptions and purposes underlying the set of indicators. In this regard, varying conceptual perspectives on community indicators are discussed in the next section.

In the remainder of this paper I use the term "community area" to refer to the unit of geography that has been chosen, be it a census tract, neighborhood, or town. I use the term "community indicator" to refer to measures that are made on these units of geography.

PERSPECTIVES ON COMMUNITY-LEVEL MEASUREMENT

Two quite different perspectives can be taken on community indicators for families and children. One I will label *outcome orientation*, the other *contextual orientation.*

The *outcome orientation* views community areas as valuable units for measuring the status of children on various social, health, and developmental outcomes. Comparing the status of children across community areas can reveal inequalities that suggest levels of need and indicate where resources should be targeted. Such comparisons also can point to differences in program effectiveness or practices across community areas. Those are the purposes for which community indicators are often obtained, and outcomes do indeed vary considerably across community areas within counties or metropolitan areas (Coulton and Pandey 1992).

This outcome orientation makes few assumptions about the relationships between community areas and their families and children. The outcome measures represent the status of a population of children who live in specified local areas. The ways in which the local communities themselves affect these outcomes remain unspecified.

An alternative view of communities, though, is to measure them as environments for families and children. This *contextual orientation* is based on the assumption, for which there is some empirical support, that community areas (for example, neighborhoods) can affect children and their families positively or negatively. Some of those effects are reflected in higher or lower rates of health, social, and developmental outcomes. But from this perspective it is the community structure and processes that are the relevant focus of measurement.

The contextual orientation makes some strong assumptions about how communities affect families and children. I have reviewed the several extant lines of research on the effects of neighborhoods on families and children in another paper (Coulton 1994), but I will summarize them here. For convenience, this summary discusses the research under four broad headings that are not mutually exclusive: compositional effects, community context of effective parenting, effects of stressful neighborhood environments, and community social organization.

First, recent interest in extreme-poverty neighborhoods has spawned a series of studies designed to determine whether neighborhood socioeconomic composition affects life chances of children over and above family background factors. Although not adopting any uniform theoretical perspective, these studies can be loosely classified as subscribing to a model of socialization processes within neighborhoods through adult, peer, or institutional influences (Jencks and Mayer 1990). Research on the socioeconomic composition of communities reveals that having sufficient affluent families in a neighborhood promotes school achievement, cognitive development, and the avoidance of teen childbearing (Brooks-Gunn et al. 1993; Clark 1992; Crane 1991; Duncan 1993). These studies have found that the positive effects of middle-class and affluent neighbors are more important as a context for children than the negative effects of having poor neighbors.

Second, the community context for parenting has been explored in several important studies. These studies shed light on how social networks, resources, local institutions, and environmental stressors shape parenting style. Parents adapt to dangerous and depleted environments by restricting their children's activities and isolating themselves from the surrounding area (Furstenberg 1993). These adaptations, while understandable and necessary for safety, may not promote academic achievement and future economic success. Also, individual parents who adopt effective childrearing styles will not be as successful when they are surrounded by less effective parents. The distribution of effective parents differs across types of communities (Steinberg et al. 1992; Steinberg and Darling 1994).

Third, the negative effects on families and children of stressful conditions in poor, urban environments have been explored in many studies. Getting most attention in recent years has been the negative impact of chronic exposure to violence in the community (Martinez and Richters 1993; Garbarino et al. 1992; Zapata et al. 1992). Daily hassles, though less dramatic, have been found to be a significant cause of parental distress in poor neighborhoods, too (Caspi, Bolger, and Eckenrode 1987; Garbarino and Sherman 1980). Considerable work on how resourceful parents adapt to these stressful conditions is contained in this line of research as well. Kinship networks and neighbors are used quite effectively by some parents (Lee, Campbell, and Miller 1991; McAdoo 1986). For others, network relationships can actually be a further source of strain (Riley and Eckenrode 1986).

Fourth, community social organization is proving to be a useful framework for understanding the relationship between macro-structural change and the experience of families and children within neighborhoods

(Sampson 1992). As neighborhoods decline economically, experience population turnover, and begin to contain large numbers of children in female-headed families, the community's internal control is diminished. Studies of crime and delinquency, in particular, support the contention that this diminishing control occurs through the effects of the macro-structure on processes within the community such as friendship networks, institutional participation, normative consensus, and monitoring of the environment (Bursik and Grasmick 1993; Sampson and Groves 1989; Sampson 1991). Dimensions of community structure such as economic resources, residential mobility, family structure, and age distribution of the population have been linked to varied childhood outcomes including child maltreatment, delinquency, teen childbearing, and low-birthweight rates (Coulton et al., forthcoming).

Regardless of whether an outcome orientation or contextual orientation is chosen, caution must be exercised in interpreting differences among communities. Community selection processes are complex and difficult to isolate but can be important explanations for variation among local areas (Tienda 1991). On the one hand, self-selection of families into particular communities and forced selection of communities by families due to discrimination, affordability, or public policy may be responsible for variation in outcomes or community context. On the other hand, pre-existing differences in social, economic, and institutional structures and processes can affect children within communities regardless of the selection processes that lead to their presence in a particular community in the first place.

Even with these caveats in mind, community-area boundaries need to be consistent with the orientation that is chosen. The outcome and contextual orientation also call for somewhat different types of indicators to represent the well-being of children in communities. Examples of such indicators are provided in the next section.

COMMUNITY INDICATORS OF CHILDREN'S WELL-BEING

Community indicators are measures of child and family well-being tied to local community areas. Indicators that reflect an *outcome orientation* include social, health, and developmental outcomes for the population living in local areas. Indicators that reflect a *contextual orientation* include measures of the community structure and process that are believed to affect children and family life.

Neighborhoods and other community areas can change rapidly. Thus, community indicators from either orientation should be calculated and available annually or bi-annually.

Outcome Indicators

Outcome indicators that are useful at the community level include many of those that have been proposed for use at the national and state levels. However, data sources and availability differ at the community level, placing limitations on what is practical. In particular, large-scale surveys seldom have sufficient sample sizes to make estimates for small areas. Furthermore, the base rates of some outcomes useful at the state or national level are too low to allow valid measurement at the local community area level.

Table 1 offers a list of indicators that we have used in Cleveland's neighborhoods and the surrounding metropolitan area as an illustration of what is currently possible. This is not an exhaustive list. The indicators are organized according to the general categories suggested by Zill (1991). Our system in Cleveland allows calculation of the indicators for block groups, census tracts, neighborhoods officially designated as planning areas, or any other sub-areas of the county that can be aggregated from block groups such as areas defined by residents or neighborhood leaders. This type of flexibility is highly desirable in local indicator work.

Measures of health and safety of children are the types of outcomes most readily available at the local level. Local health departments, hospitals, police jurisdictions, child welfare agencies, and coroners are all potential collaborators for developing indicators in this area. Infant death rates and low-birthweight rates and other measures of infant and child health can be calculated from birth and death certificates that are readily available and can be geo-coded for aggregation into small areas. Rates from year to year are quite labile in small areas and three-year averages are preferred.

Child maltreatment rates can be calculated from official reports and are reasonably comparable in terms of definitions and criteria within one agency jurisdiction. However, over- and under-reporting biases may differ across community areas and must be assessed carefully. (See Reporting Bias and Error, below.)

Table 1
Examples of Community Outcome Indicators for Children Available in the Cleveland Metropolitan Area

Indicator	Measure	Data Sources
Health and Safety		
Infant death rate	Infant deaths/live births	Vital Registrar
Low-birthweight rate	Births <2,500 grams/live births	Vital Registrar
Child maltreatment report rate	Reports of abuse or neglect/population <18	County Children's Services
Trauma rate[a]	Children's injuries/population <18	Hospital emergency rooms
Child homicide rate	Child homicides/population <18	County Coroner
Child suicide rate	Child suicides/population <18	County Coroner
Social Behavior		
Teen childbearing rate	Births to teens/females 12–17	Vital Registrar
Delinquency rate	Delinquent filings/population 10–17	County Juvenile Court
Teen drug violation arrest rate	Drug arrests of teens/population 12–17	Municipal Police Departments
Cognitive Development and Achievement		
High school graduation rate	Persons graduating/persons entering 9th grade	Board of Education
Performance in math and reading	Mean performance score	Board of Education
Youth employment rate	Employed persons 16–25/total population 16–25	U.S. Census, STF-4
Economic Well-Being		
Family poverty rate	Poor families/total families	U.S. Census, STF-3
Child poverty rate	Children in poor families/children in all families	U.S. Census, STF-3
Child public assistance rate	Public assistance recipients <18/total population <18	County Entitlement Services

[a]Planning and development of this data source is currently under way.

Trauma rates can be calculated for children if trauma registries exist in the emergency departments of most major hospitals serving the communities of interest. We are currently in the planning stages for such a registry system for Cleveland. The trauma events will be geo-coded using the home address of the patient and aggregated by age to yield rates for children. A seriousness threshold for inclusion in this indicator will need to be developed.

Child homicide rates and suicide rates as well as gun-related deaths for community areas can be calculated from the coroner's data. Because these are rare events, multiple years need to be averaged and rather large community areas must be used for analysis.

Measures of what Zill (1991) labels moral and social development and emotional development are more difficult to obtain at the local level without resorting to impractical neighborhood surveys. One useful measure, though, is the teen childbearing rate, which is based on births to teens per 1,000 females ages 12 to 17.

The delinquency rate is another possible indicator of moral and social development and is derived from court records that are classified as to level of offense and age of offender and then geo-coded. Delinquency filings are counted per 1,000 males and females ages 10 to 17. Further refinements of this indicator can include separate rates for males and females, separate rates for violent offenses, and direct age standardization.

Teen drug violation arrest rates are also available and can be calculated from arrest records of the police departments. Caution must be exercised when comparing these rates across police precincts or municipalities because police practices may differ. While these rates do suggest the communities in which youth are interacting with the criminal justice system as a result of drug-related activities, they cannot be used as valid measures of drug use or involvement as a whole.

Measures of cognitive development and academic achievement can be developed for communities in collaboration with local school systems. High school graduation rates require student-level data from the schools that are geo-coded so students can be assigned to neighborhoods. If multiple years of data files are available, counts of students entering the ninth grade in each community area can be divided into counts of students graduating four years later. Unfortunately, this only measures students' graduation rates and does not include persons who obtain a general educational development (GED) credential or who complete high school later.

Student performance is measured as the mean grade level achieved by students at selected grade levels on standardized achievement tests. These scores can be usefully compared across neighborhoods even though the role of standardized testing in education is undergoing rapid change. Nevertheless, longitudinal comparisons should be made cautiously.

These school-based measures are more practical in neighborhoods where most of the children attend public schools. We have found some neighborhoods in Cleveland, though, in which fewer than 50 percent of the children are enrolled in public schools. A valid school graduation indicator for those areas would require obtaining student data with home addresses from more than 30 private and parochial schools, all of whom have differing methods of data collection and storage. Such a task has been impractical thus far.

Youth employment can also be considered an indicator of achievement. It uses the decennial census to calculate the labor force status of young men and women, ages 16 to 25, who are not in school. Unfortunately, we have not yet found a measure of youth employment at the community level that is available more frequently than each decade. However, the use of the state reporting system related to unemployment compensation is being explored.

The economic status of families, a final category suggested by Zill (1991), is available at the community level from the decennial census. Family poverty rate, child poverty rate, and family median income can all be calculated easily. However, we know that the actual economic status of families in a neighborhood can change rapidly during a decade. Therefore, we are developing a model for estimating these rates in each subsequent year using variables derived from Aid to Families with Dependent Children (AFDC) and food-stamp recipients in each community area. Our previous experience in estimating overall poverty rates for census tracts between 1980 and 1990 showed fairly high accuracy. Public assistance counts for various programs were benchmarked to census counts of poor persons and the model was used as an estimator in intercensal years.

The child public assistance rate is an additional indicator of the economic status of families that is available yearly. Public assistance families typically have income that is well below the poverty threshold. This indicator reflects, therefore, the children with the most extreme economic deprivation. It can be calculated using the monthly average caseload of children receiving public assistance in each community area divided by the number of children living in the area. The monthly public assistance case files are geo-coded and counts are produced for the desired units of geography.

Contextual Indicators

The search for practical measures of community environments has an extended history (Rossi 1970). However, the identification of indicators of community context that may be important factors in the well-being of children requires either scientific research or a set of assumptions that link aspects of community structure and process to effects on families and children. Unfortunately, research that pinpoints those aspects of community that affect children and families has yet to yield definitive connections. (See Connell, Aber, and Walker in this volume.) Nevertheless, the research described earlier (in the section entitled "Perspectives on Community-Level Measurement") can be used to suggest a set of indicators of community context that are worthy of experimentation.

Table 2 presents a set of indicators of community context for children that we have been exploring in Cleveland's neighborhoods. At the aggregate level, they have been linked to rates of child maltreatment, teen childbearing, low birthweight and delinquency (Coulton et al., forthcoming). Ethnographic studies conducted in selected neighborhoods representing varying levels of risk for children generally confirm that these factors coincide with residents' perceptions of the neighborhood as "good or bad places for raising children" (Korbin and Coulton 1994). The data sources for these contextual indicators are much more limited at the community level than they are for the outcome types of indicators. Since many come from the decennial census they only are available at ten-year intervals.

Economic status of neighbors is suggested as an important contextual indicator for the well-being of children both in the compositional effects and the community social organization research. The compositional research, though, emphasizes that measurement needs to reflect not only overall economic status, such as median income or poverty rate, but must also include an indicator of the presence of middle-class or affluent neighbors (Brooks-Gunn et al. 1993; Clark 1992; Crane 1991; Duncan 1993).

The importance of the age and family structure of a community is also implicated as an important factor in the well-being of children. Specifically, community areas with a higher percentage of elderly persons, a more balanced ratio of men to women, a greater percentage of two-parent

Table 2
Examples of Indicators of Community Context for Children
Used in Cleveland Metropolitan Areas

Indicator	Measure	Data Sources
Socioeconomic Composition		
Middle-class neighbors	Percent families with income > $35,000	U.S. Census, STF-3
Affluent neighbors	Percent families with income > $50,000	U.S. Census, STF-3
Managerial and professional workers	Percent managerial and professional workers	U.S. Census, STF-3
Poverty rate	Percent persons below poverty threshold	U.S. Census, STF-3
Poverty estimates	Est. percent persons below poverty threshold	Estimates using public assistance counts
Age and Family Structure		
Female-headed families with children	Percent families with children headed by female	U.S. Census, STF-1
Non-marital birth rate	Percent births to unmarried mothers	Vital Registrar
Elderly population	Percent population > 65	U.S. Census, STF-1
Male/Female ratio	Adult males (21–64)/ adult females (21–64)	U.S. Census, STF-1
Child/Adult ratio	Population 0–12/ population 21+	U.S. Census, STF-1
Residential Mobility		
Population gain or loss	1990 population–1980 population	U.S. Census, STF-1
Movers in <5 years	Percent who moved between 1985 and 1990	U.S. Census, STF-3
Residential tenure <10 years	Percent in current residence <10 years	U.S. Census, STF-3
Environmental Stress		
Vacant and boarded houses	Percent housing units vacant or boarded	Municipal housing departments
Housing code violations	Percent units substandard	Municipal housing departments
Personal crime	FBI index crimes against persons/1,000 population	Municipal police departments
Drug arrests	Drug arrests/1,000 population	Municipal police departments

families, and a more favorable adult–child ratio are found to correlate with lower rates of poor outcomes and to be perceived by residents as promoting a better environment for children (Coulton et al., forthcoming; Korbin and Coulton 1994).

Several indicators of residential mobility are deemed important because population turnover has been repeatedly connected to aspects of community process (Freudenburg 1986). Most important as a context for children is the negative effect of residential mobility on parent-to-parent networks and support for institutions serving children.

Indicators of environmental stress are potentially useful because they may directly affect parents' ability to protect and nurture their children and because of the negative effects of these factors on community social organization. Substandard and abandoned housing is associated with growing disorder and fear of crime (Skogan 1990). High levels of personal crime and drug selling are seen by residents as a source of anxiety and distraction that affects their parenting (Furstenberg 1993; Korbin and Coulton 1994).

On the positive side, some contextual supports for effective parenting are also suggested. Parental involvement with social institutions, neighbor-to-neighbor relations, and community resources for families are but a few of the features of community that seem important (Zill and Nord 1994; Garbarino and Sherman 1980). Unfortunately, few data sources are readily available for measuring resources at the local community level. Community resources for children have been studied in national and local surveys, but surveys are seldom practical for local indicators. New sources of data need to be developed to measure these aspects of community context.

Relationship of Contextual and Outcome Indicators

The distinction between contextual and outcome indicators is not as clear as may be implied by the discussion thus far. A given indicator could be viewed as contextual or outcome depending upon the circumstances. For example, decreasing the number of children in poverty is often an outcome objective of community initiatives, especially those that include job creation and workforce development components. Yet, a similar indicator, the economic status of the families in a neighborhood, is thought to represent an important aspect of the context for child-rearing. Improvement in this aspect of context would presumably benefit children even if their own families remained poor.

Contextual and outcome indicators may also have complex and difficult-to-detect relationships with one another. While it might generally be assumed that context affects outcome, the direction of the influence may be the other way around. For example, the presence of large numbers of vacant and boarded houses may be viewed as an indicator of declining community social organization, and drug trafficking by teens a consequence that can flourish in such a context. However, heavy drug trafficking may actually be a reason that owners abandon their property and police often close and board homes of known drug dealers.

Because of these complications, monitoring both types of indicators is desirable. Panel studies can help to unravel the reciprocal relationships among processes and outcomes (for example, Pandey and Coulton 1994) but undoubtedly there are unique stories that need to be told within specific communities. Ethnographic and observational studies can be useful in interpreting changing indicators in specific locales (Korbin and Coulton 1994).

METHODOLOGICAL CONSIDERATIONS
FOR COMMUNITY-LEVEL INDICATORS

There are numerous methodological problems pertinent to making measurements of child and family well-being for small geographic areas such as communities. While they are formidable, many can be managed through careful definition and interpretation.

Assignment of Geographical Location
Because definitions of community areas typically have some geographic boundaries, data used for community indicators must be suitable for assignment to geographic units. Administrative agency data, which are often the preferred source for local community indicators, must be obtained with the street addresses intact. The addresses can be geo-coded using the TIGER files (census files containing street addresses) and aggregated to the desired geographic boundaries—for example, block groups, census tracts, resident-defined neighborhoods, wards, catchment areas, school zones, and so on.

In our experience, agencies differ considerably in the accuracy and validity of their addresses for this purpose. Problems include the timeliness of the address, whether it is verified or not, and administrative conventions that can be misleading. For example, some agencies overwrite addresses when there is a move so the address is the most current one. The most current address, however, may differ from the address at which an event of interest occurred, such as an arrest or a child abuse incident. Also, the address given may not be a home address, which is usually the one desired for community analysis, but an office or agency where a service was delivered. Finally, when the address is obtained by the agency for informational rather than service delivery purposes, accuracy may be low and a substantial number of addresses may not be codable without considerable effort expended to correct errors.

Finally, for some indicators, there may be ambiguity as to which geographic area to assign a case. For example, infant deaths are ordinarily assigned to the community area in which the death occurred. However, since infant death is highly related to conditions in the prenatal period, it may be more useful to assign the death to the community area in which the birth occurred.

Small Area Limitations
The geographic units for community indicators are typically fairly small. Block groups vary considerably in their population size but may have anywhere from just a few to hundreds of housing units. While census tracts have an average population of 4,000, many are quite a bit smaller, especially in central cities that have been losing population. Designated neighborhoods can be of any size depending on the methodology used for drawing the boundaries. This small geography poses several limitations.

Unavailability of Survey Data. No national surveys are available with sample sizes that are adequate to provide valid estimates for small areas such as neighborhoods and census tracts. Even statewide or metropolitan-wide surveys are seldom adequate for these purposes. Only the decennial census, in which 15 percent of the households complete the long form, provides some estimates of family structure and economic status that can be used for small geographic areas. The Public Use Microdata (PUMS) 5 percent sample from the census can be used to make estimates at the sub-city level, but these areas of 100,000 minimum population seldom correspond to any meaningful definition of community area.

Surveys are periodically undertaken locally that are capable of generating measures of child and family well-being for small, geographically defined communities. However, it is seldom feasible to draw adequately sized samples for all neighborhoods in a region so a multi-stage sampling method can be used. Thus, these surveys do not provide measures for all community areas but only for a sample, selected randomly or otherwise. Furthermore, these expensive surveys are seldom repeated and so they do not yield measures over time, which is desirable for indicators.

Low Base Rates. Outcomes of significant interest such as childhood deaths from trauma can show extreme variation in rates because they are rare. Since aggregating geography to achieve sufficient population size would often negate the purpose of community-area analysis, multi-year averages must be used to obtain a stable trend. The disadvantage, of course, is that important changes in conditions may be obscured in the short run.

Unequal Population Sizes. A third problem is the fact that meaningful geographic units often have widely differing population sizes. The stability or reliability of an indicator will be better in larger areas than in smaller areas. An extreme rate in a smaller area must be viewed with considerable caution. For some purposes, such as statistical modeling, the geographic units can be weighted for their population size, but such weighting does not typically make sense when the indicators are being used for local planning or evaluation purposes.

Reporting Bias and Error

Although error and bias must be considered in all work on indicators, two problems are particularly troubling at the local community level. First, because local community indicators rely so heavily on administrative agency data, they are beset by the reporting bias and error in those data sources. The nature of these problems is likely to vary from one indicator to another. Birth and death certificates, for example, are known to be quite complete. However, cause of death on death certificates and information about the mother's health contained in birth certificates are prone to error. These errors differ depending upon the hospitals and physicians involved in their completion. Thus, the degree of error will differ in an unknown way across community areas.

Reports of criminal or deviant acts are subject to the most severe and troubling sorts of bias. Police reports and court records are known to underestimate the true levels of criminal and violent events (O'Brien

1985). More importantly, they are also biased by differences that may exist across jurisdictions in victims' or observers' tendencies to report (Sampson 1985) and government officials' tendency to file reports and take action (Sherman 1989; O'Toole, Turbett, and Nalpeka 1983). Unfortunately, the direction of the bias in each of the community areas cannot be known but could account for some part of the observed differences.

The problem of errors and bias in administrative records requires careful investigation in each instance. Few generalizations can be made across regions. Generally, though, errors will be fewer when the data element used serves a mandated function or vital purpose of the agency. Information gathered by the agency for descriptive purposes only can often be misleading due to large amounts of missing data or coding errors. Reporting bias is particularly troubling when the direction of the bias is not the same in all community areas.

It is desirable, therefore, that efforts be made to validate widely used indicators based on administrative records against other data sources. Specially designed community surveys can be useful for establishing the validity of indicators derived from administrative agencies or other sources. For example, Jill Korbin and I have a study in the planning stage that will use a survey instrument to measure aspects of child abuse and neglect. The survey will be conducted in a random sample of neighborhoods whose rates of child abuse and neglect have been calculated based on official reports to the county authorities. These two sources of data can be compared to illuminate the issue of reporting bias and error in both the survey and administrative agencies.

Another example of validating administrative data with another source are the infant mortality reviews that are being carried out as a part of Cleveland's Healthy Start Program and are being performed in other Healthy Start cities. In Cleveland, the infant mortality review has revealed considerable variation across hospitals and physicians in classifying causes of death and in deciding what is a live birth. When corrected, the quality of this source of administrative data will be improved.

An additional issue that is pertinent to local community indicators is the amount of undercounting and missing data. This problem has received considerable attention with respect to the decennial census. Most troubling for community indicators is that the amount of undercounting and missing data is not uniform across community areas. Census counts are more likely to be undercounts when they pertain to young men and minorities in central city neighborhoods, for example. Furthermore, the amount of missing data that the census bureau imputes is greater in low-income, minority neighborhoods leading to differential reliability of census indicators (White 1987). Adjusting for the estimated undercount in some neighborhoods may be necessary but also introduces another source of error since the true undercount cannot be known in each location.

Small Area Population Estimates and Change

Community indicators are often reported as rates in which the area's population is used as the denominator. Rates may be reported per 100, 1,000, or 100,000 persons. Unfortunately, population estimates are not universally available at the block group or census-tract level between censuses, so rates in non-census years will be less valid. While established methods of population estimation are used at state and county levels, their application to areas as small as block groups, census tracts, or neighborhoods has not been widespread (Heeringa 1982).

Nevertheless, the sources of data needed to perform these population estimates can generally be obtained for community areas through geocoding. The housing unit method of population estimates, for instance, can use building and demolition permits, utility hookups and disconnections, or county assessor tax records to update housing unit counts postcensally. The component-cohort method relies on birth and death certificates. While estimating small-sized areas results in greater error, there is evidence that useful estimates are possible (Smith and Cody 1994).

Equally important as changes in the size of the population are shifts in the composition of the population. For example, the poverty rate of residents of a neighborhood may rise due to declining wages of existing residents, in-migration of disadvantaged residents, out-migration of more affluent residents, or departure of previously poor residents who recently became more affluent, perhaps as a result of an initiative. Tracking changes in population size or poverty rates will not reveal what combination of processes are operative, yet the processes themselves are important to understanding comprehensive community initiatives. For example, using a method developed by Jargowsky and Bane (1990), we estimated that approximately one-third of Cleveland's growth in extreme-poverty neighborhoods in the 1980s was due to the flight of the middle class as opposed to actual decline in earnings of area residents or in-migration of poor from elsewhere (Coulton, Pandey, and Chow 1990). More sensitive and precise methods of decomposing population changes are needed to properly assess the impact of interventions on these types of indicators.

Standardization

Community-level indicators are applied to areas of widely differing demographic makeup. In some instances, therefore, it may be useful to apply age or gender standardization. Small geographic areas often display marked variability in age and gender distribution. Some childhood indicators are sensitive to the particular age distribution that is present in the community. For example, teen births are concentrated in older teens and occur with less frequency in younger teens. Therefore, if two communities have a similar number of teens but the teens in one community tend to be older, the community with older teens would be expected to have a higher teen birthrate. Age standardization can compensate for differing age distributions and is probably worth the extra computational steps when children's ages put them at greater or lesser risk for particular outcomes.

Certain indicators may also be sensitive to gender distribution in the community. For example, delinquent behavior is known to be more frequent among boys. Gender-specific rates should be calculated for these types of indicators.

Other forms of statistical adjustment have been suggested for indicators, such as adjusting outcome indicators for the economic status or ethnicity of the population (Zill 1991). Such adjustment must be done cautiously, since it can obscure important ways in which more affluent communities differ from lower-income communities or ways in which some communities may be favored over others in resource distribution.

However, where community indicators are being used for evaluating specific programs, known risk factors for a particular outcome that are not amenable to the effects of the intervention would be suitable factors to use in adjustment. For example, mothers' age, ethnicity, and educational attainment are known risk factors for infant mortality. Community area rates of infant mortality could be adjusted for these factors in an evaluation of an infant mortality prevention program.

Corruption of Indicators

Many of the community indicators mentioned in this paper are collected by agencies of government for their own purposes. Indicators can become corrupted when the employees within the agency believe they are being judged by an indicator and act to change the indicator itself but not the underlying phenomenon it is supposed to measure. Indicators can also be affected when an initiative leads to less underreporting, such as increased reports of child abuse as community residents become more aware of the problem.

A careful examination of each community indicator is needed to determine the extent to which corruption could become a source of invalidity. To the degree that the indicator data come from agencies not directly involved in the comprehensive community initiative, direct corruption by employees is unlikely. However, more subtle influences within each agency may result in corruption or changes in reporting rates, and it is important that these be taken into account when interpreting trends in the indicators at the community level.

ROLE OF COMMUNITY INDICATORS IN EVALUATING COMPREHENSIVE COMMUNITY INITIATIVES

Community indicators can contribute to understanding comprehensive community initiatives, but they must be used very carefully. It is most important that they be interpreted within a framework of metropolitan and regional dynamics. A neighborhood that is the target of an initiative cannot be viewed in isolation because it will be affected by the trends in surrounding areas. Furthermore, changes in a target neighborhood may affect contiguous areas and this fact, also, cannot be ignored.

The application of community indicators to comprehensive community initiatives should also be embedded within a long-term perspective. Specifically, target neighborhoods have experienced a history of change. The patterns and rates of past changes must be taken into account when prospectively tracking changes into the future. Expectations regarding improvement in key indicators must be based on the reality of past experience and trends.

Analysis and Interpretation of Community-Level Indicators
The analysis of community indicators can take several forms. First, each target neighborhood and surrounding areas can be examined over time to determine the amount and direction of change in each indicator. When

areas are small, multi-year averages must be used and a fairly long-time trend is needed to detect significant variation. Nevertheless, for practical purposes neighborhood residents and organizations are often interested in monitoring these types of trends to get a sense of whether they are making desired progress.

Second, target neighborhoods and surrounding areas can be compared with one another cross-sectionally on each indicator. Areas can be ranked on selected indicators and maps can be used to determine the location of communities that are relatively high and relatively low on the various indicators. Cross-sectional analyses of this type are often useful for planning purposes such as choosing locations for programs or deciding which issues should receive priority. Also, they allow areas that are performing poorly to identify areas that are performing better and seek their advice and assistance for improvement. These cross-sectional comparisons must be made cautiously, though, due to differences in reporting biases and an expected amount of random variation at any given period in time.

Third, community areas can be grouped according to their similarities on a set of indicators. Such clusters can aid community leaders in recognizing the interrelationships among several aspects of children's well-being. The recognition that several troubling outcomes or conditions are concentrated in a few areas can lead to greater collaboration and service integration. Maps that allow overlaying of several indicators can be powerful visual aids in this process and promote community approaches to problem solving.

Fourth, panel studies of change in multiple indicators across multiple community areas are possible (Pandey and Coulton 1994). Such analyses can suggest the degree to which change in an indicator leads or lags behind change in other indicators. This knowledge can allow communities to anticipate improvement or deterioration and to react accordingly.

Finally, indices that capture the metropolitan-wide distribution of community indicators are quite useful for understanding the regional context for a comprehensive community initiative. For example, an important concern today is that poor children and their families are often isolated from the rest of the population in inner-city enclaves and this concentration of families at risk is particularly detrimental (Wilson 1987). A commonly used method of determining this level of concentration is to establish a threshold that is considered detrimental. With respect to poverty, census tracts with poverty rates of 40 percent or more are considered extreme-poverty areas (Kasarda 1993). A resulting index of concentration pertinent to child well-being is the percentage of all children in a county or metropolitan area who live in these extreme-poverty neighborhoods.

Another method of determining the local distribution of child well-being is to calculate a D index of dissimilarity (Lieberson 1980) for selected child outcomes. For example, the degree to which low-birthweight babies are segregated from babies whose weights are in the normal range could be calculated for a metropolitan area. The D index varies from 0 to 1 and represents the proportion of those babies who would have to be moved to achieve an even distribution of low-birthweight babies throughout the metropolitan area. It reveals the amount of segregation of childhood outcomes within the metropolitan area.

Reducing concentration and segregation could be an explicit objective of comprehensive community initiatives. Even if not an official target of change efforts, such concentration and segregation may be impediments to community improvement that are important to understand.

Community Involvement and Dissemination of Indicators

The development of community indicators requires involvement of local residents and leaders. They need to be involved in designating the appropriate geographic units to be studied as well as setting priorities regarding the types of indicators to be sought. Because of the demands of data cleaning and geo-coding, the generation of community indicators can be quite expensive and the community needs to influence the choices that are made.

Community residents and leaders also play an important role in interpreting trends and patterns that are observed in the indicators. They are aware of changes that are occurring in their communities that may account for the findings. They are also the vehicle for converting the information that indicators provide into action.

Since local and state administrative agencies are the source of much community indicator data, their involvement is essential, too. Collaborative relationships need to be established so that the agency as well as the community can benefit from the information that is generated. Data preparation may be burdensome for the agency and there are often serious concerns about the protection of confidentiality, especially since addresses are needed for geo-coding. These barriers can be overcome when all parties see the benefit of producing the information.

Getting community-level indicators into the hands of the public in a useful format is not a trivial problem, though. Because so many units of geography are of potential interest, the indicators need to reside in a system that can be quickly and easily manipulated, preferably by users as well as analysts. Taking Cleveland and its suburbs as an example, there are 1,535 block groups, 495 census tracts, 35 city neighborhoods, and 58 suburban municipalities. Indicators for each of these units need to be readily available if comprehensive community initiatives in target neighborhoods are to be properly examined within their metropolitan and historical contexts.

To accommodate these hierarchically structured units of geography and over 80 indicators for a thirteen-year period, we have created an interactive information system that is available to community-based organizations and initiatives (Chow, forthcoming). Using the system that we have named CANDO (Cleveland Area Network for Data and Organizing), leaders and ordinary citizens can generate their own geography and trend analyses for indicators of their choice. We also produce a hard-copy report of selected indicators each year for one unit of geography, Cleveland's thirty-five city neighborhoods.

Conclusion

Community indicators have a place in planning and evaluating comprehensive community initiatives. They are important adjuncts to other methods for monitoring progress and determining whether desired objectives are being achieved. To be interpretable, however, they must be available not only for target neighborhoods but also for surrounding areas. Historical trends must be linked to projections into the future as well.

The use of community indicators in isolation presents a danger because they are sensitive to a variety of economic and demographic processes that occur along with deliberate actions of any initiative. Also, it may appear that an initiative has not met its stated objectives when key indicators do not improve, but it is difficult to determine what the trends would have been in the absence of the initiative. Furthermore, because general knowledge about community change is sparse, expectations regarding the speed and amount of change in indicators may be unrealistic. Nevertheless, the availability of a comprehensive set of community indicators that can describe metropolitan trends will aid in the interpretation of findings from within target neighborhoods and contribute to the overall process of evaluation.

NOTE

Portions of this paper were prepared for a Conference on Indicators of Children's Well-Being, November 17–18, 1994, sponsored by The Office of the Assistant Secretary for Planning and Evaluation in the U.S. Department of Health and Human Services; Child Trends, Inc.; and the Institute for Research on Poverty, The University of Wisconsin-Madison.

REFERENCES

Brooks-Gunn, J., G. J. Duncan, P. K. Klebanov, and N. Sealand. 1993. "Do Neighborhoods Influence Child and Adolescent Development?" *American Journal of Sociology* 99: 353–95.

Bursik, R. J., and H. G. Grasmick. 1993. *Neighborhoods and Crime.* New York: Lexington Books.

Caspi, A., N. Bolger, and J. E. Eckenrode. 1987. "Linking Person and Context in the Daily Stress Process." *Journal of Personality and Social Psychology* 52: 184–95.

Chow, J. Forthcoming. *CANDO (Cleveland Area Network for Data and Organizing) Users Guide.* Cleveland: Case Western Reserve University, Center for Urban Poverty and Social Change.

Clark, R. 1992. *Neighborhood Effects on Dropping out of School among Teenage Boys* Washington, D.C.: The Urban Institute.

Coulton, C. 1994. "Effects of Neighborhoods in Large Cities on Families and Children: Implications for Services." In *Children and Their Families in Big Cities.* Ed. A. Kahn and S. Kammerman. Seminar held at the Columbia University School of Social Work, New York.

Coulton, C. J., and S. Pandey. 1992. "Geographic Concentration of Poverty and Risk to Children in Urban Neighborhoods." *American Behavioral Scientist* 35: 238–57.

Coulton, C., J. Korbin, J. Chow, and M. Su. Forthcoming. "Community Level Factors and Child Maltreatment Rates." *Child Development.*

Coulton, C., S. Pandey, and J. Chow. 1990. "Concentration of Poverty and the Changing Ecology of Low-income, Urban Neighborhoods: An Analysis of the Cleveland Area." *Social Work Research and Abstracts* 26: 5–16.

Crane, J. 1991. "Effects of Neighborhoods on Dropping out of School and Teenage Childbearing." In *The Urban Underclass,* ed. C. Jencks and P. E. Peterson, pp. 299–320. Washington, D.C.: The Brookings Institution.

Duncan, G. J. 1993. *Families and Neighbors as Sources of Disadvantage in the Schooling Decisions of White and Black Adolescents* Ann Arbor: University of Michigan.

Entwisle, B. 1991. "Micro-Macro Theoretical Linkages in Social Demography: A Commentary." In *Macro-Micro Linkages in Sociology*, pp. 280–86. Newbury Park, Calif.: Sage Publications.

Freudenburg, W. R. 1986. "The Density of Acquaintanceship: An Overlooked Variable in Community Research." *American Journal of Sociology* 92: 27–63.

Furstenberg, F. F. 1993. "How Families Manage Risk and Opportunity in Dangerous Neighborhoods." In *Sociology and the Public Agenda*, ed. W. J. Wilson, 231–58. Newbury Park, Calif.: Sage Publications.

Galster, G. C. 1986. "What Is Neighborhood? An Externality-Space Approach." *International Journal of Urban and Regional Research* 10: 243–61.

Galster, G. C., and G. W. Hesser. 1982. "The Social Neighborhood: An Unspecified Factor in Homeowner Maintenance?" *Urban Affairs Quarterly* 18: 235–54.

Galster, G. C., and R. B. Mincey. 1993. "Understanding the Changing Fortunes of Metropolitan Neighborhoods: 1980 to 1990." *Housing Policy Debate* 4: 303–48.

Garbarino, J., and D. Sherman. 1980. "High-risk Neighborhoods and High-risk Families: The Human Ecology of Child Maltreatment." *Child Development* 51: 188–98.

Garbarino, J., N. Dubrow, K. Kostelny, and C. Pardo. 1992. *Children in Danger.* San Francisco: Jossey Bass.

Heeringa, S. G. 1982. "Statistical Models for Small Area Estimation." *Readings in Population Research Methodology* 5: 126–32.

Jargowsky, P. A., and M. J. Bane. 1990. "Ghetto Poverty: Basic Questions." In *Inner-city Poverty in the United States*, ed. L. E. Lynn and M. G. H. McGeary, 16–67. Washington, D.C.: National Academy Press.

Jencks, C., and S. E. Mayer. 1990. "The Social Consequences of Growing up in a Poor Neighborhood." In *Inner-city Poverty in the United States*, ed. L. E. Lynn and M. G. H. McGeary, 111–86. Washington, D.C.: National Academy Press.

Kasarda, J. 1993. "Inner-city Concentrated Poverty and Neighborhood Distress: 1970 to 1990." *Housing Policy Debate* 4: 253–302.

Korbin, J. E., and C. J. Coulton. 1994. *Final Report: Neighborhood Impact on Child Abuse and Neglect.* Washington, DC: National Center for Child Abuse and Neglect.

Lee, B. A., K. E. Campbell, and O. Miller. 1991. "Racial Differences in Urban Neighboring." *Sociological Forum* 6: 525–50.

Lieberson, S. 1980. *A Piece of the Pie: Blacks and White Immigrants since 1880.* Berkeley, Calif.: University of California Press.

Lyon, L. 1987. *The Community in Urban Society.* Chicago: Dorsey Press.

Martinez, J. E., and P. Richters. 1993. "The Nimh Community Violence Project: Children's Distress Symptoms Associated with Violence Exposure." *Psychiatry* 56: 22–35.

McAdoo, H. P. 1986. "Strategies Used by Black Single Mothers Against Stress." *Review of Black Political Economy* 14: 153–66.

O'Brien, R. M. 1985. *Crime and Victimization Data* Beverly Hills, Calif.: Sage Publications.

O'Toole, R., P. Turbett, and C. Nalpeka. 1983. "Theories, Professional Knowledge, and Diagnosis of Child Abuse." In *The Dark Side of Families: Current Family Violence Research*, ed. D. Finkelhor, R. Gelles, G. Hotaling, and M. Strauss. Newbury Park, Calif.: Sage Publications.

Pandey, S., and C. J. Coulton. 1994. "Unraveling Neighborhood Change Using Two-Wave Panel Analysis: A Case Study of Cleveland in the '80s." *Social Work Research* 18: 83–96.

Riley, D., and J. Eckenrode. 1986. "Social Ties: Subgroup Differences in Costs and Benefits." *Journal of Personality and Social Psychology* 51: 770–78.

Rossi, P. 1970. *Community Social Indicators* Baltimore: Johns Hopkins University.

Sampson, R. J. 1985. "Neighborhood and Crime: The Structural Determinants of Personal Victimization." *Journal of Research in Crime and Delinquency* 22: 7–40.

————. 1991. "Linking the Micro- and Macro-level Dimensions of Community Social Organization." *Social Forces* 70: 43–64.

————. 1992. "Family Management and Child Development: Insights from Social Disorganization Theory." In *Advances in Criminological Theory*, vol. 3: 63–93. New Brunswick: Transition Press.

Sampson, R. J., and W. B. Groves. 1989. "Community Structure and Crime: Testing Social-Disorganization Theory." *American Journal of Sociology* 94: 775–802.

Sherman, L. 1989. "Hot Spots of Predatory Crime: Routine Activities and the Criminology of Place." *Criminology* 27: 27–56.

Skogan, W. G. 1990. *Disorder and Decline* Berkeley, Calif.: University of California Press.

Smith, S. K., and S. Cody. 1994. "Evaluating the Housing Unit Method." *APA Journal* 60: 209–21.

Steinberg, L., and N. Darling. 1994. "The Broader Context of Social Influence in Adolescence." In *Adolescence in Context*, ed. R. Silbereisen and E. Todt. New York: Springer.

Steinberg, L., S. D. Lamborn, S. M. Dornbush, and N. Darling. 1992. "Impact of Parenting Practices on Adolescent Achievement: Authoritative Parenting, School Involvement and Encouragement to Succeed." *Child Development* 63: 1266–81.

Taylor, R. B., S. D. Gottfredson, and S. Brower. 1984. "Block Crime and Fear: Defensible Space, Local Social Ties, and Territorial Functioning." *Journal of Research in Crime and Delinquency* 21: 303–31.

Tienda, M. 1991. "Poor People and Poor Places: Deciphering Neighborhood Effects on Poverty Outcomes." In *Macro-Micro Linkages in Soci-ology*, ed. J. Huber, 244–62. Newbury Park, Calif.: Sage Publications.

White, M. 1987. *American Neighborhoods and Residential Differentiation* New York: Russell Sage Foundation.

Wilson, W. J. 1987. *The Truly Disadvantaged: The Inner City, the Underclass, and Public Policy*. Chicago: The University of Chicago Press.

Zapata, B. C., A. Rebolledo, E. Atalah, B. Newman, and M. C. King. 1992. "The Influence of Social and Political Violence on the Risk of Preg-nancy Complications." *American Journal of Public Health* 82: 685–90.

Zill, N. 1991. *Improving KIDS COUNT: Review of an Annual Data Book on the Condition of Children in the 50 States of the U.S.* Washington, DC: Child Trends.

Zill, N., and C. W. Nord. 1994. *Running in Place: How American Families Are Faring in a Changing Economy and Individualistic Society.* Washington, DC: Child Trends.

The Role of the Evaluator in Comprehensive Community Initiatives

Prudence Brown

The use of the term "evaluation" has undergone considerable expansion in its purpose, scope, and methods over the last twenty years. This expansion is reflected in the range of roles that evaluators currently play, or attempt to play, in carrying out their work: scientist, judge, educator, technical assistant, facilitator, documenter/historian and repository of institutional memory, coach, manager, planner, creative problem solver, co-learner, fund-raiser, and public relations representative. While the field has moved toward a view of evaluation that is fundamentally normative rather than technical, political rather than neutral or value-free, many unresolved questions remain about how evaluators should operationalize such a view as they select and shape the role(s) they play in any particular evaluation enterprise.

Evaluators of comprehensive community initiatives (CCIs) face a particularly wide and complex array of roles available to them. It is often the case, however, that different stakeholders in an initiative prioritize these roles differently, generate expectations that are unrealistic or difficult to manage simultaneously, and/or define the evaluator's role in a way that limits substantially the learning potential and, some would maintain, even the likelihood of the initiative's success. The goal of this paper is to explore how evaluators' roles are being defined, and with what consequences, in terms of the lessons we are learning and what we need to learn in the future about comprehensive community initiatives. The paper begins by reviewing the CCI characteristics that create special challenges for the evaluator, the existing social science context in which evaluations are being developed, and the different purposes and audiences for such evaluations. That is followed by sections on the current status of evaluations in this field and on the different options and strategies—both their limits and possibilities—open to evaluators. The paper ends with some thoughts on how evaluators can maximize the learning opportunities comprehensive community initiatives present through increased innovation and experimentation and through the opportunity to structure disciplined cross-site learning.

COMPREHENSIVE COMMUNITY INITIATIVES

The characteristics of CCIs were described in depth earlier in this volume. However, the qualities that contribute to the particular challenges for evaluators are briefly reviewed here in order to set a context for a discussion of evaluation roles:

- They have "broad, multiple goals, the achievement of which depends on complex interactions" through which they aim to promote "an ongoing process of 'organic' or 'synergistic' change" (Chaskin 1994).

- They are purposively flexible, developmental, and responsive to changing local needs and conditions.

- To varying degrees, they conceptualize devolution of authority and responsibility to the community as a necessary though not sufficient aspect of the change process. While the terms may be operationalized in quite different ways, all the current CCIs refer to some combination of community empowerment, ownership, participation, leadership, and/or capacity-building as central to their mission.

- They recognize the long-term nature of fundamental community change or neighborhood transformation and tend to have longer time frames than more narrowly defined categorical approaches.

- While they are intended to produce impacts at different levels in different spheres, their theories of change are generally unspecified or specified in the form of broad guiding principles rather than specific causal relationships. The empirical basis for these principles is generally lacking.

These qualities create evaluation challenges that are both methodological and political in nature, ranging from the problems of establishing attribution in a saturation design and of developing markers of progress for assessing short- and medium-term change, to balancing different stakeholders' needs for information and feedback and weighing the goals and values of rigor and relevance. Such questions are not unique to CCIs, nor do they pose entirely new challenges for program evaluators,[1] but in combination they forecast the need to develop new ways of thinking about evaluation in this field.

The social science context in which these challenges need to be addressed is also shifting and developing. Michael Patton writes that the traditional distinction between formative and summative evaluation may not be a helpful way to think about evaluation of "cutting edge" approaches in "uncharted territory." Formative evaluations have been directed toward the process of program implementation, while summative evaluations aim at "making a fundamental and generalizable judgment about effectiveness and replicability." Patton argues that "it is the nature of uncharted territory and the cutting edge that there are no maps. Indeed, in the early stages of exploration there may not even be any destination (goal) other than the exploration itself. One has to learn the territory to figure out what destination one wants to reach."[2] Most of the comprehensive initiatives that are under way are so exploratory and developmental that premature specification of concrete, measurable outcomes can be seen as antithetical to the notion of ongoing course corrections and the discovery of creative new paths, possibly even new destinations. Corbett (1992, 27) echoes these concerns: "The old form of discrete, impact-focused evaluations, awarded to firms on a competitive basis, may be counterproductive. Longer time lines, less obsession with what works, and a more collaborative evaluation industry may be needed. The days of the short sprint—one-shot summative evaluations—may be ending. A new paradigm, where the marathon constitutes the more appropriate metaphor, may be emerging."

The conception of multiple exploratory paths and marathons conforms with the emerging philosophy that questions the utility of the "techno-rational, logical-positivist approach toward theory and practice" and moves toward a "relativistic, heuristic, postmodern perspective" (Bailey 1992; Lather 1986). In this framework, there is less emphasis on discovering the one, objective truth about a program's worth and more attention to the multiple perspectives that diverse interests bring to judgment and understanding. Such a framework is consistent with a CCI that is designed to stimulate a process of change that is likely to be defined and experienced in many different but equally valid ways by many different community constituencies. The differences between the positivist and interpretivist paradigms tend to "play out as dichotomies of objectivity versus subjectivity, fixed versus emergent categories, outsider versus insider perspectives, facts versus values, explanation versus understanding, and single versus multiple realities" (House 1994, 16). House argues, however, that the "choice does not have to be between a mechanistic science and an intentionalist humanism, but rather one of conceiving science as the social activity that it is, an activity that involves considerable judgment, regardless of the methods employed" (19). The fact that these issues are being debated at present in the evaluation field creates a context more open to experimentation and new combinations of paradigms and methods than might have existed a decade ago. In a social science context that acknowledges multiple perspectives and realities, it is easier to discuss the advantages and disadvantages of the role of evaluator as co-learner rather than expert, conveyor of information rather than deliverer of truth (Weiss 1983), educator rather than judge.

Finally, related to this notion that we do not know enough about the expectable developmental trajectories of these initiatives, let alone the realistic outcomes that can be anticipated within certain time frames, are the potentially disempowering consequences of committing too early to specific goals and criteria for success. As discussed above, one of the assumptions of these initiatives is that they are driven by a process in which community residents play key roles in identifying and implementing development strategies. For the process to work, the evaluator is often an "enabling partner," helping the initiative's participants articulate and frame their goals in ways that can be assessed over time. This in itself is "one of the outcomes of the process rather than one of the up front, preordinant determinants of the process."[3] Furthermore, the goals may change as evaluators come to better understand the lay of the land. "When clear, specific, and measurable goals are set in stone at the moment the grant is made, the struggle of community people to determine their own goals is summarily pre-empted and they are, once again, disempowered—this time in the name of evaluation."[4] In sum, the characteristics of CCIs shape the learning opportunities, constraints, and needs presented to the evaluator and help define the broad parameters of the evaluator's role. Another major determinant of the particular role(s) the evaluator selects is the purpose of the evaluation as defined by the primary client—that is, who is paying for the evaluation—and/or by the primary audience: who wants to do what with the evaluation findings?

PURPOSE AND AUDIENCE FOR EVALUATION

The purpose of an evaluation is often, though not always, determined by the funder, sometimes in negotiation with the various stakeholders and the evaluator. Most evaluations of CCIs serve one or more of the following overlapping functions:

1. They provide information about the ongoing implementation of the initiative so that its progress and strategies can be assessed and mid-course corrections instituted.

2. They build the capacity of the initiative participants to design and institutionalize a self-assessment process.

3. They draw some conclusions or judgments about the degree to which the initiative has achieved its goals.

4. They support a collaborative process of change that combines creating knowledge with mutual education and mobilization for action.

5. They hold those conducting the initiative accountable to the funder, the community, and/or other stakeholder groups.

6. They contribute to the development of broad knowledge and theory about the implementation and outcomes of comprehensive community initiatives.

7.   They promote a public relations and fund-raising capacity.

These different purposes for evaluation put different premiums on the kind of data the evaluator needs to collect, the relationship the evaluator establishes with the initiative's designers and participants, and the nature of the products the evaluator is expected to generate, both during and at the end of the initiative. In addition, the learning produced to serve these different evaluation functions has distinct primary audiences: funders, practitioners, policymakers, and community members, all of whom tend to place a different value on particular kinds of information and evaluation lessons. Also, they can be driven by different priorities and investments: there are those whose major goal (and often passion) is to improve the quality of life in the targeted community; those who want to know how successful strategies can be adapted and brought to scale in other communities; and those whose priorities are to develop for scholarly purposes a theory and body of knowledge about community change initiatives. As discussed later, an evaluator's success depends a great deal on the clarity and consensus with which the relevant parties define the purpose and intended products of the evaluation early on in the process.

CURRENT STATUS OF EVALUATIONS
OF COMPREHENSIVE COMMUNITY INITIATIVES

The current status of evaluations of CCIs seems to mirror the sense of frustration and confusion, as well as excitement and hope, within the initiatives themselves. What we see so far is a range of expectations, often implicit and sometimes conflicting, about what is to be achieved and how that achievement is to be assessed. As Corbett (1992, 26) describes, part of the discontent is characteristic of the natural life cycle of new programs:

> [P]rograms are launched with great fanfare and exaggerated claims, to sell them in the first place; the pace and scope of implementation conform more to political cycles than to the hard work of program development; outcomes are (intentionally?) unclear or overly complex, thereby difficult to operationalize and measure; and the investment in program evaluation is insufficient given the complexity of underlying theoretical models (or the lack

of them) and the fiscal and human costs at stake. Given this life cycle, it is all too easy for excitement to evolve into disenchantment and ultimately despair. . . .

Political imperatives for solutions seem to overwhelm the patience and integrity that are required for good long-range policy/program development.

The signs of this discontent are widely manifest among those associated with CCIs. Evaluators produce interim reports that elicit such responses as: "Is that all we learned? We could have told you that at the start," or "Why didn't you give us feedback earlier so we could have done things differently?" Community members believe the reports are abstract or inaccessible, not timely, and/or irrelevant to them, and they often respond with anger because they feel over-studied without getting any useful feedback (or respect) in return. Learning is limited substantially by weak implementation. Funders can be intolerant of failure, unimpressed by partial successes and impatient with fine-tuning, unclear whether they are getting enough "bang for their buck." Decision-makers want a quick fix and are disappointed that the "bottom line" is so murky and takes so long to assess. Implementers worry that "truth" will make it hard to raise money, win elections, or maintain momentum or hope in the community. All the parties involved are looking for reassurance that unguided process is not replacing accountability and long for some well-accepted standards with clear timelines against which to assess an initiative's progress. Evaluators recognize the limits of traditional roles and methods but feel caught between standards that will bring them rewards in the academy and credibility in the funding and policy community, and the risks of trying out new ways of learning. Do their clients want "experiments or stories" (Smith 1994), and is there any creative middle ground between the two?[5] Finally, the evaluation becomes the arena in which conflicting expectations and interests among all the parties involved inevitably get focused but are not always worked out. Issues of power and control concerning such questions as who defines the pace and criteria of success, how funding decisions are related to interim evaluation findings, and who shares what information with whom, can make it extremely difficult for evaluators and initiative operators and participants to establish relationships of trust and open communication. Evaluators may be called upon to "educate" both parties about what evaluation can and cannot do, the scale of investment required to address various kinds of questions, and the realistic time frame needed for examining initiative outcomes.

Evaluators can find themselves in the middle of an awkward, sometimes contentious, process between foundations and communities that are trying to operationalize an empowerment orientation in the context of a grantor–grantee relationship. Foundations may aim to establish new partnerships or collaborations with "community-driven" initiatives, while falling back on traditional dominant and subordinate roles and practices in the face of uncertainty or disagreement. This power dynamic is complicated by issues of race and class, given the players, who are largely white foundations and frequently distressed minority communities.

In addition, given their dependency on foundation support, both evaluators and community initiative leaders may be ambivalent about giving honest feedback to foundation staff who can be highly invested as the primary architect of the particular change model being implemented and less than receptive to "bad news." A culture of grantee accountability and foundation authority may serve to undermine a culture of learning, innovation, and partnership. This situation can be exacerbated when foundation staff do not recognize the power of the funds and ultimate authority they possess to affect the dynamics of CCI relationships and implementation. Documenting the role of the foundation as an actor in CCI planning, implementation, and evaluation is an important task for the evaluator notwithstanding its potential to generate discomfort on both sides.

Despite pervasive uncertainty and some outright unhappiness about the role of evaluation in current CCIs, there exists simultaneously among funders, policymakers, and practitioners a sense of urgency and need to know whether and how these initiatives can succeed. We know more than we did in the 1960s, both in terms of effective program models and in terms of program evaluation methods and approaches. On the one hand, there is a sense of hope that these initiatives are on the "right track" and a belief that we can't "give up" on persistently poor urban neighborhoods. On the other hand, there is a deep-seated fear that nothing short of structural changes in the economy can "transform" distressed urban neighborhoods. But still believing in the democratic values of individual and community potential, we also still believe in the value of experimentation in the broad sense, hence the many different community initiatives under way. This makes the role of knowledge development all the more pressing.

So . . . what's an evaluator to do?

OPTIONS AND STRATEGIES FOR THE EVALUATOR

Given the demands of the initiatives themselves and a social science context that provides more support than it has historically for the notion that "science is not achieved by distancing oneself from the world" (Whyte et al. 1991), it is not surprising that most of the new roles that evaluators have taken on in their work with comprehensive initiatives are strategies of engagement; that is, they serve to bridge the traditional distance between the evaluator and the activities under study. Chavis, Stucky, and Wandersman (1983, 424) talk about this distance in terms of the basic philosophical conflict that exists between some of the "values of scientists and citizens":

> The citizen or professional practitioner is often under pressure to act immediately, to solve complex problems with the incomplete information on hand, and to make judgments based on the knowledge available. The scientist is trained to reserve judgment until the data are complete, to test and refine hypotheses, to isolate variables and to hold conditions constant, and to reinterpret observations and revise theories as new data become available. Whereas the citizen needs to develop complex strategies in a confounded, changing environment, the scientist is cautious in generalizing from the data and controlled conditions of research. At the extreme, scientific objectivity may be seen to require separation between the researcher and subject. . . .

The authors argue that both the evaluator and the community initiative benefit from reducing this separation and "returning research to the citizen": it can "enhance the quality and applicability of research, provide an opportunity for hypothesis generation and hypothesis testing, and facilitate planning and problem solving by citizens" (433).

While most evaluators of CCIs aim to reduce the traditional separation between themselves and the initiatives under study, they operationalize their roles and construct their relationships with the "citizens" in a range of different ways, presumably with different consequences for what is learned on both sides. Research models of engagement can take multiple forms. Many comprehensive community initiatives call for evaluations that provide ongoing feedback to the initiative's designers and operators, clearly taking the evaluator out of the role of a "faceless judge" and into the action in one way or another. By providing such feedback, the evaluator becomes part of the dynamic of the initiative. If he or she attaches recommendations to the feedback and supports the initiative's implementation of such recommendations, the evaluator moves into a coach role. Other initiatives define one of the evaluator's central roles as helping to build the capacity of the initiative to carry out its own ongoing evaluation or self-assessment. Here the evaluator plays an educational or technical assistance role. Some evaluators call this "facilitated problem-solving" in which the evaluator helps the group explore design alternatives but does not advocate for a particular position.

A different approach to bridging the gap between the evaluator and the initiative is to engage community members as advisory or steering group participants, key informants, and/or volunteers or paid staff as part of the evaluation team. A variant on this approach is "utilization-focused evaluation" in which the evaluator brings together decision-makers and information users in an "active-reactive-adaptive process where all participants share responsibility for creatively shaping and rigorously implementing an evaluation that is both useful and of high quality" (Patton 1986, 289). At the "close" end of the spectrum is the role of evaluator as a participatory action researcher. In this role, which is discussed in more depth later in the paper, the evaluator joins the initiative in a "collaborative, co-learning process which integrates investigation with education and collective action" (Sarri and Sarri 1992). The next sections describe the rationale for drawing upon various engagement strategies in evaluating comprehensive community initiatives, the skills required, and the debates that exist about their strengths and weaknesses as methodologies.

Rationale for Engagement

Although some of the roles described above are commonly assumed and others have yet to be fully embraced by evaluators of comprehensive community initiatives, they are rationalized to varying degrees by many of the same related arguments. First, when evaluators assume roles like coach, collaborator, or capacity-builder, they help to demystify and democratize the knowledge development process. The active involvement of participants in the process of knowledge generation creates the research, problem analysis, group problem-solving, technical skills, and leadership necessary for identifying and solving problems on an ongoing basis. Second, when evaluators become embedded in the initiative's implementation (to varying degrees depending on the roles they play), they help position the evaluation less as a discrete activity that can be "dispensed with as a cost-cutting measure" (Patton 1988) and more as an integral part of the initiative's core activities. Indeed, a developmental and responsive evaluation is seen as generating ongoing information that becomes a tool for reviewing current progress, making mid-course corrections, and staying focused on the primary goals of the initiative. Third, by engaging an initiative's operators and participants in its assessment, evaluators can enhance community understanding, stakeholder commitment, and utilization of the results. Fourth, reducing the distance between the evaluator and the community can serve to bridge the cultural gaps that may exist, enable the evaluator to draw upon the "popular knowledge" of participants, "explicate the meaning of social reality" from the different participants' perspectives, and increase the likelihood that the findings are experienced by participants as relevant (Patton 1988).

New Demands on the Evaluator

While debate exists about the wisdom of adopting these new evaluation roles in comprehensive community initiatives, it is clear that these new roles bring increased demands on the evaluator. The first and perhaps most important is that evaluators need to have a much broader range of skills than they might have needed to be "distant observers." Besides methodological and technical competency based on their training in systematic inquiry and analysis, evaluators are likely to need skills in communication and team building, group process, and negotiation (Guba and Lincoln 1989).[6] The researcher's ability to facilitate a process that allows participants to contribute their expertise and develop new competencies is often critical to the success of the evaluation enterprise (Israel et al. 1992). Evaluators may also need:

- pedagogical skills so they can teach both about evaluation and through evaluation (Wise 1980; Cousins and Earl 1992);

- political skills to help them assess multiple stakeholder interests and "incorporate political reality into the evaluation" (Palumbo 1987); and

- the ability both to gain stakeholder's cooperation and trust and to sustain their interest and involvement over an extended period of time (Fitzpatrick 1989, 577).

Additionally, evaluators who take on more engaged roles inevitably find them more labor-intensive than expected. Involving multiple stakeholders at every stage in the research process, for example, takes a significant commitment of time and energy. The intended benefits to the evaluation process, however, are many. Such an approach can help participants become tuned to the complexities and priorities of the enterprise; clarify and focus goals; appreciate the strengths and limitations of various methods and measurement strategies; and develop realistic expectations for what questions can and cannot be addressed. This type of collaborative relationship also tends to reduce participants' suspicions and fears about the evaluation process because they know what decisions are being made and who is involved in making them. Establishing and sustaining such relationships takes time.

In sum, apart from their methodological strengths and weaknesses, which are discussed below, the new roles that evaluators are being asked to play in CCIs create new demands, some of which evaluators may not feel comfortable or competent in addressing. Traditionally trained evaluators may lack the technical skills, the temperament, and/or the desire to adopt these new roles. Some may experience a conflict between their legitimate need to be perceived as credible and their sense that taking on some roles traditionally considered outside of the evaluation enterprise may produce important and useful learning. It is their credibility, in fact, that makes it possible to even try out certain kinds of new research roles.[7] Clearly, these issues have implications for the curriculum and culture of training programs in the academy, for the value foundations place on different kinds of learning, and for the role of knowledge in the policymaking process.

Methodological Strengths and Weaknesses

There are obvious risks involved when the evaluator becomes positioned inside the action rather than at a distance from it. One critique is simply that such roles no longer constitute evaluation. Instead, evaluation becomes primarily an intervention tool (Israel et al. 1992), and the evaluator takes on a management consultant role, not a role charged with making judgments about the "efficiency and effectiveness" of a program (Rossi

1994). Questions of bias and lack of reliability are also raised. Or the evaluator may become an advocate for positions espoused by the respondents with whom he or she feels the most sympathy. Being part of a process of mutual learning gives the evaluator access to information in a form that contributes to a particular way of understanding the dynamics and effects of the initiative, which may have both limitations and strengths. By becoming so engaged in the planning and implementation process, the evaluator may not be able to assess outcomes with an open view or may encounter the danger of being used as a public relations tool. Perhaps more risky than the evaluator's own loss of "objectivity" may be a reduction in the credibility he or she is perceived to have in the eyes of some initiative constituencies. No longer seen as neutral, the evaluator's access to some sources of quality data may be decreased (although increased for others).

Many of these concerns stem from two larger questions: Can the term "evaluation" be defined broadly enough to encompass multiple ways of generating and using knowledge? Or should we call these new ways of learning something other than evaluation? And, second, what does empirical rigor mean in a post-positivist context (Lather 1986, 270)? What are the "scientific" standards against which evaluators should assess the quality of their work in comprehensive community initiatives?

There is still considerable debate within the field of evaluation about how broadly or narrowly evaluation should be defined, let alone what value should be placed on different methods and approaches. For example, Gilgun (1994) makes a good case for "thickly described" case studies that "take multiple perspectives into account and attempt to understand the influences of multilayered social systems on subjects' perspectives and behaviors." Scriven (1993, 62), however, concludes that rich (thick) description is "escapist and unrealistic" because instead of helping the client make hard decisions, "it simply substitutes detailed observations for evaluation and passes the buck of evaluation back to the client." Scriven seems to be setting up an argument with only the most extreme of constructivists who take the position that the best evaluators can do is produce journalistic narratives, a stance that "begs the questions of rigor and rationality, effectively takes evaluators out of the conversation, and obviates the necessity to do good. It is an escape from responsibility and action" (Smith 1994, 42). However, the acknowledgment of multiple perspectives and truths that evolve over time does not by definition release the evaluator from the right or obligation to both maintain high standards of scientific inquiry and to make judgments and recommendations as warranted.[8] Having a more complex appreciation of the realities of life and dynamics of change within a distressed neighborhood should add a richness and force to evaluators' assessments rather than either undermine their ability to make judgments and/or contribute to a paralysis of action. As Smith (1994, 41) notes, "although objectivity, reliability and unbiasedness have been amply demonstrated as problematic, rationality, rigor and fairness can still be sought." Patton (1987, 135) proposes fairness as an evaluation criterion in place of objectivity, replacing "the search for truth with a search for useful and balanced information, . . . the mandate to be objective with a mandate to be fair and conscientious in taking account of multiple perspectives, multiple interests, and multiple realities." He also stresses the importance of keeping a focus on the empirical nature of the evaluation process, upon which the integrity of the evaluation ultimately depends. He conceptualizes the evaluator as the "data champion" who works constantly to help participants adopt an empirical perspective, to make sure that rival hypotheses and interpretations are always on the table, and to advocate the use of evaluation findings to inform action.

Another commonly adopted strategy to balance the weaknesses or narrow yield of any one method or data source is the use of multiple methods, types of data, and data sources. "Perhaps not every evaluator can or is willing to take on multiple approaches within a study, but he or she can promote, sponsor, draw on, integrate the findings of, negotiate over, and critique the methods and inferences of multiple approaches" (Smith 1994, 43). If data are to be credible, the evaluator has some responsibility to triangulate data methods, measures and sources in a way that allows for "counter patterns as well as convergence." In a related vein, Weiss (1983, 93) suggests that there may be benefits to funding several small studies (as opposed to a single blockbuster study) and sequencing them to respond to the shifting conditions and opportunities that emerge during implementation. Although problems of continuity and overall integration may arise, different teams of investigators, using different methods and measures, may be able to enrich understanding of the initiative in a way that is beyond the scope of a single evaluation team.

Whyte et al. (1991) make the case that the scientific standards that must be met to conduct more "engaged" approaches to evaluation are daunting, but have several built-in checks to enhance rigor that are not present in the standard model of evaluation. For example, in the standard model, the subjects usually have little or no opportunity to check facts or offer alternative explanations. Evaluators of comprehensive initiatives often devise mechanisms to feed back and test out the information they are collecting on a continuous basis, as well as in the form of draft interim and final reports. They also have the opportunity to test the validity and usefulness of the findings when they are fed back and become the basis for future action (insofar as some form of action research is adopted). Stoecker (1991) expands on the issue of establishing validity in the following ways: by seeing whether the findings lead to accurate prediction, by comparing findings derived from different methods, and by involving the "subjects" themselves in a validity check. The resulting knowledge is validated in action, and it has to prove its usefulness by the changes it accomplishes (Brunner and Guzman 1989, 16). Although "we are still low in the learning curve regarding our knowledge as to how action and research cycles can benefit from one another—and from greater participation," it is generally accepted that "broader participation can lead to stronger consensus for change and sounder models—because models arrived at through broader participation are likely to integrate the interests of more stakeholder groups. Participation also promotes continual adjustment and reinvention. . . ." (Walton and Gaffney 1991, 125).

Engagement also provides an evaluator with certain opportunities for the development of social science theory, one of the vital ingredients of the research process. Elden and Levin (1991) write about how a collaborative model rests on "'insiders' (local participants) and 'outsiders' (the professional researchers) collaborating in cocreating 'local theory' that the participants test out by acting on it. The results can be fed back to improve the participants' own 'theory' and can further generate more general ('scientific') theory" (129). Ideally, this approach improves the quality of the research as well as the quality of the action steps and becomes a strategy to advance both science and practice.

FUTURE NEEDS: INNOVATION AND DISCIPLINED CROSS-SITE LEARNING

Evaluations of CCIs now under way seem to suffer as a group from the lack of at least two phenomena that might contribute to accelerated learning in the field: innovation and experimentation, and disciplined comparative work. To address what they recognize as significant methodological and conceptual challenges that call out for new approaches, evaluators tend to respond by trying almost everything (but the kitchen sink) in their current tool kit: surveys, ethnographies, community forums, examination of initiative records, structured interviews, analysis of demographic data, file data extraction, and so forth. But few are developing new methods or defining their roles in substantially new ways, and few have the opportunity to develop a comparative perspective across initiatives. Thus the field is benefiting from neither innovation nor cross-site learning. This is in part because of insufficient resources for adequate evaluations of these initiatives, let alone support to experiment with new methodologies and roles. Few funders seem to have an investment in promoting the development of the field of evaluation, even though the current challenges facing evaluators constrain the learning possibilities and opportunities to improve the design and practice of initiatives that these funders currently support.

Many innovations are possible to enhance the learning that is being generated by evaluators of CCIs. One, participatory research, is described below because it seems to have a potentially interesting fit with the philosophy and operations of many comprehensive initiatives. The focus on this one example, however, should not detract from the overall need for more innovation and experimentation with a range of approaches and new learning strategies.

Participatory Research

Different disciplines and traditions within the field of evaluation— sociology, psychology, organizational development, education, international development—have spawned a range of related approaches variously known as participatory research, action research, participatory action research, and participatory evaluation (Brown and Tandon 1983; Brunner and Guzman 1989; Whyte 1991; Hall 1993).[9] While they differ significantly in their relative emphasis on action compared with research and theory building, in the role the researcher plays in the action, and in their political orientations, they constitute a group of approaches "committed to the development of a change-enhancing, interactive, contextualized approach to knowledge-building" that has "amassed a body of empirical work that is provocative in its implications for both theory and, increasingly, method" (Lather 1986). A number of the characteristics of participatory research described below apply to the other approaches as well.

Nash (1993) explains,

> Participatory research [PR] links knowing and doing through a three-part process of investigation, education, and action. As a method of social investigation, PR requires the active participation of community members in problem posing and solving. As an educational process, PR uncovers previously hidden personal and social knowledge and develops skills which increase "people's capacity to be actors in the world." Finally, PR is a process of collective action which empowers people to work to transform existing power structures and relationships that oppress them.

The approach is explicitly normative in its orientation toward redressing inequity and redistributing power: it involves initiative participants as "researchers" in order to produce knowledge that could help stimulate social change and empower the oppressed (Brown and Tandon 1983). It is built on a "cyclical, overlapping and often iterative" process of data gathering, analysis and feedback, action planning and implementation, and assessment of the results of the action through further data collection (Bailey 1992).

The approach seeks to "reduce the distinction between the researcher and the researched" (Sarri and Sarri 1992). The role of the evaluator in participatory research is one of co-learner, member of the "co-inquiry" team, methodological consultant, collaborator, equal partner. While the researcher brings certain technical expertise and the community participants bring unique knowledge of the community, neither side uses these resources to "gain control in the research relationship" (Nyden and Wiewel 1992).

There are several interesting parallels in the goals and (sometimes implicit) theories behind participatory research and many comprehensive community initiatives. Both articulate a strong belief in individual and collective empowerment. Israel et al. (1992, 91) define empowerment as the "ability of people to gain understanding and control over personal, social, economic, and political factors in order to take action to improve their life situations." The participatory research approach can be conceptualized as a way of developing knowledge that enhances the empowerment of initiative participants and, as a consequence, furthers the goals and agenda of the community initiative.[10] Both participatory research and comprehensive community initiatives depend on the iterative process of learning and doing. Both recognize the power of participation and strive to develop vehicles to enhance and sustain that participation. Both have at their core a conception of the relationship between individual and community transformation, between personal efficacy and collective power. Both view the creation of knowledge as an enterprise that is both technical and includes other forms of consciousness. And both rely on the release of energy and hope that is generated by group dialogue and action.

All the cautions expressed earlier about any research approach that positions the researcher in a more interactive/collaborative relationship with the initiative being evaluated are amplified with participatory research. Such an approach may be particularly "cumbersome and untidy to execute" (Park 1992) because it is so labor-intensive and because it is unlikely to have much yield unless the evaluator brings a certain personal commitment to community change. It has yet to develop much legitimacy in the academy and has yet to be implemented in enough cases to identify its full limits and possibilities.[11] So it is an approach to be used selectively, possibly along with other methodologies. It is a misconception, however, to characterize it as completely impractical for evaluating today's comprehensive community initiatives. Bailey's (1992) initial research with a community-based consortia in Cleveland and Sarri and Sarri's (1992) work in Detroit (as well as in Bolivia) illustrate the specifics of implementing participatory research in distressed urban communities.[12] Weiss and Greene (1992) make a strong conceptual case for empowerment-oriented participatory evaluation approaches in the field of family support and education programs and describe several examples of such evaluations. Israel et al. (1992) provide a detailed account of the implementation of a six-year action research study within an organizational context. Whitmore (1990) describes six strategies she used as an evaluator to support participant empowerment in the process of evaluating a comprehensive prenatal program.

While participatory research should not be portrayed as the major answer to all the research challenges facing comprehensive community initiatives, it makes sense to add this underutilized approach to the array of evaluation strategies currently being tested. Others working in the field may have their own "personal favorites" that seem promising to them. What is important is that a research and demonstration context is created in which evaluators are provided with the resources they need and are encouraged to work with community initiatives to develop and try out new ways of learning about how these initiatives work and how their long-term impacts might be enhanced. This is more likely to occur if funders can conceive of these resources as integral to the initiative's implementation rather than competitive with the initiative's operational funding needs. Fawcett (1991, 632) outlines ten values for community research and action that may help "optimize the rigors of experimentation within the sometimes chaotic contexts of social problems." The goal is to support efforts that combine research and action in more "adventuresome" and functional ways so that the dual purposes of applied research—contributing to understanding and improvement—can be served.

Cross-Site Learning

Despite the sense of urgency about developing credible approaches, innovative tools, and useful theories to bring to bear on the evaluation of comprehensive community initiatives, little cross-site learning is actually taking place among the group of initiatives under way. Often, foundations supporting demonstrations are unenthusiastic about close external scrutiny of their models before those models have a chance to evolve and be refined. Evaluators are set up to compete with each other for evaluation contracts, making the sharing of experience with different tools and approaches a complex and variable enterprise. Initiatives feel a need to put the best light on their progress in order to obtain continued support. Community leaders recognize that any "bad news" delivered in an untimely and destructive fashion can undermine their efforts at community mobilization. And all parties are aware of a context in which the media and the taxpayer, as well as policymakers, are all too ready to conclude that "nothing works" in distressed urban communities.

Overcoming these barriers to cross-site learning will require a variety of strategies, all of which must be constructed to satisfy in one way or another each party's self-interest. The Roundtable is presumably one vehicle for supporting such efforts. It may be helpful, also, to think about the current initiatives as a series of case studies around which some comparative analyses could be conducted. An example of an issue that might benefit substantially from a comparative perspective is community participation: What place does it have in the different initiative's theories of change? "[I]s the purpose of community participation to improve the efficiency of project implementation or to contribute to the empowerment of politically and economically weaker communities or groups" and are these complementary or competing objectives (Bamberger 1990, 211)? And how can this evolutionary process—whose impacts may only be evident after a number of years—be measured in ways that provide "sufficient quantification and precision to permit comparative analysis between communities, or over time, while at the same time allowing in-depth qualitative description and analysis" (Bamberger 1990, 215)? While most challenging, selecting for comparative work some of the major concepts (such as community participation, program synergy, and build-ing social fabric) that appear central to the underlying theories of change governing community initiatives may have the most payoff for the evalu-ator at this point in the development of the field.

When full-scale comparative longitudinal evaluation is unrealistic, a low-cost methodology suggested by Wood (1993) is *practitioner-centered evaluation*, a qualitative technique that focuses on the informal theories of behavioral change that underlie a program as implemented. It relies on the ability of program implementers to document success and failure in the context of their own theories about "various cause and effect linkages set in motion by program activities" (Wood 1993, 97). This approach focuses on the theory of action being tested by the people actually implementing it, encouraging them to define change strategies and anticipated outcomes more concretely than they often do and then to refine their theories on the basis of experience, including unintended as well as intended conse-quences. Wood characterizes this approach as a flexible model-building methodology that encourages initiatives to "build up a repertoire of suc-cessful cause-and-effect sequences" (98), some of which will be suitable for application elsewhere and all of which should contribute to cross-initiative learning. It is not a substitute for more rigorous evaluation methods but begins to explore systematically "the ambiguous realm between feeling that a program is good and knowing that it is" (91). The more such practitioner-centered evaluations can be set in motion, the more compara-tive learning an evaluator will have to draw upon to advance the field.

◊   ◊   ◊   ◊   ◊

In sum, comprehensive community initiatives present evaluators with a host of methodological and strategic questions about how to define their roles and to prioritize the lessons they are asked to generate for different audiences. Some would frame the central concern for evaluators as finding the appropriate balance between scientific rigor and social relevance. Others would limit the definition of evaluation to quite a narrow enterprise, but then reframe questions that are too "messy" to be included in this enterprise as subject to "systematic study" that draws upon a broader range of methodologies and roles for the "evaluator." Still others, though a smaller group, would either aim to redefine the fundamental nature of the scientific approach, citing its limited ability to yield knowledge that is useful for CCI participants, or would reject CCIs as unevaluable and therefore unworthy of any evaluation role. This paper suggests that CCI implementers, sponsors, and evaluators work collaboratively to create a learning culture that encourages a range of strategies for generating knowledge and improving practice.

NOTES

1. See, for example, Peter Marris and Martin Rein, *Dilemmas of Social Reform: Poverty and Community Action in the United States* (Chicago: University of Chicago Press, 1967).
2. Letter of August 14, 1991, from Michael Patton, then of the American Evaluation Association, to Jean Hart, Vice President of the Saint Paul Foundation.
3. Patton, as cited in note 2.
4. Ibid.
5. Phillip Clay, Associate Provost and Professor of City Planning at the Massachusetts Institute of Technology, in an October 24, 1994, review of this paper suggests that documentation may constitute a middle ground. "Documentation is a way of going well beyond description because documentation sets a milestone and offers some benchmarks against which to assess program implementation. By its nature it then looks back at the framing of the problem and the design of the intervention. Yet it is short of evaluation because it does not force the question, 'Does this program work for the purpose for which it was intended?'"
6. Guba and Lincoln (1989) characterize the first three generations in evaluation as measurement-oriented, description-oriented, and judgment-oriented. They propose that the key dynamic in the fourth generation is negotiation.
7. Phillip Clay, as cited in note 5.
8. Personal communication with Avis Vidal, July 19, 1994.
9. Participatory research has its roots in adult education and community development in Tanzania in the early 1970s and in the libratory tradition of

Friere in Latin America. Hall (1992) reports that Friere made a trip to Tanzania in 1971; his talk was transcribedand became one of his first writings in English on the subject of alternative research methodologies. Participatory *action* research emerged from a very different tradition, that of organizational development, and represents a strategy for innovation and change in organizations. The term "participatory research" is used in this paper in its broadest sense in order to encompass the philosophy of participatory action research.

10. "In addition to transformations in consciousness, beliefs, and attitudes, empowerment requires practical knowledge, solid information, real competencies, concrete skills, material resources, genuine opportunities, and tangible results" (Staples 1990, 38). Consistent with this definition of empowerment, both research methodologies place an emphasis on building the capacity—in individuals, groups, and communities—for effective action.

11. A number of articles have been written about the conflicts between activist research and academic success, participatory research in the community and life in the university (Reardon et al. 1993; Cancian 1993; Hall 1993). Bailey (1992, 81) sees a role for academics in participatory research, noting that her own experience suggests the importance for the "outside other" to acknowledge his or her own values, biases, and interests that may "go beyond the community to include academic interests regarding the methodology and outcomes of the research."

12. A personal conversation in July 1994 with Darlyne Bailey, now Dean of the Mandel School for Applied Social Sciences at Case Western Reserve University, revealed that it appears that the Department of Housing and Urban Development (HUD) will support some participatory research, as well as the establishment of a client tracking system, in its recent HOPE VI grant in Cleveland.

REFERENCES

Bailey, Darlyne. 1992. "Using Participatory Research in Community Consortia Development and Evaluation: Lessons from the Beginning of a Story." *The American Sociologist* 23: 71–82.

Bamberger, Michael. 1990. "Methodological Issues in the Evaluation of International Community Participation Projects." *Sociological Practice*. 208–25.

Brown, L. David and Rajesh Tandon. 1983. "Ideology and Political Economy in Inquiry: Action Research and Participatory Research." *Journal of Applied Behavioral Science* 19: 277–94.

Brunner, Ilse, and Alba Guzman. 1989. "Participatory Evaluation: A Tool to Assess Projects and Empower People." In *International Innovations in Evalu-*